The Role of Birds in World War One

The Role of Birds in World War One

How Ornithology Helped to Win the Great War

Nicholas Milton

Forewords by Beccy Speight & Professor Ben Sheldon

First published in Great Britain in 2022 by
Pen & Sword History
An imprint of
Pen & Sword Books Ltd
Yorkshire – Philadelphia

Copyright © Nicholas Milton 2022

ISBN 978 1 39907 056 0

The right of Nicholas Milton to be identified as Author of this work has been asserted by him in accordance with the Copyright, Designs and Patents Act 1988.

A CIP catalogue record for this book is available from the British Library.

All rights reserved. No part of this book may be reproduced or transmitted in any form or by any means, electronic or mechanical including photocopying, recording or by any information storage and retrieval system, without permission from the Publisher in writing.

Typeset by Mac Style
Printed in the UK by CPI Group (UK) Ltd, Croydon, CR0 4YY.

Pen & Sword Books Limited incorporates the imprints of Atlas, Archaeology, Aviation, Discovery, Family History, Fiction, History, Maritime, Military, Military Classics, Politics, Select, Transport, True Crime, Air World, Frontline Publishing, Leo Cooper, Remember When, Seaforth Publishing, The Praetorian Press, Wharncliffe Local History, Wharncliffe Transport, Wharncliffe True Crime and White Owl.

For a complete list of Pen & Sword titles please contact

PEN & SWORD BOOKS LIMITED
47 Church Street, Barnsley, South Yorkshire, S70 2AS, England
E-mail: enquiries@pen-and-sword.co.uk
Website: www.pen-and-sword.co.uk

Or

PEN AND SWORD BOOKS
1950 Lawrence Rd, Havertown, PA 19083, USA
E-mail: Uspen-and-sword@casematepublishers.com
Website: www.penandswordbooks.com

Contents

Acknowledgements — v
Forewords by Beccy Speight & Professor Ben Sheldon — vii
Preface — xi

Chapter 1 The Charm of Birds — 1

Chapter 2 The Great War on Birds — 32

Chapter 3 The Best Birdwatching Army Ever Sent to War — 52

Chapter 4 Birds at the Front — 75

Chapter 5 Birds and Enemy Aliens — 97

Chapter 6 The First Flying Corps — 125

Roll of Honour — 147
Appendix: The Ornithological Roll of Honour — 148
Notes — 221
Bibliography — 228
Index — 229

Acknowledgements

I would like to thank Beccy Speight and Professor Ben Sheldon for so kindly writing a foreword for this book. Both are great ambassadors for birds and I really appreciate them contributing to it. I would also like to thank the Biodiversity Heritage Library whose digital archives made much of the research for this book possible. Similarly, the Lives of the First World War digital archive run by the Imperial War Museums was an invaluable source of information for the Ornithological Roll of Honour. Finally, I would also like to thank the fantastic team at Pen and Sword, especially Chris Cocks, Laura Hirst, Lucy May and Claire Hopkins. This book is dedicated to my two grandfathers who both fought in the First World War. Herbert Reginald Milton was in the Royal Flying Corps and as a Member of the Magic Circle performed a variety of card tricks in the mess to entertain his fellow pilots and pay his bar bills. Herbert Albert Sweet was with the 1/4th Battalion, the Wiltshire Regiment and fought in Palestine, helping to capture Jerusalem under General Allenby.

Forewords

The Royal Society for the Protection of Birds has a long and proud history of campaigning for nature. In 2021 we celebrated the 100-year anniversary of the 1921 Plumage (Prohibition) Act, the result of the RSPB's first and long-running campaign against 'murderous millinery'. It was spearheaded by three female founders, their original all-woman movement being born out of frustration that the male-only British Ornithologists' Union (BOU) was not acting on the issue. So, I was fascinated to read in this book of the sad irony that it was the number of their members being killed in the First World War which finally forced the BOU to admit women, following a stormy Annual General Meeting in 1916. This was a small but significant step in women's historic struggle for equality.

The next year the Women's Army Auxiliary Corps was formed in response to the shortage of workers and the conscription of men a year earlier. Although women could not fight, they served in a wide variety of roles on the front line from doctors to ambulance drivers and on the home front from tram drivers to munition workers. Like the BOU, the War Office found out the hard way that women were indispensable to the war effort.

While the Plumage Bill had to be put on hold during the conflict, this book reveals that throughout the war the Society championed the plight of the humble house sparrow. At the start of the war, the Board of Agriculture and the National Farmers' Union announced a national cull of house sparrows, falsely accusing them of destroying the nation's wheat and oat crops. To do this, they resurrected Rat and Sparrow Clubs, formerly popular during Victorian times, and they rapidly spread throughout Britain. These cruel clubs placed a bounty on the head of every sparrow, the killing soon extending to tree sparrows and then all small birds in the countryside.

From the outset the clubs were vociferously opposed by the RSPB who fought a long running battle to ban them, slowly winning over the public to the cause. Eventually in 1918 the government told the Board of Agriculture to stop supporting the clubs after the RSPB had organized an impressive letter writing campaign and mobilized Members of Parliament. Sadly, in the century since the war, house sparrows have declined by over 70 per cent and tree sparrows by a staggering 95 per cent, in part the result of modern farming policy and methods. Consequently, both birds are now priority conservation species for the RSPB, Red-listed as Birds of Conservation Concern.

At the start of the First World War the RSPB was also presented with a very practical problem: all its tree-hole nest boxes were made in Germany. Overcoming all the obstacles of supply in wartime, it led the way in manufacturing 'British Boxes for British Birds' and distributing them to its members. The RSPB's new industry came at a time when other feathers were being increasingly seen on the streets: white feathers. Many women, barred from fighting, saw joining the White Feather Brigade as their patriotic duty, supporting their men fighting at the front by shaming those who refused to enlist. Like society as a whole, women were split on the issue of supporting the war which was reflected in the rank and file of organizations like the Women's International League of Peace and Freedom. One male victim perceptively asked why some women would shame men into joining the army while their pacifist sisters were campaigning with precisely the opposite aim of stopping the war.

From the outset of the conflict the RSPB published a series of remarkable bird reports coming back from the front in its magazine, *Bird Notes and News*. Many of these reports form the basis of this moving book. They showed only too clearly how birdwatching helped to bring joy, solace and above all hope to a generation of young men who had everything to live for but who died in their droves on the battlefields. The Ornithological Roll of Honour at the back of the book bears testimony both to their contribution to ornithology and their bravery in making the ultimate sacrifice. At a time when conflict is once again happening in Europe, it is a fitting reminder of the hope that birds can bring even in the most challenging of conditions – and that our love of birds and the fight for their survival can take different forms in different times, but above all persists.

Beccy Speight
Chief Executive Officer
Royal Society for the Protection of Birds
Sandy, May 2022

I write this in the spring of 2022 when armed conflict in Ukraine has brought sharply to mind the great wars in Europe of the twentieth century, after a sustained period of relative peace. Much has changed in the intervening period, including our understanding of bird movements and migrations. The technology that enables us to receive news and images of dreadful scenes in Ukraine almost in real time has also revolutionized our ability to understand the lives and movements of birds. Small, lightweight GPS tags enable the movement of migrating birds to be tracked by satellite. In March 2022, birdwatchers in Europe were amazed to learn that a rare Ring-billed gull, a vagrant from America that had been tagged in Poland, and then spent the winter in the Netherlands and Belgium, had made a sudden move eastward, along the Dnieper River, into the heart of the part of Ukraine that had been invaded by Russian Forces.

This small anecdote serves as an illustration of how birds, and an interest in birds, can link us to armed conflict in unexpected ways. Thinking about a Ring-billed gull migrating through the Ukraine war zone from Western Europe both reminds us about how small the globe is, and how connected we are, but also about how nature and natural processes often continue despite ongoing human events.

Nicholas Milton's fascinating book explores these themes in the light of the First World War – the Great War – from the perspective of British involvement in the conflict. He explores the role of birds in the lives of the armed forces engaged in the conflict, where observing birds and reflecting on the similarities and differences with the familiar British birds enabled some distraction from the long weeks and months at the front. A fascinating chapter deals also with the role of the Royal Society for the Protection of Birds – at the time a much smaller and younger organization than the million-member conservation powerhouse of today. The impact of birds on agriculture and food production is also explored – a serious issue a century ago when numbers of seed-eating birds in our country landscapes were much higher. Milton also spends some time exploring the impact that the life and role of birds had on some of the 'great men' of those times, notably Viscount Grey of Fallodon, Foreign Secretary at the time of the outbreak of war. Edward Grey's interest in birds sustained him through difficult times, and even enabled some gentle pre-war diplomacy when Grey led Teddy Roosevelt on a birdwatching walk in the New Forest. Grey later became Chancellor of the University of Oxford (despite his less than distinguished academic record as an undergraduate) and his life-long interest in birds meant that it was natural that a new Institute of Ornithology at the University was named after him when it was founded in 1938. That was, of course, just before another great conflict, and one of the first tasks of the fledgling institute was to carry out research into 'economic ornithology' and assess the potential impact of birds on food production as war loomed.

Nicholas Milton has written a book that illuminates the role of birds in the lives of individuals as well as encouraging contemplation of the links between today's times and those of more than a century ago: much has changed, but we still have much in common with those who lived through such turmoil.

Professor Ben Sheldon
Luc Hoffmann Professor of Field Ornithology
Edward Grey Institute
Department of Zoology
University of Oxford
Oxford, May 2022

Preface

Over a century has now passed since the end of the Great War, 'the war to end all wars', but the conflict continues to exert a powerful influence on our national consciousness. With modern technology grainy black and white images have been transformed into high-definition colour film bringing the war to life, a process exemplified by Peter Jackson's extraordinary documentary, *They Shall Not Grow Old*. This archive footage highlighted not just the senseless slaughter on the battlefield but also soldiers relaxing behind the lines and the long periods of boredom in the trenches which were so characteristic of the conflict. It was during these periods that many Tommies turned to birdwatching as a way of whiling away the long hours spent on guard duty or watching over no man's land. As a result, the hobby ranked as one of the most popular past-times for soldiers at the front, on a par with smoking, writing, games, gambling, sport and shooting rats.

The British Expeditionary Force sent to France in the late summer of 1914 has been referred to as the 'Best British Army Ever Sent to War' as it was one of the most highly trained and disciplined forces in the world. It was also the 'Best Birdwatching Army Ever Sent to War' for among its ranks were hundreds of both amateur and professional ornithologists. Many of these were officers whose interest in ornithology had been started at home or public school but all the ranks from private upwards contained experienced birders who swapped their local patch for the battlefield. With the war soon descending into stalemate, the soldiers started sending back remarkable bird reports from the field with the letters home to their families. These accounts movingly show how birdwatching helped to bring joy, solace and above all hope to a generation of young men, many of whom would never see England's 'green and pleasant land' again.

The role of birds in maintaining morale at the front was extensively reported in the newspapers, magazines and ornithological journals of the day. The list of birds seen by soldiers serving in all the theatres of war was truly impressive, ranging from the common like sparrows, skylarks and swallows to the exotic like golden orioles, hoopoes and bee-eaters. It also included many enigmatic species like nightingales whose own explosive song often competed with the guns at dawn. Remarkably, one soldier, Christopher James Alexander, who died at the Battle of Passchendaele on 5 October 1917, counted 107 species for the year, his brother writing in his obituary that it was 'a wonderful total under such conditions'.

On the battlefield birds turned up in the most unexpected places from dug outs to the woods directly in the firing line. One blackbird even built her nest on a howitzer which was being used to pound the German lines while robins, swallows and sparrows built theirs in the trenches, living cheek by jowl with the troops. Many soldiers recorded with amazement birds like partridges and harriers flying over no man's land, seemingly oblivious to the rifle fire and shell explosions all around them. The skylark in particular carried on singing regardless, its beautiful ascending song often being the last sound many mortally wounded Tommies heard above the din of battle.

It was not just on the battle front that birds found themselves in the firing line but also on the home front. As well as declaring war on Germany on 4 August 1914, the government also declared war on the humble house sparrow, farmers falsely accusing it of destroying Britain's dwindling wheat and oat supplies. To exterminate them Rat and Sparrow Clubs were resurrected by the Board of Agriculture and a bounty was put on the tiny head of every house sparrow. Clubs were formed across Britain with schoolboys and clergymen competing to see who could kill the most birds, the slaughter soon extending to all small birds in the countryside. From the outset the clubs were opposed by the fledgling Royal Society for the Protection of Birds (RSPB) who fought its own battle against the powerful Board of Agriculture, accusing it of ignoring the economic value of birds and encouraging cruelty among children. Slowly winning over the public to its cause by its campaigning work, the society finally emerged victorious and, in the process, came of age, becoming the powerful voice for conservation we know today.

Aside from the war on sparrows, birds featured in a variety of campaigns on the home front. They were used extensively in war time propaganda from cigarette cards to Christmas cards, helping to remind the troops of home and what they were fighting for. On the streets white feathers from chickens, ducks, swans and exotic birds like egrets were used by women to publicly shame young men who had not signed up, members forming the so-called White Feather Brigade. Lamentably many men were labelled as cowards or war shirkers when they were exempt on medical grounds or doing essential war work. A similar campaign was waged against anyone with a German-sounding surname, 'enemy aliens' being subject to increasing hostility like the ornithologist William Teschemaker. He bravely wrote an astonishing article on the contribution of German aviculture at the height of the war but subsequently found himself ostracized by the ornithological elite.

Birds were the subject of much war-related research; their sentient ability to detect aircraft and Zeppelin airships long before they could be seen being investigated as an avian early warning system. Seagulls underwent extensive trials as a way of detecting U-boats, championed by an eccentric Australian inventor called Thomas Mills who was so convinced it was a war-winning idea that he funded his own trials when he was rejected by the Admiralty. In the air pigeons carrying messages under fire played a crucial part in winning battles while canaries in the trenches used to detect poisonous gases often became regimental pets. In honour of their contribution and that of all the wild birds on the battlefield, the RSPB christened them 'The First Flying Corps'.

Birds provided inspiration for politicians, poets and artists who carried on despite the terrible conflict raging all around them. For the Foreign Secretary Edward Grey, who worked tirelessly to preserve the peace but ended up convincing the House of Commons to go to war, birds were his hinterland. His weekends were spent communing with nature at his cottage on the river Itchen near Winchester with his wife Dorothy. Together with his own collection of wildfowl at his ancestral home, Fallodon Hall in Northumberland, birds were his way of coping with the huge political demands placed upon him. Similarly, birds were the catalyst for some of the most evocative literature of the war, from the poems of Edward Thomas who is commemorated in Poets' Corner in Westminster Abbey to the satirical novels of Hector Munro, one of the most popular authors of Edwardian Britain. The war also inspired artists like Henry Edward Otto Murray-Dixon, a protégé of the world-famous artist Archibald Thorburn, who excelled at illustrating the RSPB's Christmas cards until he, like so many others, was killed in action.

When the guns finally fell silent on 11 November 1918 and the Great War came to an ignoble end, a generation of birdwatchers lay dead. Among them were scientists, researchers, lords, librarians, artists, authors, professors, poets, lawyers, surgeons and explorers, many young men with great promise. Had they lived, the science of ornithology and the hobby of birdwatching would have undoubtedly been much the richer. A selection of them is included in the Ornithological Roll of Honour at the back of this book, their names now engraved on cold stone in the many cemeteries and memorials to the dead scattered through Europe, the Middle East and Asia. These long lists of the fallen, while showing the scale of the sacrifice and honouring the dead, cannot tell their tales which have mostly been lost with the passage of time. By piecing together a small number of their stories, I hope to give their brief lives meaning once again and inspire a new generation of birdwatchers to tread in their footsteps.

Chapter 1

The Charm of Birds

As dusk gathered across Westminster on Monday, 3 August 1914, the Foreign Secretary, Edward Grey, stared down at the darkening street below him lost in thought. From his office window he could just about make out a man dressed in a flat cap and dirty overalls carrying a ladder over his shoulder. Stopping in front of the imposing façade of the Foreign Office, the man put his ladder up against a gas lamp. Squinting to get a better view, Grey's eyes struggled to make out the shadowy figure in the failing light.

What Grey knew that late summer evening was that Britain stood on the cusp of war. What he didn't know was that over the next four years he would witness a whole generation of young men slaughtered in the bloodiest conflict in British history. Grey's anguish over the coming conflict was heightened by the fact that he was hiding a dark personal secret. Suffering from advanced macular degeneration, he was slowly but surely going blind in the service of the country he loved.

As Grey stared out of his window, across the road a flock of gulls landed on the island in the centre of St James's Park. There they squabbled noisily, jockeying for position at that evening's roost. At the lake margin a skulking moorhen, unnerved by the commotion, gave out its short, sharp alarm call. In the middle of the water over twenty different species of wildfowl, including mallards, tufted ducks, pochards and shovelers, tried to settle down for the night. With the light fading, their calls echoed eerily around the park, competing with its most famous residents, the pelicans, who had been given to King Charles II as a gift by the Russian ambassador in 1664.

All the birds in St James's Park were familiar to Grey who had his own unique wildfowl collection at his home, Fallodon Hall, in Northumberland. It was a bird collection he had started in his youth and was his pride and joy. So, when he was in London, he was a regular visitor to the park and the picturesque lodge belonging to the Bird Keeper, Thomas Hinton, appropriately enough called Duck Island Cottage. That evening, though, his mind was far from the birds he loved. Instead, it lingered on the historic speech he had given earlier that day in Parliament.

In the face of German aggression, he had made the case for Britain honouring its Entente Cordiale with France. To a packed and solemn House of Commons, he had declared:

> Last week I stated that we were working for peace not only for this country, but to preserve the peace of Europe. Today events move so rapidly that it is exceedingly difficult to state with technical accuracy the actual state of affairs but is clear that the peace of Europe cannot be preserved. Russia and Germany, at any rate, have declared war upon one another.[1]

The dilemma facing the House of Commons that fateful day was whether or not Britain should stand by its neighbour and friend France. If it did war with Germany would be inevitable. Members were divided on the issue so to make the government's case Grey skilfully appealed to their consciences, stating, 'How far that friendship entails obligation – it has been a friendship between the nations and ratified by the nations – how far that entails an obligation, let every man look into his own heart, and his own feelings and construe the extent of the obligation for himself.'[2]

Yet he left members in little doubt what, in his opinion, that obligation meant. As MPs looked on in silence, he added:

> My own feeling is that if a foreign fleet engaged in a war which France had not sought, and in which she had not been the aggressor, came down the English Channel, and bombarded and battered the undefended coasts of France, we could not stand aside and see this going on practically within sight of our eyes, with our arms folded, looking on dispassionately, doing nothing!

At this the Commons broke into applause, many members waving their order papers. Summing up the government's efforts to secure a peaceful settlement with Germany, he concluded:

We worked for peace up to the last moment, and beyond the last moment. How hard, how persistently, and how earnestly we strove for peace last week the House will see from the papers before it. But that is over, as far as the peace of Europe is concerned. We are now face to face with a situation and all the consequences which it may yet have to unfold.[3]

By the time of his speech Grey had been Foreign Secretary for nearly nine years, the longest tenure of any politician who had occupied that great office of state. In the debate that afternoon he had used all his political experience to make the case for standing by France in a way which would bring together a divided House of Commons. It was widely recognized as the greatest speech of his political career but as he was addressing members that afternoon Germany had declared war on France and the next day German troops would invade Belgium.

Now back in his office Grey watched on in silence as the lamplighter climbed up the ladder, unhooking the cast-iron shade and putting a flame to the gas, lighting up the street below. Despite all his efforts to maintain peace, Grey knew Britain would soon be at war. In the office with him that evening was John Spender, the editor of the *Westminster Gazette*. Turning to his friend, Grey lamented, 'The lamps are going out all over Europe; we shall not see them lit again in our lifetime.'[4] The phrase would later ensure Grey's place in history but at the time his mood darkened still further as he contemplated the forthcoming conflict. Later that evening when a member of the Foreign Office staff came into his office and praised his speech, Grey turned on him angrily, pounded his fist on the table, and shouted three times, 'I hate war'.

Grey's reputation had been built on his ability to pursue British interests while keeping a fragile peace but now that lay in tatters and he was bereft. A tall, handsome man with aquiline features, he was known for speaking in a steady, passionless voice. The American ambassador, Walter Hines Page (1855–1918), described him as 'a moderate, patient, wise man'. Yet to his critics Grey was out of his depth in the emergency, lacking the diplomatic skills to reconcile the warring sides. Theodor Wolff, the German editor of the liberal *Berliner Tageblatt* newspaper, wrote:

But the idea of bringing the two estranged nations together, and so assuring the peace of Europe, was too odd for Sir Edward Grey to entertain; every weekday he industriously attended to business, with no plan and little imagination, and he did not observe the current of the times with the same loving comprehension as he did his trout stream on Sunday.[5]

To Grey his speech that day to the House of Commons was a long and agonizing admission of diplomatic failure. But if Grey found himself wanting, it was not a view shared by his Prime Minister. Afterwards Herbert Henry Asquith commended his Foreign Secretary's efforts to keep the peace with sincere words of praise rarely heard in the House of Commons:

> the papers which have since been presented to Parliament, and which are now in the hands of honourable Members, will, I think, show how strenuous, how unremitting, how persistent, even when the last glimmer of hope seemed to have faded away, were the efforts of my right honourable friend to secure for Europe an honourable and lasting peace ... If his efforts upon this occasion have, unhappily been less [than] successful, I am certain that this House and the country, and I will add posterity and history, will accord him what is, after all, the best tribute that can be paid to any statesman: that, never derogating for an instant or by an inch from the honour and interests of his own country, he has striven, as few men would have striven, to maintain and preserve the greatest interest of all countries – universal peace.[6]

With the outbreak of war many parliamentary bills were put on hold including one that was very close to Grey's heart – the Plumage Bill. Introduced by Lord Avebury in 1908, it had returned to the House of Commons in 1913 and sought to outlaw the trade in plumes or feathers which were then widely used to adorn women's hats. Having passed both its first and second reading, the bill only required one more stage to become law. For the RSPB the delay caused by the onset of war was a bitter blow and it called a meeting to discuss it. Grey sympathized but due to pressures of work gave his apologies, stating:

> I am very sorry that it is impossible for me to come to the meeting; I must be in the House of Commons that afternoon at the time

when the meeting is to be held. I am, of course, strongly in favour of the Plumage Bill. I cannot see that any of the suggestions that have been made for alternative measures would be as effective as this Bill: indeed, it seems to me that they would all be ineffective. The need for some step to be taken to stop the wholesale killing of birds for the sake of their plumage, especially in the breeding season, is urgent, and the Plumage Bill is the best contribution that we ourselves can make to this object.[7]

Grey could not attend the meeting because all his time and energy was focused on preventing war. For years he had been trying to maintain the peace of Europe against a backdrop of steadily escalating tension in Western Europe and the Balkans. Now in his own eyes he had failed and the following day, Tuesday 4 August 1914, Asquith declared war on Germany. After the start of the war, Grey's diplomatic skills would be less and less in demand by a country which was fighting for its very survival. Mentally and physically drained by the conflict, he would eventually step down just over two years later, in December 1916. Like the destruction wrought on the countryside of Belgium and northern France, the declaration of war would also devastate Grey's wildfowl collection and his favourite birdwatching haunt, St James's Park.

* * *

Edward Grey was born in 1862, the eldest son of seven children born to George Henry Grey and his wife Harriet Jane Pearson. The family were wealthy and well connected, coming from a long line of Greys who had served their country at the very highest levels of government. His father was a colonel in the Rifle Brigade, serving in both the Crimea and West Indies before later becoming an equerry to the Prince of Wales. His deeply religious mother was the daughter of an army officer, her family coming from generations of clergy. So Grey was born into a dynasty, one forged by empire, religion and service.

After Edward was born a succession of children quickly followed over the next twelve years, Alice in 1865, George in 1867, Jane in 1869, Alexander in 1870, Mary in 1872 and Charles in 1874. The Grey family lived at Fallodon Hall, near Alnwick in Northumberland, a stately home with large, sprawling grounds covering 2,000 acres. Located in the northeast of Northumberland, Grey described it as being:

> on stiff clay soil, at no great altitude above sea-level, from which it is separated by some two miles of exposed land, now mostly grass. A high ridge of moor lies three miles to west. Near the house are sheltering woods, and in the grounds are two ponds and plenty of shrubs: in short, a place attractive to birds, but with no unusual characteristics.[8]

Fallodon Hall was also the birthplace of Grey's most famous relative, Charles Grey (1764–1845), who became Prime Minister in 1830 and gave his name to Earl Grey tea (Charles was his great-great-uncle). In 1838 a statue and a road were named after him in the centre of Newcastle upon Tyne. It commemorated his greatest achievement, the passing of the Great Reform Act of 1832. The statue, Grey's Monument, has Charles Grey standing on top of a 130-feet-high column clutching the Act; erected at the head of Grey's Road, the main inscription on the pedestal reads:

> THIS COLUMN WAS ERECTED IN 1838
> TO COMMEMORATE
> THE SERVICES RENDERED TO HIS COUNTRY BY
> CHARLES EARL GREY K.G. [KNIGHT OF THE GARTER]
> WHO, DURING AN ACTIVE POLITICAL CAREER OF
> NEARLY HALF A CENTURY, WAS THE CONSTANT
> ADVOCATE OF PEACE AND THE FEARLESS AND
> CONSISTENT CHAMPION OF
> CIVIL AND RELIGIOUS LIBERTY.
> HE FIRST DIRECTED HIS EFFORTS TO THE
> AMENDMENT OF THE REPRESENTATION OF THE
> PEOPLE IN 1792,
> AND WAS THE MINISTER
> BY WHOSE ADVICE, AND UNDER WHOSE GUIDANCE,
> THE GREAT MEASURE OF PARLIAMENTARY
> REFORM WAS AFTER AN ARDUOUS AND
> PROTRACTED STRUGGLE
> SAFELY AND TRIUMPHANTLY ACHIEVED
> IN THE YEAR 1832.[9]

The Great Reform Act or Representation of the People Act 1832 introduced wide-ranging changes to the electoral system of England and Wales and is generally credited with launching our modern democracy. The Act was highly controversial because it sought, in the words of the day, to 'take effectual Measures for correcting divers Abuses that have long prevailed in the Choice of Members to serve in the Commons House of Parliament'. The Act granted seats in the House of Commons to large cities that had sprung up during the Industrial Revolution and removed seats from some of the smaller boroughs which were controlled by wealthy landowners. The Act also increased the electorate from about 400,000 to 650,000, making about one in five adult males eligible to vote.

Charles Grey died in 1845, seventeen years before Edward Grey was born, but his proud father would take Grey and his siblings to see the statue and discuss how their family had helped to extend voting to great industrialized cities like Newcastle which were the heart of Victorian Britain. However, Grey showed little interest in the illustrious past of his family and instead loved nothing more than roaming the grounds of Fallodon Hall where he would spend hours playing by the ponds and exploring the surrounding woods. This happy childhood came to an abrupt end when, at the age of just 12, his father died of pneumonia while Grey was away at preparatory school. It then fell to him and his grandfather, Sir George Grey (1799–1882), the 2nd Baronet of Fallodon, to become the 'men of the family' and look after his mother and his six siblings. As a result, Grey grew up quickly and learnt early on in his life that even money and privilege cannot buy happiness.

Grey's grandfather was a devout Christian and an MP for forty years who rose to become home secretary three times. In Parliament he championed the plight of the poor, introducing a Private Members' Bill requiring the building of public baths and wash houses in all major towns. He also took part in all the popular rural pursuits of the day including hunting, shooting and fishing. Without a father figure, Grey took his grandson under his wing, and taught him everything there was to know about estate management. Recalling the relationship much later on in life, Grey singled out his grandparents love of rural life and the long country walks they enjoyed together as being his happiest childhood memories.

Despite growing up in the countryside, Grey's love of birds did not come from either his parents or his grandparents who knew little about ornithology. Reflecting on their lack of knowledge during his childhood, Grey wrote:

> Nevertheless though my father lived a country life and was fond of all sorts of country sport, of farming and of woods and fields, I do not remember that he had any individual knowledge of bird songs ... No one seemed interested in the songs of birds. My parents or grandparents would perhaps remark, 'How well the blackbirds and thrushes are singing' or take some favourable notice of the fact that birds were singing, but it would be quite a general remark, and it is not probable that they knew the distinction between the song of a thrush and that of a blackbird, which they classed together.

Instead, Grey taught himself about a few of the common birds 'by appearance or name' but still 'arrived at the age of manhood knowing only two songs of individual birds: one was the robin, whose tameness and persistence in singing when there is hardly another song to be heard force everyone to know his voice: the other was 'thrushes-and-blackbirds', between which I could not distinguish and which for the purpose of song represented to me one species.'[10]

During his long school holidays Grey developed a passion for fishing and whenever the opportunity arose, he would disappear with a short line to catch firstly sticklebacks, then eels and later brown trout in the cold, fast-flowing burns and rivers near his home. In one of his books, the *Fallodon Papers*, Grey recalled fondly his early obsession with fishing:

> As a boy the real angler will fish for sticklebacks or eels, if he can get nothing better; the watching of a float will be to him a matter of undeviating attention and interest; the bobbing of the float when a fish bites will cause him excitement; the thrill that he will feel when a fish is hooked and being played is indescribable; and the capture of a fish of relatively large size will produce exhalation; the loss of such a fish after hooking it will afflict him with intolerable anguish. After a successful day, he will be in a glow of beatitude, but blank days will not dull the edge of keenness.[11]

After prepatory school Grey was sent to Winchester College, arriving there in September 1876. Here he cut a somewhat solitary figure, taking little interest in his studies and struggling academically. However, he took like a duck to water to the fly-fishing on the meandering chalk streams of Hampshire with their crystal-clear water and abundant fish life, writing, 'Many things are taught at public schools, but Winchester is probably the only school at which the most scientific and highly developed form of angling can be learnt.'[12] He also excelled at sport, playing cricket, fives and racquets, later becoming a champion tennis player.

Following Winchester, in 1880 Grey was accepted by Oxford University where he studied the classics at Balliol College. Among its former pupils was the future Prime Minister Herbert Henry Asquith (1852–1928) who Grey would much later serve under with such distinction. Although a decade separated them, an important part of the close bond that both men shared came from their time and experiences at the college. At Balliol Grey again struggled with his studies so when he returned home during the summer holiday, his grandfather organized for him to see a tutor by the name of Mandell Creighton (1843–1901). He was a local vicar in the nearby village of Embleton and was a historian, prolific author and a radical Liberal who would go on to be the first Professor of Ecclesiastical History at Cambridge University and the Bishop of London. As well as teaching Grey about the classics, Creighton also discussed politics and soon Grey, who had exhibited no real interest in politics until this point, became fascinated by the big political issues of the day, later adopting his mentor's radical liberal views.

The next year, 1882, Grey suffered another sad loss when his grandfather Sir George Grey died. It left him as the sole head of the household and he inherited the viscountcy, becoming the 1st Viscount of Fallodon. Despite his grandfather's wish that Grey study hard, he still found the classics dull and instead would spend his time fishing or playing sport. Often truant, he would bunk off lectures and frequently fail to hand in his assignments on time. Finally, in January 1884, his indolence and contempt for academic life resulted in Balliol expelling him for 'idleness', a process known at Oxford University as 'rustication'. To his mother's consternation, Grey was sent down for three months to consider his future and returned cap in hand to Fallodon Hall. However, far from being crestfallen, Grey decided it was an ideal opportunity to pursue his hobbies and gain some valuable political experience.

With his mentor's encouragement Grey now aspired to be a politician but he lacked any experience or understanding of Westminster politics. To get some Creighton suggested he get in touch with his great-uncle, Lord Northbrook. He was then serving in Prime Minister William Gladstone's government as the First Lord of the Admiralty. During Grey's rustication, Northbrook arranged for him to be private secretary to Sir Evelyn Baring, the colonial administrator of Egypt and his second cousin. Later he got him an even more prestigious role as secretary to the Chancellor of the Exchequer, Hugh Childers (1827–1896). The experience proved invaluable and confirmed to Grey that he wanted to pursue a career in politics.

Creighton was not only his academic mentor but also became Grey's close personal friend, confidant and matchmaker. Believing the boy needed a steadying influence in his life, he set Grey up with his future wife, Dorothy Widdington. Arranging for him to go on a first date with her, they met at a hunt with the Percy foxhounds and from the outset there was a strong mutual attraction. She came from a long line of Conservatives but was a good match for Grey, both in temperament and interests. Dorothy's first great love was the countryside and by the time they met she was already an experienced ornithologist who knew many birds by their song.

Grey also became involved with his local Liberal Party who were campaigning in favour of extending the vote from the towns to the countryside. Well aware that the Grey family name was still closely associated with the Great Reform Act of 1832, they invited him along to their meetings where he joined in discussing the great political issues of the day from the economy to foreign policy. In 1880, William Gladstone (1809–98) had been re-elected as prime minster for a second time and his government had put forward the 'Representation of the People's Bill' which proposed extending voting to rural areas but it had proved extremely controversial. In particular, the move was deeply opposed by the House of Lords whose stance caused widespread protests throughout the countryside.

One of these demonstrations was held in the market town of Alnwick near Fallodon where a large crowd had gathered to hear the debate.

Grey went along to the meeting to show his support and being well known locally was asked to speak in favour of the bill. The speech he made in favour of extending the vote so impressed those present that afterwards he was asked to stand as a Liberal candidate at the next general election. Believing his name would be a great asset on the doorstep, he was duly selected to fight the seat of Berwick-upon-Tweed against the incumbent Conservative MP, Henry Percy (1846-1918), the 7th Duke of Northumberland.[13]

Percy had first entered Parliament in 1868 and over the years had built up a formidable reputation among the electorate based on his family name and connections. His family derived from a long line of Earls of Northumberland, one of the most powerful dynasties in northern England. His connections ensured he was an influential, if aloof, MP who from 1874/5 held the prestigious position of Treasurer of the Royal Household. In the previous general election in 1880 he had easily beaten the Liberal candidate John Clay, polling 2,163 votes to Clay's 1,509. However, Percy opposed extending the vote and this put him firmly at odds with Grey who believed strongly that the Lords were seeking to deprive ordinary rural people of the vote.

Grey's expulsion from Balliol, as well as being good for him politically, was also to be the start of his lifelong passion for birds. He had first become interested in wildfowl in his youth when like many other wealthy landowners he would shoot ducks in his grounds and the surrounding countryside. But one day he had picked up a dead bird and instead of putting it into his bag decided to examine it in detail. Spreading out its wings, Grey marvelled at the perfection of each feather which was made from keratin, the same material his nails and hair were made from. Running his fingers slowly through the barbs radiating from the central quill, Grey saw that each was held in place by tiny velcro-like fasteners. Bowled over by its beauty, Grey made a vow to himself to give up shooting birds and instead to conserve them.

So Grey decided to start his own wildfowl collection during his rustication, buying his first five pairs of ducks from local wildfowlers. He brought them back to Fallodon Hall and released them on the two ponds in the grounds. To keep the ducks safe he surrounded the ponds with a foxproof fence, also planting shrubs around the outside to ensure the birds were not disturbed, writing:

In the enclosure you must have quiet, because waterfowl spend, in the early spring when they are in pairs, some weeks looking about for nesting-places, cautiously and quietly by themselves, and if they find that they are watched, or you should come suddenly upon them, and they are disturbed, they will not select that nesting-place, and will not nest at all.[14]

Grey realized that birds, like other animals, would only stay if there was a constant food supply so he also made sure that they were fed every day. At the end of his expulsion Grey entrusted the care of his precious collection to his faithful gardener, Mr Henderson.

By the time Grey returned to Oxford in the late summer of 1884, he had found the two great loves of life: Dorothy and birds. During the time he was away Grey had successfully argued the case for changing his course from the classics to law, the master of Balliol, Benjamin Jowett, hoping it would help him to get a good degree. Despite this, Grey found the change of course difficult academically and finished his troubled time at Balliol college by scraping a third-class honours degree in law.

While he was finishing university, the political landscape had been transformed. The Representation of the People Act, which the Gladstone government had passed in December 1884, had extended the vote to all counties throughout the United Kingdom, including Northumberland. Like the Reform Act of 1832, it ushered in great changes to the political system. It meant that for the first time a majority of adult males could vote and established the modern one-member constituency for Parliamentary elections.

The next year, 1885, was a pivotal one in Grey's life, both personally and politically. That year he married Dorothy although they had a far from conventional relationship. Dorothy did not enjoy sex and didn't want or couldn't have children. So, despite being very close to Grey, she eschewed the physical side of their marriage. Instead, they had an open relationship with a mutual understanding that if Grey had affairs, he would keep them private. Although their marriage was celibate, it was a happy one born out of their shared love for each other and the countryside (friends believed Grey had several serious affairs during his marriage and fathered a couple of illegitimate children but always remained committed to Dorothy). She was also supportive of his political career although she had no interest in politics helping Grey run a general election campaign championing the new rights of the majority of the adult population to vote. It was a message which resonated well with young voters and also had the desired effect of castigating his political opponent, Earl Percy, as being out of touch and unrepresentative.

When the election finally came, from 24 November to 18 December 1885, Grey polled over 4,600 votes easily beating Percy who received just over 3,500 votes. It was a stunning victory and at the tender age of just 23, Grey became the Liberal MP for Berwick-upon-Tweed and the second-youngest member of the House of Commons (Grey would hold on to the seat throughout his political life for 31 years until he entered the House of Lords in 1916). However, for the Liberal Party the general election result was less joyous, they winning the largest number of seats but remaining bitterly divided over Irish Home Rule. As a result, another election quickly followed the next year, Grey winning again but the Liberals losing power to the Conservatives who then governed with a breakaway unionist wing of the Liberal Party.

As his political career flourished, so Grey was able to invest more money in his wildfowl collection at Fallodon. Over the years he would build up an impressive collection of ducks from Britain and around the world, listing them with great pride in his book, *The Charm of Birds*. Resident birds included the mallard, wigeon, pintail, shoveler, garganey, teal, tufted duck, common pochard and red-crested pochard. Internationally the collection included the spotted-bill duck from India, the blue-winged and Carolina wood ducks from North America, the Bahaman pintail, the Chinese Mandarin duck, the Japanese teal, the Siberian falcated duck and from South America the Brazilian teal, Chilean wigeon, pintail and teal, rosy-billed pochard and the versicolor teal.[15]

From 1886 until 1905, Grey would meticulously record their breeding success in *The Fallodon Green Book*, documenting the number of young reared by each species and their nesting habits. It would be a passion matched only by his love of reading, particularly the works of the romantic poet William Wordsworth. Later on in life, Grey recalled how character-forming being expelled from Balliol had been and the joy that birds had brought him, commenting:

I bought my first five pairs of waterfowl, which afterwards became a great interest in life, and I remember finding it extraordinary the opinion of one of my Oxford friends that I should have been bored at home, when on the contrary I had not been conscious of one dull moment. This fact was the first thing that gave me some idea that I was different from other people in this respect.[16]

When Grey took up his seat in the House Commons in 1885, he and Dorothy moved to Hereford Square in Kensington where she was expected to move in political circles, organize meetings and attend parties with other aspiring Westminster wives. However, Dorothy found political life tedious and missed more and more the countryside where she had grown up. Consequently she shunned the high life, instead telling Grey she wanted to return to her rural roots. So, in 1890, Grey decided to build his own angling cottage on the River Itchen near Winchester, his old fishing grounds from his time as a pupil at Winchester College. It was an astute move which probably saved both his marriage and his sanity, here Dorothy finding a rural idyll which reminded her of home and Grey a place where he could escape the pressures of political life.

Michael Waterstone, Grey's biographer, described how pivotal the cottage was in both their lives:

The Cottage provided for her [Dorothy's] every need: peace, solitude, breathtaking scenery, invigorating walks and abundant wildlife ... She adored the water meadows in the valley facing the Cottage, spending much of the early summer months alone on the Itchen, reading and enjoying the myriad of birds. For Grey, The Cottage began as a base camp for his fishing, but in time it also became a welcome weekend refuge from the stresses of office. It was in this lush valley that he received his education on birdlife from Dorothy and honed his skills in deciphering the songs of the summer warblers.[17]

'The Cottage' was a rather grandiose name for what was actually a glorified cabin, its walls covered in creepers and climbers like honeysuckle and clematis. But it was comfortable and provided a base from which they could explore the river and the surrounding countryside while enjoying the wildlife on their doorstep. For Grey this included following the fortunes of a pair of long-tailed tits as they raised a family. Gregarious and noisy birds, they are easily recognized because of their distinctive undulating flight and tails which, as their name suggests, are much longer than their bodies.

Grey had first come across them during the winter roving through the woods and hedgerows in small, excitable flocks. By the spring the long-tailed tits had paired off and a couple had begun nest-building right outside his door. 'One Sunday morning before the middle of March I observed from the window a pair of long-tailed tits building their nest in a sweet-briar hedge,' Grey wrote in the *Fallodon Papers*.[18] 'If you will look closely you will see about that time they have some little nesting material in their beaks and if you watch them you will see them going to the nest and you can locate it.' Recording how the birds built their intricate cup-shaped nest, Grey took great pleasure in watching the pair flying back and forth to line it with feathers, moss, spider's webs and lichens. Described it as being 'like a bag with a hole near the top', he wrote, 'I have been told that the feathers used in the lining of a long-tailed tit's nest have been counted to number more than nine hundred. That seems incredible.'

What Grey particularly admired about the long-tailed tits was that they seemed oblivious to his presence, so he could follow their fortunes without disturbing them. 'Whether they think they are so small that you do not see them or whether they are so intensely busy in their work,' he wrote, 'it so happens that they are not at all shy, and you can stand at a distance of three yards from the nest quite openly and watch them build.' Grey closely followed the success of the brood until all the young finally fledged, writing, 'During all those weeks, when I could be there, the nest was a subject of interest to me, and many of you living in the country may have the same experience provided that you will yourselves, and are able to induce other people to observe the rule, not to disturb or destroy.'

After a while both Grey and Dorothy began to keep a detailed diary of their life at The Cottage chronicling the changing seasons and the wildlife they encountered in the surrounding countryside. His entries would be marked by an E, hers by a D. Their cottage year would start in early March with the onset of spring and carry on until the end of summer in late August, after which they would spend the winter at Fallodon and in London. One of the first entries in 1894 tells how they found the nest of the kingfisher. Grey wrote on 7–9 April:

> E: On Saturday I walked from Winchester in the afternoon and saw wheatears, a redstart, a whichat and heard my first willow wren [willow warbler]. We heard two kingfishers making a great noise behind a willow blown up by the roots at the other side of the meadow opposite the cottage. On Monday, after I had gone to London, D. found the nest and saw small fish brought to the hole: she says that only one bird feeds and the other watches.[19]

For Grey The Cottage was a hinterland where he could retreat from political life; for Dorothy it was a wonderland where she could commune with nature unhindered by the troubles of the world. Grey would often arrive there very late on Friday evening, having taken the last train from London and would then depart on a Sunday evening back to the House of Commons, only spending longer periods there while on holiday. In contrast, during the spring and summer Dorothy would spend protracted periods at the cottage on her own, finding nests along the River Itchen or identifying the plants which grew in profusion in the surrounding water meadows. Visitors were rare, Grey and his wife preferring their own company and the solitude which their cottage offered.

The diary paints a picture of a rural idyll rich in wildlife, much of which has been lost today and is also a wonderfully evocative account of the peace and solace that studying nature can bring. The birds Grey found there included the now rare nightingale, whose explosive and exquisite song has inspired so many writers and poets. However, unlike John Keats whose 'Ode to a Nightingale' waxes lyrical about its celebrated song, Grey thought there was room for improvement in its repertoire. 'A nightingale's song is the most wonderful, but the most imperfect, of songs,' he wrote on 28 April 1894. 'The long notes are divine, but they come seldom, and never go on long enough: the song continually breaks out with a burst, which promises a fine spell, but it is always broken off in the most disappointing way.' Later on in the season, though, Dorothy helped to revise his opinion about their musical abilities, he writing on 5 May, 'They seem to sing more continuously now than when they first came, which makes the song more satisfactory than when there were such long intervals between the notes.'

He concluded 'The song of birds, the set performance, variety, and musical quality, for instance of a nightingale or a song-thrush or a starling, surpass similar efforts in all other orders of life, excepting only that of mankind.'

Occasionally both Grey and Dorothy would take in injured or young birds, trying to give nature a helping hand. On 19 May 1894, Grey updated the diary about the long-tailed tits which he had watched nest build in March, writing:

> The female did not bring the young ones out till the 17th of May. D found them all in a row on a branch in the hedge, except one weakling, which was in the grass calling. There were nine altogether; we caught the weak one and fed it with flies and aphids. It had no fear, but no idea of feeding itself, and we think it certainly lost the others and died.

Although the cottage was his refuge from the stresses of Westminster life, Grey could never entirely escape from politics and he would sometimes have to rush back early to the House of Commons to make a statement on foreign affairs. In contrast, Dorothy refused point blank to go back to London, even for state occasions. Mostly though they had weekends to themselves and revelled in the tranquillity of their rural retreat, whiling away the days discovering the wildlife that was all around them. On 11–13 May 1895, Grey wrote:

> The great find however of this week is a cuckoo's egg in a dunnock's nest in the wild park: it is a brown sort of egg not the least like the dunnock's and larger. Close to it is a finished nest, just like the whitethroats, but so much in the nightingale part that we have faint hopes of finding nightingales eggs in it, when we come back.

Both Grey and Dorothy would dedicate many hours to looking for nests of different species but they took particular pride in being able to find the elusive nightingale's nest. However, sometimes the bird was so secretive that it would elude even Dorothy, much to her frustration. 'Have not succeeded in finding a nightingale nest and felt very low about it,' she wrote on 20 May 1895, adding, 'I was sitting on a tree root in a wet place watching wagtails when a stoat put its head out of a hole about two inches off my dress, hissed and made a noise like a loud harsh water-hen several times and then got quiet.'

Grey so enjoyed his time at The Cottage that he would even turn down great political occasions that fell on weekends so he could be with Dorothy and explore the wildlife along the river. On 25 and 26 May, he wrote 'Hawthorn fully out. Chestnuts passing away. Our garden warblers have left us. I refused the Queen's birthday in London and came here and have been rewarded by two splendid days, bright and up to 68 [degrees].' Although enchanted by all the wildlife, they would particularly revel in finding rare species, he writing on 7 June, 'the great event in bird life for us this year has been the nesting of a pair of red-backed shrikes in the chalk pit. D. found the nest, there are five eggs and the cock visits the nest occasionally, I suppose to find the hen.'

As a result of Dorothy's expert tutelage, over time Grey became an accomplished ornithologist in his own right, as witnessed by his entry from The Cottage diary dated 15–18 May, 1896: 'A little bird with a monotonous and rapid note has plagued me all these days: I have spent hours sitting opposite or under it without ever getting a really good sight of it, but I think it is a lesser whitethroat [The lesser whitethroat is a frustratingly difficult bird to identify in the field, it rarely emerging from deep cover. Its song is also rarely heard, unlike its much more common relative the whitethroat].'

Grey and his wife kept a detailed diary of their forays and wildlife observations from 1894 until the end of 1905 when the entries became more sporadic. Grey's last entry was on 20 November 1905 when he fatefully wrote, 'It is not known why our book has been so much neglected. I haven't had many days here, only weekends, but there has been a lot of these and D. has been here continually. Perhaps we are too well and strong to be properly grateful.' Three months later in February 1906 the Greys' idyllic rural life came to a tragic end when Dorothy was thrown from a horse-drawn carriage she was travelling in and killed. Following her untimely death, Grey stopped writing in the diary, finding the experience too painful. However, in memory of her he published it privately three years later with the title *The Cottage Book*, printing a limited number of copies for family and friends.

* * *

In December 1905, just a few months before Dorothy's premature death, Grey had become Foreign Secretary, following Arthur Balfour (1848–1930), the Conservative leader, resigning as Prime Minister. As a result, Grey's Liberal Party who had not been in government since the election of 1885 suddenly found themselves returned to power when at the prompting of the King, Edward VII, Henry Campbell-Bannerman (1836–1908) formed a minority government. On taking up the premiership, Campbell-Bannerman or 'C. B.' was already aged 69, having previously served as Secretary of State for War twice. The First Lord of the Treasury to be officially called 'Prime Minister', due to his age, he remains the only person to hold both the positions of Prime Minister and Father of the House (the member with the longest continuous service) at the same time.

From the outset Grey believed Campbell-Bannerman lacked the leadership skills to modernize the country. In turn Campbell-Bannerman was reluctant to make Grey Foreign Secretary because of 'his ignorance of foreign countries and foreign languages', a judgment derived from his belief that Grey's only continental trip had been 'two glum days in Paris'. So, Grey controversially decided to stage a coup against the elderly Prime Minister, hoping to replace him with his fellow Balliol student Henry Herbert Asquith. Conspiring with Asquith and another close ally, Richard Haldane, they came up with a plan to force a vote of confidence in Campbell-Bannerman, hoping he would retire to the House of Lords. Together the three conspirators became known as the Relugas Compact, named after a Scottish village where the plotters met in a fishing cottage owned by Grey. However, the plot failed after Bannerman got wind of it and to appease the conspirators offered them all Cabinet positions, Grey eventually accepting and becoming Foreign Secretary, Asquith Chancellor of the Exchequer and Haldane Secretary of State for War.

When he was appointed Foreign Secretary, Grey was the first person holding the office to sit in the Commons, rather than the Lords, since 1868. It was a huge honour and a great personal achievement, his only regret being that his mother who had died earlier that year was not there to witness it. Months later Campbell-Bannerman led the Liberal Party to a landslide victory over the Conservatives at the 1906 general election, the last time the Liberals would gain an overall majority in the House of Commons. However, he was dogged by ill health during his term of office, suffering a series of heart attacks. He finally resigned from office on 3 April 1908, dying just over two weeks later on 22 April 1908. Asquith then became Prime Minister, Campbell-Bannerman going down in history as the only Prime Minister ever to die in 10 Downing Street.

Grey's tenure as Foreign Secretary under Asquith would be the pinnacle of his career, he helping to keep a fragile peace against the backdrop of escalating tension with Germany, France, Russia, Morocco and Austria-Hungary. However, it wouldn't be his diplomatic but his birdwatching skills which would be called upon two years later when Britain had to host a very special visit from one of the great statesman of the age, the former US President Theodore Roosevelt (1858–1919). The 26th President of the United States, Teddy or 'T. R.', was just 42 years old when he occupied the White House, the youngest person ever to hold the presidency. Serving from 1901 to 1908, he had been elected on a platform of peace, prosperity and conservation, encompassed in his so-called 'Square Deal'. Like Grey, Roosevelt was a passionate conservationist and during his time in office established many new national parks, forests and monuments to preserve America's natural heritage.

Roosevelt arrived in England in the summer of 1910 as part of a long foreign tour combining politics and pleasure. The visit was widely covered in the British press where he was still admired as one of the great reforming US presidents and a key ally of the British Empire. However, the trip proved a diplomatic challenge for the British government because Roosevelt was no longer in office but his stay still needed to have all the trappings of an official state visit. For his part as a keen ornithologist Roosevelt had complicated the trip further by requesting a day birdwatching at the end of the visit so he could familiarize himself with Britain's birds. The usual diplomatic dilemma facing the British government was easily solved as there was only one Cabinet member with the skills and knowledge to pull it off: Edward Grey. After prevaricating about how it would play with the sitting president, Asquith eventually asked Grey if he would host Roosevelt's visit. Recalling the trip in his autobiography, *Twenty-Five Years*, Grey wrote:

> He had not heard the songs of British birds and would time his visit so as to be in England at the time of the singing of the birds. He would like it to be arranged that someone, who knew the songs of

birds, should spend a day walking with him and naming the songs as they were heard. In youth I had spent much time in identifying the songs of different species; hearing and recognizing them had been a pleasure kept up every year, and all the common songs were familiar to me. I therefore replied that I should be glad to do this service, and probably I named May as the best month for the purpose.[20]

Grey prepared for the visit by honing his birdwatching skills but was told Roosevelt's arrival had been delayed until June. On the tour, which took in Africa and Europe, Roosevelt had greatly enjoyed a big-game expedition to British East Africa (now Kenya), hosted by the 'great white hunter', Frederick Selous (1851–1917), who would later be killed in the war (see Ornithological Roll of Honour). He had then taken longer than expected travelling up through the Sudan and Egypt before finally arriving in Europe. On his eventual arrival, Roosevelt's private office had decided that his itinerary was too full to include the birdwatching trip. However, the former president was adamant that it must go ahead. 'It required a whole day to be set apart for it, and the last day of his visit was the only opportunity,' recalled Grey. 'That postponed the walk till well into June, but the weather was good singing weather, grey and moist, and not hot and dry, and the birds sang well.'

The location chosen for the walk was the New Forest, home to a wide variety of British birds including rare species like the Dartford warbler, the crossbill and the woodlark. Roosevelt was keen to see as many species as possible and in particular to see if the songs of British birds were similar to American ones. Grey recalled:

His knowledge of birds was very remarkable. With few exceptions, the birds of the North American States are different from ours; there are more thrushes and larks, for example, in the United States than in Britain, but the species there are not the same as ours. For example, they are without the skylark. Of all the songs that Roosevelt and I heard that afternoon and evening of our walk, there was only one song, that of the golden-crested wren [goldcrest] that he recognized as being practically the same as the song of an American bird, and when I consulted the late Mr. Ogilvie Grant [1863–1924, Curator of Birds at the Natural History Museum in London] afterwards, he told me that the resemblance in this instance was correct, and that it was the only one we could have heard in that walk [Roosevelt was mostly correct, the British goldcrest being similar in appearance to the golden-crowned kinglet which is widespread in North America. Both belong to the same family and the contact calls of the two are the same. Although some consider them to be the same species, they are still classified as separate ones].

Roosevelt writing afterwards in his autobiography published in 1913 said of the visit:

> The bird that most impressed me was the Blackbird. I had already heard Nightingales in abundance near Lake Como, and had also listened to Larks, but I had never heard the Blackbird, the Song Thrush, or the Blackcap Warbler, and I did not know what really beautiful singers they were. Blackbirds were very abundant, and they played a prominent part in that chorus which we heard throughout the day on every hand, though perhaps loudest the following morning at dawn. In its habits and manners the Blackbird strikingly resembles the American Robin, and indeed looks exactly like a Robin with a yellow bill and coal-black plumage. Its song has a general resemblance to that of our Robin, but many of the notes are far more musical, more like those of our Wood-Thrush; and the highest possible praise for any song-bird is to liken its song to that of the Wood-Thrush or Hermit-Thrush.[21]

The former president was particularly impressed with the musical abilities of the blackbird, blackcap and robin writing, 'I certainly do not think that the Blackbird has received full justice in the books. I knew that he was a singer, but I really had no idea how fine a singer ... It is a fine thing for England to have such an asset of the countryside, a bird so common, so much in evidence, so fearless and such a really beautiful singer.' Of the blackcap he said, 'The most musical singer we heard was the Blackcap. To my ear its song seemed more musical than that of the Nightingale. It was astonishingly powerful for so small a bird; in volume and continuity it does not come up to the songs of the Thrushes and of certain other birds, but in quality, as an isolated bit of melody, it can hardly be surpassed.'

And of the Robin he noted, 'Among the minor singers the Robin was notice-able. I was prepared to find him as friendly and attractive as he proved to be, but I had not realized how well he sang. It is not a loud song, but very musical and attractive.'[22]

As a result of their shared love of birds and their walk in the New Forest on that summer day in 1910, Grey and Roosevelt became lifelong friends exchanging correspondence with each other for many years. Writing to the former president from the Foreign Office on 24 October 1912, Grey said:

> My thoughts went back to our bird talk; indeed, I often think of that with pleasure, and great desire to do something of the same kind with you again. Soon I suppose that I must be free; for this Government has lasted so long that a change cannot be very far off, though the means of bringing it about are not yet apparent. You apparently may be in for another spell of office, though we know little of the chances in the Presidential contest, and I can't in an official position comment upon the issues. The account of your wound [Roosevelt had been shot and wounded on his way to a public meeting which he still insisted on addressing despite his injury] stirs me with a curiosity to know whether, if the experience had been mine, I should have had the nerve to make the speech, and whether my body would have proved as healthy. You have a great gift, moral and physical, of stimulating other people, and I never hear of you without wishing to see you again.[23]

Roosevelt in turn replied on 15 November, from his residence in New York, stating, 'My dear Grey, I greatly appreciate your letter. I am glad you sometimes think of our bird walk, because it was one of the incidents I shall always remember. I cannot help hoping that sometime I shall have the chance to get you over here and repay in kind.'[24]

Sadly, politics and the onset of war would prevent the two great friends from arranging their return birdwatching trip to America [Roosevelt contended the 1912 Republican nomination but lost and contested the 1912 presidential election as a 'progressive' coming second]. However, following the success of Roosevelt's visit, Grey would enter the most influential part of his career, helping to keep a fragile peace through a series of treaties which owed much to his diplomatic skills. An intensely loyal and honourable man, Greys' friendship with Roosevelt would be matched only by his unwavering commitment to his Prime Minister, Herbert Henry Asquith (known as H. H. Asquith) for the remainder of his career. Their relationship was born out out of their shared desire to keep the peace of Europe but not at the expense of abandoning Britain's ally France in the face of German aggression. Following Grey's historic speech on 3 August 1914 H. H. Asquith would give Germany an ultimatum to withdraw their troops from Belgium, the next day declaring war. Two years later his government fell, Grey also stepping down on 10 December 1916, exactly eleven years to the day he took office on 10 December 1905.

The onset of war, as well as signalling the beginning of the end of Grey's career, would also destroy his precious birdwatching haunt, St James's Park. To mobilize the country for the coming conflict, the War Office and the government expanded rapidly, the number of civil servants in Whitehall nearly doubling in just a few months. With office space at a premium, in 1915, His Majesty's Office of Works turned to London's royal parks and green spaces to provide the accommodation it so desperately needed. Flying in the face of centuries of history, it ordered that all the wildfowl in St James's Park be moved and its magnificent lake drained so the land could be built upon. In the place of the lake with its island and unique wildfowl collection was constructed a temporary War Pensions office, a War Trade Intelligence Department and a Ministry of Shipping (in the buildings the Admiralty would draw up plans to use the Royal Navy to blockade Germany and starve her into submission). The lake and its birds, so beloved of Grey, would become just another casualty of war and neither would be returned to their rightful home until 1920 when the buildings would be finally demolished. By this time, however, Grey would no longer be able to appreciate the return of the wildfowl he loved so much as he would be almost blind.

The declaration of war would also devastate Grey's own precious wildfowl collection, which like St James's Park, would also fall foul of the conflict. Among his collection Grey was particularly proud of the silver or veriscolour teal, a species he bred at Fallodon which, 'as far as I know, [are] the only birds reared in this country.' A dabbling duck which breeds in South America, Grey managed to raise one brood of eight but following a fox getting into one of his enclosures he found himself left with just five drakes. He wrote:

> Then came the War. Of course, during the War I made no attempt to buy any birds or replace losses by purchase. Two drakes I sent to the Zoological Gardens. They had not the species at all and were glad to have them. I had then three drakes. I heard of one female of the species being in the collection at Kew. I thought it worth while to send one of my drakes to Kew to mate with the female which had no mate, so I did that. In the next air-raid a piece of our own shrapnel fell and killed the female at Kew. Soon after that food became impossible to get, and what remained of my veriscolor drakes, in common with several other rare things, perished.[25]

At the outset of the war Grey's role was celebrated, his portrait being one of sixteen VIPs included in the 'John Bull' portfolio of war 'celebrities' together with King George V, H. H. Asquith and Lord Kitchener. The biographical notes said of him, 'The critical affairs which led up to this, the Great War of 1914, have probably brought out the finest that was in him, and made his name one of the best known to the man in the street. He has always engendered respect from all parties at home, while his firmness and fearlessness have made him dreaded by the enemies of this country.'[26]

However, as the war progressed Grey found himself less central to a government whose foreign policy was now not determined by diplomacy but by destruction of the enemy. He again sought consolation and healing in nature, memorably writing:

> In those dark days I found some support in the steady progress unchanged of the beauty of the seasons. Every year, as spring came back unfailing and unfaltering, the leaves came out with the same tender green, the birds sang, the flowers came up and opened, and I felt that a great power of Nature, for beauty was not affected by the War. It was like a great sanctuary into which we could go and find refuge.

Following stepping down from office Grey entered the House of Lords in 1916 and briefly became ambassador to the United States between 1919 and 1920, a position he only held for five months due to his rapidly deteriorating eyesight. Afterwards, he became Leader of the Liberal Party in the Lords between 1923 and 1924 and following that from 1928 until his death in 1933 chancellor of his old alma mater, Oxford University. The irony of the student who was expelled for idleness and only managed to scrape a third in law being appointed to the most prestigious position at Oxford would have particularly appealed to his old tutor Mandell Creighton who had died over twenty years earlier in 1901.

In his later life Grey found himself in increasing demand by the next generation of ornithologists. In 1925, he wrote the preface to the second book by Captain Charles William Robert Knight (1884–1957) called *Aristocrats of the Air*. Knight was a sniper in the Great War with the Queen's Own Royal West Kent Regiment; who afterwards took up falconry as a living and became a celebrated explorer, author, photographer and lecturer (through his books and films featuring his golden eagle, Mr Ramshaw, Knight became a household name in Britain and America). In the preface to the book Grey made it clear how important ornithology was in his life:

> Anyone who is fond of outdoors life will find the most lasting pleasure in observation, especially in observing the habits of birds ... Birds interest most people chiefly from three points of view: eating, shooting, or collecting. Observation of bird-life has this especial advantage – that it does not, as these three aspects do, imply any destruction ... And to cultivate a liking for birds will produce one source of happiness. Captain Knight has not only, I hope, secured this for himself; he has done even better than that, by enabling us who see his photographs to share his own interest and pleasure. In doing this we shall realize that the wild bird-life of this country is a valuable national possession, and should be preserved, both for our own sakes to-day, and for the sake of the generation that will succeed us.

Despite all that he had achieved in politics and conservation, Grey could never escape tragedy in his personal life. After Dorothy's death all his brothers died young in tragic circumstances. George was killed by a lion while big-game hunting in British East Africa in 1911. Charles, having lost an arm and won the Military Cross in the First World War, died after being stampeded by a buffalo in Tanganyika (Tanzania) in 1928. Grey's remaining brother, Alexander, became a vicar in Trinidad but died aged 44, probably from the long-term effects of a childhood cricket injury.[27] Grey also suffered the heartache of his ancestral home, Fallodon Hall, burning down in May 1917. Although it was subsequently rebuilt, he could not afford to replace the top floor and the building was never the same again.

Grey would find brief personal happiness when in 1922 he married his second wife, the writer Pamela Adelaide Genevieve Wyndham (1871–1928, the daughter of the Honourable Percy Wyndham MP and widow of Lord Glenconner). However, tragedy again followed him when a year later his precious cottage in Hampshire where he had enjoyed so many happy years burnt down, never to be rebuilt. To crown it all, five years after that Pamela died suddenly leaving Grey a widower for the second time. So, Grey dedicated the rest of his life to his other great love: his wildfowl collection. Replacing some of the birds he lost during the war, he would spend the remainder of his years at Fallodon enjoying the 'Charm of Birds'.

Reflecting on his life collecting waterfowl in his book the *Fallodon Papers* published in 1926, Grey said:

> My collection is not what it was. I lost a great many birds during the War owing to bad food. I did not attempt to replace the losses, and could not have done so in some cases had I tried. I have got a lot of birds still, mostly bred on the place, but I have not the same number of species that I had; and now, partly because my sight is so much impaired, I find most interest in having as many as I can unpinioned, as tame as possible, and yet at perfect liberty. There is a sort of romance in having naturally shy birds, perfectly free and unpinioned, coming, as some of my widgeon and pintail do, to feed with perfect confidence out of my hand, while I know all the time that any day they may join the wild ones to go south in the winter or far north in the spring.[28]

A conservationist far ahead of his time, Grey in his breeding of ducks blazed a trail for the likes of Sir Peter Scott who forty years later would build up one of the world's greatest collections of wildfowl at Slimbridge in Gloucestershire. In his final years Grey was completely blind but would find great pleasure in simply being surrounded by the birds he loved so much. The most famous picture of Grey is of him in his finest tweed sporting jacket and deerstalker hat with a robin on his head. Another shows him sitting alone on a bench at Fallodon Hall, a mandarin duck perched on his head and one eating out of his hand. Commenting on the wonder of a wild bird overcoming its natural fear of man, he said, 'They are naturally shy things, yet, when they are in this particular sanctuary, they are perfectly tame and have perfect confidence. If they should go away with the wild birds, they will be wild outside like others of their own species, and yet any morning I may go round the pond and find they are back quite tame again.'

For Grey the fact that a wild bird should trust him enough to perch on his head or eat out of his hand was a beautiful and almost divine experience. He concluded:

> There is interest, almost romance, in these happenings, and I know of no greater satisfaction for people interested in birds or animals than having wild things altogether free from control, naturally wild and shy, yet perfectly tame, so that they show you confidence and trust. You can observe their natural habits going on in your presence, which you could not do with the same species in the wild state, because their exceeding shyness and fear of man make it impossible freely to observe their habits till on some way or another you have convinced them that in one place at any rate man is not an enemy. Then you can have the great pleasure of watching close to you the colour of their plumage, their movements, their courting, their flight, and all the things that make them beautiful and interesting.

Grey summed up all that birds meant to him when he said at an RSPB conference 'The love of birds and pleasure of seeing and listening to them is in the long run a happier thing than personal success.'

Despite his many achievements in the field of conservation, Edward Grey will probably always be remembered as the man whose phrase about the lamps going out across Europe captured the darkness and coming slaughter of the First World War. One of the greatest politicians of the

Edwardian era, his political legacy lives on through his tenure as the longest serving Foreign Secretary in the House of Commons, a record which stands to this day. Grey wrote on and off throughput his adult life, his achievements in politics being recorded in *Twenty-Five Years*, his biography published in 1925. His contribution to fishing and nature conservation is also enshrined in the books he wrote: *Fly Fishing* was published in 1899, *The Cottage Book* in 1909, *Recreation* in 1920, the *Fallodon Papers* in 1926 and lastly *The Charm of Birds* in 1927 when he was 65 years old. A highly accomplished fly fisherman, ornithologist and author, Grey dedicated much of his life outside politics to studying nature. During his final years he was completely blind and became increasingly frail but his passion for natural history never dimmed. Though he could no longer see his beloved birds, the bird song that he had learnt at The Cottage came into its own giving him solace, pleasure and peace in his old age.

Summing up Grey's love affair with birds, the Scottish photographer, naturalist and author Seton Gordon (1886–1977) wrote in an obituary in the *Scottish Field*:

> Of his many friends, none will miss him more than his birds. Like St Francis of old, he was the kindly genius of the place, whose first and last thought was of the happiness of his feathered friends. And so I like to recall him as I saw him last – seated on the white seat with a mandarin drake perched on his head and two others standing as if on guard, one on either side of him, on the back of the seat.[29]

Grey's favourite birdwatching haunt in Westminster, St James's Park, would soon become the ornithological refuge from the pressures of high office for another politician, the Chancellor and Prime Minister Neville Chamberlain (1869–1940). On reading Grey's book *The Charm of Birds*, Chamberlain wrote to his sister Hilda:

> I have started on Grey's 'Charm of Birds'. If you have not read it I really must lend it to you for I am sure you would enjoy it. To me it is especially delightful in its description and analysis of the songs of common birds. Grey remarks truly how few people can distinguish them or pay more than the most general attention to

them ... Grey's descriptions took me back to my youth at Highbury [the family home]. I suppose when I was 19 or 20 and I began to pay attention to the bird songs and got up at 5 o'clock in the morning to identify the singers. I remember making exactly the same discoveries as Grey – learning the difference between the blackcap and garden warbler, being astounded at the disproportion between the size of the wren and the volume and vehemence of its song, puzzling over the two utterly different voices of the woodwren. I have never seen any description which so happily conveys the quality of these songs and the impression they make on the listener.[30]

Grey's book the *Fallodon Papers* would also be cited as the single most important influence on another pivotal figure in the Second World War, Field Marshal Alan Brooke, Britain's top soldier. Brooke was an avid ornithologist for whom filming birds became his way of coping with the continual demands of Winston Churchill, a man he loathed and admired in almost equal measure. Writing in his biography, he said:

These occasional spells of bird watching did marvels as a means of 're-creation'. I was able for a short spell to forget about the war [and] all the nightmare of responsibility. For a short spell I was able to step into that Sanctuary of Nature, which Sir Edward Grey describes so well in his Fallodon papers. A sanctuary unaffected by the horrors of war.[31]

Like the First, the Second World War would also take its toll on the places that Grey loved. Duck Island Cottage, which he used to so enjoy visiting in St James's Park, would narrowly survive being hit by an incendiary bomb but Grey's Monument in Newcastle would not be so lucky: a bolt of lightning knocked off the Earl's head, the headless statue not being replaced until 1947. Unlike his most famous relative, more modest memorials would be erected to Grey after his death. In 1936, a plaque was dedicated to him by the National Trust at Ros Camp Castle in Northumberland which read: 'This height with its wide prospect was a favourite resort of Sir Edward Grey, afterwards Viscount Grey of Fallodon K.G., Foreign Secretary December 1905 to December 1916.' A year later a medallion featuring his profile was unveiled by Prime Minister Stanley Baldwin outside the Ambassador's Entrance to the Foreign Office on Tuesday, 27 April 1937.[32] The plaque is surrounded by a circular inscription which reads, 'Secretary of State for Foreign Affairs, MCMV–MCMXVI' and underneath is the following tribute: 'By uprightness of character, wisdom in council and firmness in action, he won the confidence of his countrymen, and helped to carry them through many and great dangers.' (The memorial was restored to its former glory in 2014 to commemorate the centenary of the outbreak of the First World War.) At his death over a thousand people subscribed to a memorial fund in honour of his political work, raising over £4,000. Like his public service Grey's contribution to conservation would also not be acknowledged in his lifetime. However, five years after his death, in 1938, the prestigious Institute of Field Ornithology at Oxford University would be named after him. It was a fitting tribute to a man who had dedicated his life to inspiring others about the Charm of Birds.

Chapter 2

The Great War on Birds

After the Foreign Secretary, Edward Grey, lamented that the lights were going out all over Europe, it was not just the Germans whom the government declared war on but also a far more insidious enemy at home: the humble house sparrow. It was an ornithological conflict which would rage for the entire duration of the Great War, pitching the farming lobby against the fledgling Royal Society for the Protection of Birds. At stake was not just the fate of the house sparrow but millions of other small birds which lived in the British countryside.

Intelligent, adaptable and gregarious birds, house sparrows had happily lived beside people for hundreds of years but with the outbreak of war in 1914 suddenly found themselves public enemy number one. During their brief lives, usually no more than two to three years in the wild, they rarely left the farms on which they were born. Reliant on humans for their survival, these cheerful opportunists were adept at exploiting whatever food was available. In the breeding season this was mainly composed of insects but outside of it they ate waste grain from crops like wheat and oats, a diet which brought them into conflict with Britain's farmers.

At the outset of the war farming in Britain, both technologically and in its attitude towards pests, had changed little in over a century. In 1914, Britain was completely reliant on exports from abroad, importing over 60 per cent of its food and 80 per cent of its wheat. Despite some farmers having tractors and pull combines, many fields were still tilled using a horse and plough. Bringing in the harvest was also performed by hand using scythes with the help of local villagers. As a consequence, large flocks of sparrows were common on farms, the birds making a good living off the waste grain. However, many farmers believed they also stripped fields bare and it was established rural folklore that they took 'up to a third of the harvest'. So, with the onset of war the National Farmers' Union urged the government to take drastic measures to eradicate these 'rats with wings'.

The farmers' case against the sparrow was spelt out in a Board of Agriculture booklet:

> The principal charges against the house-sparrow are that at harvest time it does serious damage to wheat and other cereals; that in the spring ... it strips currant, gooseberry and other bushes ... All these charges can be proved. As to corn, it has been suggested that sparrows take only waste grain that would not otherwise be gathered. This is not true. Sparrows do, of course, pick up quantities of waste grain, but just before harvest time cornfields all over the country are visited by flocks of these birds, and it is not unusual to see parts of fields of ripening wheat literally borne down by their weight.[1]

When war was declared on 4 August 1914, H. H. Asquith's government adopted a policy of business as usual in relation to food supplies, believing that the conflict would be over by Christmas. Confident it was only matter of time before Germany would be beaten, it made no attempt to boost agricultural production or regulate the supply of food going to the shops. However, the public didn't share the government's rosy prediction for the war and, believing there would soon be shortages, panic buying set in. Seeing the shelves empty, the government quickly changed its mind and rushed through emergency provisions under the Defence of the Realm Act. This included wide-ranging powers to safeguard the nation's food supplies and make it illegal to feed wild animals including birds, a criminal act which was punishable by a large fine.

To prevent further panic buying and protect crops the government decided to form new Rat and Sparrow Clubs. These had been popular during the Victorian period as a way of eradicating 'vermin' but by 1914 had all but disappeared. The newly resurrected clubs were instigated by the Board of Agriculture and Fisheries soon after war was declared and formalized in January 1916. It said, 'While no one wishes to exterminate the sparrow [an ironic comment given subsequent events], it is generally agreed that any good it may do in destroying harmful insects is so greatly outweighed by the damage done to crops, that a reduction in its numbers is as necessary as in the case of rats, or of any other destructive pest.'[2]

The Board of Agriculture produced a leaflet with instructions on how to reduce the sparrow population by destroying its nests and netting or shooting adult birds. It also encouraged each sparrow club to draw up rules to organize the cull, essentially giving members a free licence to kill. As a way of incentivizing clubs each farmer was asked to pay an annual subscription depending on the acreage of their holding. Points were then awarded for each sparrow killed, the bounty typically being set at ¼d or a quarter of a penny a bird.

The production of the leaflet was condemned by the Royal Society for the Protection of Birds, who decried the 'ruthless and senseless extermination in this country of our feathered friends, who deserve their name not from a feeling of sentiment but from a grateful sense of their utility'. The fledgling organization had started life twenty five years earlier as the Society for the Protection of Birds to counter the barbarous trade in feathers for women's hats, a business it called 'murderous millinery'. Founded by Emily Williamson at her home in Didsbury, Manchester in 1889, in 1904 it had received its royal charter and by 1914 was making its influence felt.

Not only did the society decide to campaign in the national press against the slaughter, it also produced a pamphlet setting out the provisions of the Wild Birds Protection Acts to remind MPs that even pests like sparrows were worthy of protection. The society helpfully produced versions in French and Flemish for war refugees living in Britain 'who, it was thought, might be expected to kill birds for the pot'.[3] The problem was that the Board of Agriculture was responsible not just for food supplies and pest destruction but also for bird conservation and education. When it came to farmland birds this made it a law unto itself, a position which the society knew only too well made it a formidable adversary.

In the winter of 1914, the society fired the opening shots in its campaign by publishing a detailed paper about the diet of the house sparrow. This appeared under the title of 'Economic Ornithology' in its quarterly journal, *Bird Notes and News*. In it the society quoted a paper published in the October 1914 issue of the *Journal of the Board of Agriculture* written by a Mr Walter E. Collinge. Called 'Some Observations on the Food of Nestling Sparrows', the paper was based on field work Collinge had carried out in fruit-growing and suburban areas in 1913 and 1914.[4] Quoting the board's paper in their magazine was a brave move by the society. On the surface it claimed to be a scientific study of the sparrow's diet but it was really an attempt by the Board of Agriculture to justify a cull of the birds. Surprisingly then, Collinge stated:

In spite of all that has been written with reference to the depredations of the House Sparrow, we do not yet possess that completeness of knowledge that justifies us in condemning it as an 'avian rat', or a bird that should be exterminated. That it is far too plentiful no one doubts, but seeing that practically all modern houses provide numerous and safe nesting places for it this is scarcely surprising.

Collinge did, however, remember who was paying his wages when he added, 'the writer is of opinion that if this species were considerably reduced in numbers, the good that it would do would probably more than compensate for the harm, especially in fruit-growing districts.'

It was not just agricultural damage that the house sparrow was accused of but also the theft of other birds' nests, particularly house martins and swallows. In the RSPB's autumn 1914 magazine one critic wrote:

For some time past I have observed that during the building of the Swallows' nests around my house the Sparrows habitually place themselves so as to watch the progress of the nest, and when it is sufficiently advanced for their purpose they take possession and begin to carry grass, etc., to form a nest in the structure, and fight off the Swallows. They even attack the Swallow when sitting, and have been known at my house actually to lay hold of the sitting Swallow and drag her out of her nest.[5]

In response the RSPB pointed out that swallows were equally guilty of this behaviour, writing:

England has not much experience of parasitic birds, for here the great majority of species decently build their own nests and hatch their own eggs but it is curious to note that in another part of the world one of the Swallow family is among the sinners. In his 'Argentine Ornithology' Mr Hudson gives an account of the manner in which the Tree Swallows take possession of the nests of the Ovenbird [a small American warbler].[6]

The RSPB's defence of the sparrow was coordinated from its office based at 23, Queen Anne's Gate in the heart of London. As a consequence, it was accused by critics of being an urban-based society telling rural farmers what to do, one writing that 'the [Bird Protection] Acts were passed by townspeople, and instigated by persons who considered only their own pleasure in seeing and hearing birds during their occasional visits to the country'.[7] The RSPB hit back:

> Farmers are entitled to their protection, and their protection in some cases involves the destruction of the birds. But is there always reason for much of the destruction that goes forward under the sanction of protection for seeds and crops? If we only made proper use of them, birds are one of the most valuable national assets it is possible to have.

The RSPB believed the Board of Agriculture's Rat and Sparrow Clubs were really just an excuse to wage a wider war on all small birds in the countryside. In its winter 1915 edition of *Bird Notes and News* it stated:

> They do not confine their activities to sparrows and rats, but accept the heads of all small birds; consequently there is probably a larger proportion of useful insect-eating finches and warblers destroyed than sparrows. If these clubs cannot be ended, they should at least be under efficient control, so that the senseless slaughter of useful birds may be stopped.[8]

Despite all the society's campaigning work, the start of the year 1917 saw the slaughter of sparrows reach new levels when German U-boats in the Atlantic threatened to starve Britain into defeat. As food shortages became widespread, David Lloyd George's coalition government, which had taken over the year before, was urged to enact even more draconian measures to safeguard supplies. So voluntary food rationing was introduced in February 1917 and shortly afterwards a flood of letters began to appear in the national press blaming 'Destructive Birds' and 'The Sparrow Pest' for the nation's dwindling food supplies. This included one particularly chilling letter from the Land Cultivation Sub-Committee calling for an unlimited war of extermination against the sparrow which was sent to the *Worcester News* and many other papers on 20 March 1917:

To the Editor

Destruction of Sparrows
Sir, a few days ago you were good enough to publish our request to the citizens to assist in the destruction of sparrows as part of the work of saving our food supply. We shall be much obliged if you will give publicity to the following remarks made by Lord Devonport on this important subject: 'Sparrows destroy many thousands of pounds' worth of grain annually, and they have increased enormously of recent years. That is probably due to the abolition of the Farmers' Sparrow Clubs which used to exist all over the country. The policy of the country against sparrows should be a practically unlimited war of extermination. They are most excellent eating.'

Yours faithfully,
The Land Cultivation Sub-Committee, Guildhall, Worcester.[9]

The letter reflected the farming fraternity's view that the killing of sparrows was a patriotic duty on a par with killing Germans. In the parish of West Farleigh, near Maidstone in Kent, it was not just house sparrows that were killed but a whole range of other wildlife deemed 'vermin'. Presenting his report in March 1917, Mr L. J. Costen, Chairman of the West Farleigh and District Sparrow and Rat Club, proudly wrote: 'In Presenting my Annual Report, I am pleased to state that the members have again done good work by destroying 1192 Sparrows, 657 Rats, 33 Bullfinches, 134 Moles, 879 Blackbirds, 1301 Queen Wasps, 1,854 Butterflies, 13 Stoats and 9 Jays.'[10]

The butterflies in the report were not named but they were probably whites which were accused of destroying cabbages and other crops. Whatever the rationale, many sparrow clubs were now being used as an excuse to destroy any wildlife considered to be pests. In response the RSPB produced the first in a series of scathing editorials in its magazine, writing in the spring of 1917:

> It cannot be too widely known at the present time that any general or indiscriminate destruction of Wild Birds would be fraught with grave danger to the Food of the People. In every country and every

district where Birds have been systematically destroyed, the result has been the same: (1) insect and vermin plagues, (2) serious losses to crops of all kinds, (3) failure of man to deal with the plagues, (4) efforts to bring back the Birds.[11]

The RSPB went on to condemn the 'startling ignorance' of those who had formulated a government policy of 'culpable indolence and laissez faire which was before the War sapping the strength of the British nation and which led to its unpreparedness for the struggle in which it is now engaged'. What it particularly objected to was that:

'Kill the birds' is shrieked in the papers by correspondents possessed of no screed of ornithological or entomological information, but who have seen or heard that 'birds' eat fish or corn or fruit. 'Start a sparrow club' is the cry of the village publican or smallholder, who supposes that the popular way to deal with a difficult problem is to send children out into the fields and lanes to destroy every nest, bird, and egg.

In response the society urged its members to write letters of their own in defence of the birds and by the middle of 1917 hundreds of people had sent letters to their local newspapers protesting about Rat and Sparrow Clubs. These came from all sections of society including from soldiers serving abroad and Tommies in hospital at home, many in particular objecting to the use of children in the killing of birds. The letter campaign resulted in a spate of supportive editorials appearing in the papers, the society quoting a selection in its magazine:

The war against wild birds which is being urged in many quarters is as reckless and ignorant as it is brutal ... The great majority of the birds of the British Isles are largely, and majority are wholly, insectivorous. They destroy the insects which are the chief foes of our grain and our green food ... If it is pursued the result is sure to be heavy damage to our food supply.
—*Saturday Review*

The utter ineptitude of many of the suggestions for destruction are obvious to every one with even a rudimentary knowledge of natural history. To reduce sparrows where their numbers have become excessive is a perfectly simple matter if the right means are adopted; to incite school children to prey upon birds' nests is little short of criminal, and fails altogether in its object.

—*Yorkshire Weekly Post*

So-called sparrow clubs are generally devised in village taprooms to revive the old cruel game. The S.P.C.A. [Society for the Prevention of Cruelty to Animals], if not the S.P.C.C [Society for the Prevention of Cruelty to Children], should swell the chorus of protest.

—*Globe*[12]

Believing that sparrow clubs encouraged children to be cruel not just to birds but also to each other, the RSPB now focused its campaign on the sparrow clubs being morally wrong and bringing out the worst in human nature. At the time egg collecting was a popular pastime, especially among young boys and many had their own collections. However, the sparrow clubs instead promoted the killing of the birds, the money being particularly attractive to working-class boys. As a result, gangs scoured the countryside in search of nests, their behaviour being given added impetus by the relentless propaganda about killing the Hun. The irony was not lost on the RSPB who contrasted the cruelty of boys in the British countryside with the slaughter of 'our boys' on the battlefields of France and Flanders.

Among those offended by the use of children was the Countess of Warwick (1861–1938). An RSPB supporter, she sent a letter to the mass-circulation *Daily Chronicle* newspaper on the 30 May 1917, writing:

What can we hope for from children who are taught that it is their duty to catch sparrows or take the fledglings from their nests and destroy them in any ugly fashion they like? Cruelty is a fearful disease to plant in a child. If it is perfectly clear and beyond the possibility of doubt that sparrows are harmful to man and must be kept in check, let the necessary steps be taken by people old enough to know what they are doing and humane enough to do it in the quickest and most effective fashion; in any case let nothing be done in the sight of children.[13]

The society was particularly incensed that teachers had been asked by the Board of Agriculture to oversee sparrow clubs in schools. Writing to schools throughout England and Wales, it asked teachers to have nothing to do with the scheme, stating, 'the proposal is a direct incentive to that cruelty and destructiveness latent in children which, during the progress of civilization, Educationists and Teachers have been trying to eradicate.'

Sensing public opinion beginning to change, the Board of Agriculture convinced the Undersecretary of State at the Home Office to increase the bounty paid for each sparrow. Writing to every local authority and parish council on 6 June 1917, he outlined the new enhanced rates which were 'one pence for a dozen house sparrows' eggs, two pence for a dozen unfledged house sparrows, three pence for a dozen adult sparrows and one shilling for a dozen rats' tails'. The board's aim was to make eradicating birds the ideal way to earn a little more money in wartime or provide something for the pot at home, sparrow pie being promoted as a popular national delicacy.

The new rates led to not just gangs of children but many working-class men clubbing together after the pub to go on house sparrow killing sprees. The bounty was paid by the parish council or the local police who were required to check the number of sparrows killed and then pay the reward out of their own budget, later claiming it back from the Home Office. Not deemed priority work in a time of war, in practice it was usually the officers' wives who had to count the gory trophies, do the paperwork and hand over the cash. Most of the sparrows ending up in the police station were destined to be turned into sparrow pie for the chief constable.

In support of the incentives for killing house sparrows, there was a particularly hefty fine waiting for anyone foolish enough to be caught feeding them. Neighbour spied upon neighbour and anyone who was suspected of feeding birds was reported to the police and then taken to court. Prosecutions soon followed, in June 1917, *The Times* reporting the case of Mrs Sophia G. Stuart, 76, who had been caught feeding sparrows with bread. In court with tears rolling down her eyes, she replied, 'I have nothing else to love since my poor boy was killed in Mesopotamia [modern-day Iraq].' The judge remained unmoved and fined her £2 (about £155 today).[14]

Despite the success of its campaign, the RSPB could not match the propaganda coming out of the Board of Agriculture due to a lack of funds. In response it asked for donations from the public so that its leaflet *Birds, Insects and Crops* could be 'put into the hands of workers on the land throughout the country, and be brought to the notice of all Agricultural War Committees, members of County and Parish Councils, schoolteachers, and clergy'. The public responded in droves, the donations allowing the society to send off thousands of leaflets in just a few weeks.

To keep up the pressure the RSPB now publicly accused the Board of Agriculture of not only eradicating the house sparrow but also many other beneficial birds including hedge and tree sparrows, related but protected species. Smaller than the house sparrow and much shyer, tree sparrows although superficially similar in plumage are quite distinctive with a chestnut brown head and nape. Nesting in old trees, hedges and farm buildings, unlike the house sparrow, they only occurred on farms. More importantly from the society's perspective was the fact they were much rarer and fully protected by law.

Finding itself on the wrong side of the law, the Board of Agriculture was forced to defend itself, producing an official notice which read:

> Some misunderstanding seems to have arisen about the action of the Board of Agriculture in recommending the destruction of sparrows. It is the common house-sparrow that does the harm ... But the house-sparrow must not be confused with the hedge-sparrow, which is an eminently useful bird to be encouraged by all possible means ... Those who pay rewards for house-sparrows or their eggs should see that they get the right article ... The Board would entirely disapprove of any general attack on small birds under the plea of sparrow hunting.[15]

The admission that it had unwittingly targeted the wrong species was a small but important victory in the RSPB's campaign. Condemning the Board of Agriculture in the most blistering terms, the society said that the clarification had come too late in the day, stating, 'The genie of bird destruction had been let loose from the bottle, and its blighting form will never again be brought back within the confines of humanity and common sense.' It remained particularly critical of the board's role in encouraging children to kill sparrows, the Board of Agriculture replying, 'If schoolchildren are set to work on the destruction of sparrows they should not be allowed to claim rewards unless the work has been done under the direct supervision of the schoolmaster or schoolmistress.'

Writing to the government, the RSPB said that the killing was being promoted at a time when almost every school was understaffed due to the war effort, the society sarcastically asking if teachers would have to participate in the 'humiliating task of superintending Johnnie and Bobbie stoning, catapulting, and decapitating small birds'. Pointing out that the supervision of such tasks during school time was 'a gross misuse of educational time', the society proudly announced that following its letter many teachers were declining to serve 'in "sparrow" clubs in or out of school hours'.

Just when it thought it was winning the argument, the war on birds entered a deadly new phase when the society learnt that as well as trapping, netting and shooting sparrows, the Board of Agriculture was also advocating poisoning them. Discovering that they were clandestinely promoting the use of strychnine to kill sparrows, the society reminded the ministry that its use was illegal and anybody found using it could be heavily fined.[16] Following the disclosure the society asked, 'if no children or larrikins [badly behaved young men] habitually persecuted birds out of sheer callous stupidity …[then] there would be no need of the Board of Agriculture to teach the rural world. The boot would be on the other foot.'

To discourage children from participating in killing birds, the society wrote again to all the national newspapers, schools and educational organizations, asking them to officially stop supporting sparrow clubs. It also approached friendly MPs about highlighting the slaughter in the House of Commons. Following this, on 25 April 1917 the Liberal MP Henry Chancellor raised the issue with the Parliamentary Secretary to the Board of Agriculture and Liberal MP, Richard Winfrey (the exchange is particularly revealing for the frivolous way some MPs treated the subject):[17]

SPARROWS (DESTRUCTION)
HC Deb 25 April 1917

40. Mr CHANCELLOR asked the Parliamentary Secretary to the Board of Agriculture if his Department has recommended the

formation of children's clubs for the destruction of sparrows; if so, whether they consider that the difference between the destruction of crops by sparrows and by the insects on which they feed is commensurate with the demoralization which the habit and practice of cruelty which the killing of birds will develop and strengthen; and whether this recommendation will be withdrawn?

Sir R. WINFREY: The loss of food owing to the depredations of sparrows is so serious that the Board have urged the formation of sparrow clubs throughout the country; but they have advised that school children should not be employed on the destruction of sparrows, except under the supervision of their school teachers. The Board see no reason to fear that demoralization to any children working under their teachers will ensue in helping to rid the country of the large excess of sparrows.

Sir TUDOR WALTERS: Is the answer to this question intended to be a joke or is it serious?

Sir R. WINFREY: I am quite serious.

Sir H. CRAIK: Is this one of the subjects recognized by the Code?

Mr CHANCELLOR: Does the hon. Gentleman contend there will be any great advantage gained by the destruction of sparrows, in view of the multiplication of insects which will feed on the same crops?

Sir R. WINFREY: I think scientific opinion really shows that sparrows do more harm than good.

Mr YEO: Will the hon. Gentleman consider the destruction of cats?

Despite the jovial response of some MPs, Richard Winfrey insisting that the loss of food was very serious meant Henry Chancellor made little headway. He did, however, have better luck later in an exchange with the President of the Board of Education, Henry Fisher MP:

Mr CHANCELLOR: Will the right hon. gentleman see that school teachers are not allowed to instruct children to destroy life?

Mr FISHER: The educational value attached to the decapitation of sparrows does not, in the mind of the Board of Education, possess any positive value, and accordingly I shall not instruct its inclusion in the curriculum of elementary schools.

The society was, against the odds, starting to win the debate, having forced the Board of Agriculture to admit it had broken the law and won over the Board of Education to its cause. In the summer of 1917 it pressed home its attack by questioning the Board of Agriculture's loyalty in a time of war. It asked, 'What is the matter with the country, or with certain of the powers that be? Is the German spirit catching ... It would almost seem as if, falling foul of the old love of the wild that lies deep in the souls of Englishmen ... they had been let by sudden panic to become Huns-in-little and to resolve to make of the Birds the Belgians of their hysterical wrath.'

Despite the society's campaign attracting increasing support, by the early summer of 1917 sparrow clubs had been established in many parts of Britain. Not satisfied with the number of birds being killed, the Board of Agriculture felt more needed to be done and asked the government to deploy the army against them. Incredibly, despite a massive shortage of troops available for the Western Front, the government agreed and in May 1917 soldiers training in England were sent on 'official bird-nesting expeditions'. As the sparrow was already deemed to be well into its breeding season, the order was given that these expeditions should start immediately 'as the season is well advanced troops are to go birds-nesting at once'.

Although Rat and Sparrow Clubs were popular, many conservation-minded people refused to join in the slaughter and shunned the clubs, including a Mr. F. F. Neill, a Belfast teacher. He wrote to the society about the very different situation in Ireland, relishing the comparison with England:

Surely old England will never be reduced so low that we must order the wholesale slaughter of any species of our feathered friends.

Compare the campaign in a certain English daily with the words of the *Belfast Evening Telegraph*, which said in the cold weather, 'Remember the sparrows; give them a crumb; the cold weather will do enough harm without our killing them.' The Sparrow Club is unknown here, and the country people treat the birds as the friends and not the enemies of man.

I do not know very much about English children, but I know that the Irish boys and girls are naturally fond of birds. I have noted in spring that the boys took quite a fatherly interest in birds and their nests that they found on their way to and from school. I teach my boys to love all birds, and I do not think one of them would take even an egg from a nest. During winter they feed the feathered flock with scraps of food useless for human consumption, knowing well, for instance, that the starling loves a bit of bacon rind and giving him what they leave at breakfast.

In our church in the city Dr Macmillan gives the children an address on the birds and flowers periodically: one of the finest addresses I have heard was based on the sentence, 'Christ watches at the deathbed of a sparrow,' and it went far in inculcating the principles of humanity and justice to the feathered world.'[18]

To help the English see the error of their ways he enclosed a leaflet from the Irish Department of Agriculture which recommended the preservation rather than the destruction of birds.

By the autumn of 1917 the RSPB had, thanks to many generous public donations, distributed over 100,000 copies of its leaflet *Birds, Insects and Crops* and written over a thousand letters on the economic value of birds and the abuse of sparrow clubs. Despite this the slaughter of small birds in the countryside continued unabated, a result of the previous severe winter hard on the heels of 'the most determined onslaught on birds and their eggs ever known'. As an example, the society stated that it had proof that many thousands of birds and eggs had been destroyed in a 'single parish by a single club' which nationally gave 'an index of the destruction'. The RSPB blamed not just farmers, schoolboys and working men but also middle-class 'ignorant persons' including some parsons, lawyers and doctors. They had made the situation worse by holding 'stubbornly to the belief that birds are their natural enemies' and dealing 'destruction all round with impunity'.

The destruction of sparrows, and on the back of them lots of other small birds, had now become the society's major preoccupation and rallying call in wartime. Despite the RSPB's spirited defence, 1917 marked the bloodiest year to date in the house sparrow's long history of living beside people. Councils competed against each other to see who could kill the most birds and in the autumn of 1917, the proud county of Yorkshire found itself well behind in the sparrow-killing league table. As a result, the secretary of the Wharfedale Agricultural Society accused local councils of not doing enough to destroy birds and protect crops, after which a furious debate took place at its November meeting about what should be done. To settle the issue the matter was brought up at the next District Council meeting, Councillor Davison advocating people should organize parties to 'shoot them or get rid of them in some other way'. In response the aptly named Councillor Wheater 'held that the good they did compensated for the corn they destroyed'. But the other councillors voted for a cull and the council started trapping them en masse, Councillor Davison boasting about a farmer who had 'already trapped 2,000 in a month'.[19]

Despite the almost psychotic obsession with the killing of sparrows among farming groups and councils, many rural people neither joined in nor approved of the slaughter. Quietly appalled at the actions of the Rat and Sparrow Clubs which had sprung up all over the country, many villagers in particular pointed out that insectivorous birds like the house sparrow are 'man's best friends, since they have been proved to be protectors of his crops'. They included Hugh Gladstone who in a book called *Birds and the War*, published shortly after the end of the conflict in 1919, stated, 'Perhaps the greatest outburst against birds in general was early in 1917, when it was urged that "shoot the birds" should be the clarion cry. The formation of "Sparrow Clubs" throughout the country was recommended, and raids against the bullfinch, hawfinch, jay, blackbird, thrush and starling were widely advocated.'[20]

The irony of the war on the house sparrow was that in the trenches of France the bird provided entertainment, solace and hope to many of the troops fighting at the front. Sparrows, perhaps more than any other bird, lived check by jowl with the soldiers, flocks of them existing on the remains of the troops' rations and the seeds uncovered by the continual digging of trenches and fortified positions. Their role was the subject of an evocative poem called 'To a Sparrow' written by the famous Irish poet Francis Ledwidge (1887–1917). He was known as the 'poet of the blackbirds' and wrote it months before he was killed on 31 July 1917 at the Battle of Passchendaele.

> Because you have no fear to mingle
> Wings with those of greater part,
> So like me, with song I single
> Your sweet impudence of heart.
>
> And when prouder feathers go where
> Summer holds her leafy show,
> You still come to us from nowhere
> Like grey leaves across the snow.
>
> In back ways where odd and end go
> To your meals you drop down sure,
> Knowing every broken window
> Of the hospitable poor.
>
> There is no bird half so harmless,
> None so sweetly rude as you,
> None so common and so charmless,
> None of virtues nude as you.
>
> But for all your faults I love you,
> For you linger with us still,
> Though the wintry winds reprove you
> And the snow is on the hill.[21]

The next year, 1918, was again marked by the familiar outcry about sparrow pests and destructive birds in the press. On 7 March 1918, the *Daily Mail* published an article with the headline 'Will someone recommend a reliable Sparrow trap and so become a public benefactor?' The *Mail* also recommended that other birds, including starlings and bullfinches, be killed but this time the government disagreed, pointing out that a slaughter of insect-eating birds would result in reduced grain, vegetable and fruit crops. It was a turning point in the campaign, the RSPB having finally made the government rein in its own Board of Agriculture.

The subject dominated the society's AGM on 12 March 1918 when the loudest applause was given to the High Commissioner for Canada, Sir George Perley. He compared 'the wireworm and other land-pests to the U-boats and the birds – the greatest masters of aviation – to the aircraft which by attacking them defend our food-ships'. Perley had been mocking the President of the Board of Agriculture, Rowland Prothero, who in the House of Commons had compared the house sparrow to the enemy submarine, causing much derision and laughter in the chamber.[22] As well as support at home the society also received correspondence from soldiers serving abroad including a letter from one of the greatest wildlife photographers of his generation. Lieutenant Oliver Pike was serving in France with the Royal Flying Corps where he was in charge of aerial photography. Prior to being called up he had produced a series of award-winning wildlife films and had been the director of photography for Pathé. Regretting that he couldn't be at the RSPB's 1918 AGM to speak about the slaughter of sparrows in person, he wrote:

> I wish a special point could be made regarding the many dangerous paragraphs and letters which are now appearing in the Press of the country recommending the wholesale destruction of Sparrows by school children and soldiers. Last year the same thing was done, with the result that thousands upon thousands of Warblers, Flycatchers, Hedge-sparrows, and other useful insect-eating birds were destroyed by the ignorant, and classed as 'sparrows'. We all know what it led to – the destruction in a wholesale manner of valuable food crops by insects; in some districts the half-grown plants of the Brassica family were completely wiped out. The indiscriminate destruction of the Sparrow in spring is doing real harm, for the young are fed almost entirely on insect food.

Following its AGM, the RSPB orchestrated a remarkable letter that appeared in *The Times*, the *Daily Telegraph* and many other papers on the 25 April 1918 with the heading 'Plea for Protection'. The letter, signed by fourteen eminent zoologists and ornithologists, read:

The serious diminution in the numbers of our resident insect-eating birds which resulted from the severe winter of 1916–17, and also from widespread destruction of birds and eggs, is a cause for grave anxiety at the present time. The continual ploughing up of old grassland multiplies insect-pests; increased crops afford increased food, and thus stimulate the hatching out of countless swarms. Owing to these circumstances the protection and preservation of insect-eating birds and of those birds which destroy small vermin is a matter of urgent necessity. It is strongly urged that, in the interests of national food supplies, this matter should be promptly taken up by Agricultural Bodies, by Gardening and Allotment associations, and in elementary and secondary schools, with a view to checking the destruction of useful birds and their nests and eggs, and the preservation of insect-eating species, both resident and migratory. All who have studied economic ornithology and entomology are agreed (1) that the great majority of wild birds are beneficial to man; (2) that the insect-eating and vermin-eating species in particular are invaluable to him in field and garden (3) that children should not be permitted to take part in the destruction of birds and eggs, even of those species deemed injurious, since useful ones inevitably suffer also.[23]

The signatories included J. Stanley Gardiner, Professor of Zoology at Cambridge University, Dr. S. F. Bermer, Keeper of Zoology at the Natural History Museum, Dr W. T. Ogilvie-Grant, the Keeper of Ornithology at the British Museum and M. Montagu Sharpe, the Chairman of Council for the Royal Society for the Protection of Birds. The letter and the formidable lineup of experts who put their name to it finally made the government change course and the Board of Agriculture was told to stop promoting sparrow and rat clubs. However, by this time the sparrow had gone from being a bird that had peacefully lived beside humans for generations to one that was absent from many farms and villages, those that were left becoming for the first time in their history urban birds. The sparrow's partner in crime, the rat, suffered a similar fate as did many other small birds from blue tits to starlings.

The changing fortunes of the RSPB's campaign were reflected across Britain in counties like Berkshire. Here Wokingham Rural District Council (W.R.D.C.) had led the way in demanding that all its parish councils sign up to sparrow clubs. The parish of Swallowfield duly complied and a sparrow club was formed on 26 May 1917, chaired by the local vicar, the Reverend P. H. Ditchfield, who coordinated the killing on behalf of the council, one member Colonel Baddock reporting with pride that he had destroyed a very large number of sparrows and rats with his shotgun. The minutes of the final Swallowfield Sparrow club held on 20 June 1918 recorded their success in killing thousands of birds, the vicar proudly boasting that it had eradicated all pests throughout the parish.

Yet thanks to the RSPB's campaign other parishes refused to join in the slaughter, Swallowfield's vicar reporting with disdain that most had refused to have a sparrow club, writing, 'In view of the undoubted success which has attended the formation of a club of this sort in Swallowfield, it is very discouraging to learn that in three quarters of the parishes in W.R.D.C., the parish councils have not been public spirited enough to take any action in the matter.'[24] The sea change represented a historic victory for the society in its battle against the Board of Agriculture and one which helped to usher in a new era where conservation finally came to the fore. In its other major campaign on 'murderous millinery', the society would also eventually win the day, securing the passing of the Importation of Plumage (Prohibition) Act in 1922 which banned the importing of feathers for women's hats.

The legacy of the Great War on birds was that the humble house sparrow and many other farmland birds almost disappeared completely from large areas of Britain, needlessly slaughtered in numbers on a par with the troops fighting in France. The irony of the Board of Agriculture's ceaseless promotion of sparrow clubs was that they made little or no difference to the nation's food supply which increased rapidly as farmers responded to the national crisis. Killing the house sparrow did nothing to win the war, it just appeased a farming fraternity who from the outset wanted to make a scapegoat of birds to deflect from their own failure to produce enough food.

After the First World War, agricultural intensification did what the sparrow clubs had failed to achieve and almost wiped out both the house and tree sparrow. In the century since the war house sparrows have declined by over 70 per cent and tree sparrows by a staggering 95 per cent on farms, the result of modern farming methods. As a consequence of postwar agricultural policy, both birds are now priority conservation species for the RSPB, red-listed as Birds of Conservation Concern.

While the First World War may have been used by the Board of Agriculture, councils, children and even clergy to exterminate the house sparrow and many other harmless species, in one location at least the conflict was more beneficial for birds. Before the war Leighton Moss on the edge of Morecambe Bay in Lancashire was prime agricultural land, known as locally as the 'golden valley' because of its barley and oat crops. Prone to flooding, the land was kept dry by coal-powered pumps, the water being drained away by a series of dykes. However, during the war in 1917 the cost of coal and a shortage of manpower meant the pumps were turned off. The land quickly reflooded, returning it to reedbed and today it is one of the RSPB's most important bird reserves in the country, being home to rare species like the bittern and marsh harrier. It is also home to large flocks of both house and tree sparrows, the RSPB actively managing the former farmland for their conservation.[25]

Chapter 3

The Best Birdwatching Army Ever Sent to War

Following the declaration of war on 4 August 1914, the British Expeditionary Force (BEF) was sent to France to halt the German advance. The BEF was established by the Secretary of State for War, Richard Haldane (1856–1928), in 1907, one of Edward Grey's fellow conspirators in the Relugas Compact to remove Campbell-Bannerman from office. Haldane had been shocked by the state of the British army prior to the Boer War in 1899 when many men sent to South Africa were badly equipped and lacked training in modern warfare. After he was appointed Secretary of State for War, he had asked the head of the army to set up the new force so that the government could respond quickly to any crisis in the world that threatened British interests. With the outbreak of hostilities in 1914 the BEF came into its own under a notorious new Secretary of State for War, Field Marshal Lord Herbert Kitchener (1850–1916).

By the time war was declared on Germany, the BEF consisted of a fighting force of approximately 120,000 men. On 6 August, the Cabinet agreed to send four infantry divisions and one cavalry division to France immediately. One infantry division was held back to follow afterwards and one was retained for home defence. Mobilization happened very quickly with embarkation beginning on 9 August and by 20 August the BEF was assembled at its concentration point of Maubeugein in France. The force was commanded by Sir John French (1852–1925) and was initially divided into two corps, each with two divisions. I Corps was led by Field Marshal Douglas Haig (1861–1928) and II Corps by General Sir Horace Smith-Dorrien (1858–1930), the infantry under their leadership later being dubbed as 'lions led by donkeys'.

Unlike other combatants, the BEF was a professional army with a majority of volunteers, over half of the men being reservists. Well disciplined and highly trained in open warfare, the soldiers were particularly skilled in the use of cover and aimed rifle fire. Morale was high and as a result the BEF has often been described as the 'Best British Army Ever Sent to War.'[1] It was also the 'Best Birdwatching Army Ever Sent to War' for among its ranks were hundreds of amateur and professional birdwatchers. This was especially the case among the officer ranks for whom birdwatching was a popular passion, their involvement ranging from being amateur birders to professional ornithologists. As a hobby it was actively encouraged by the army, British generals appreciating how important it was to keep up morale among their troops. Birdwatchers were also to be found among the rank and file, a Scottish miner, killed shortly after the start of the war on the Western Front, telling a friend, 'If it weren't for the birds, what a hell it would be! I watch them singing and something comes into my throat that makes me almost greet [cry].'

For many officers their interest in birds started early on in life at public school. Most schools actively encouraged an interest in natural history, many having bird-watching clubs as well as their own taxidermy collections. Clubs were actively encouraged by organizations like the RSPB who ran a prestigious annual essay competition with silver and bronze medals. Junior clubs were awarded a certificate of merit and an 'Owl prize', often presented by a member of the RSPB Council. The society also ran a challenge shield competition for primary schools with a different theme each year to encourage children to learn more about conservation called the Bird-and-Tree (Arbor) Day.[2]

Most officers in the BEF were members of several ornithological organizations, particularly the Avicultural Society, the RSPB, the British Ornithologists' Union (BOU) and the Zoological Society of London (ZSL). When war broke out bird records from the Western Front soon began to arrive home with the letters sent by the troops. Consequently bird 'field notes' were published in national newspapers and then began to appear in monthly publications like *British Birds*, an illustrated magazine devoted to birds on the British list, *The Field*, the world's oldest country and field sports magazine and the *Avicultural Magazine*, the journal of the Avicultural Society 'for the study of Foreign and British Birds in Freedom and Captivity'. After a delay they also appeared in quarterly ones like *Ibis*, the journal of the BOU, and *Bird Notes and News*, the magazine of the RSPB.

The outbreak of war posed a difficult dilemma for many bird organizations because among their ranks were many German ornithologists. Particularly popular in Germany was the science of aviculture or the breeding of captive and wild birds. As a consequence, the Avicultural Society had among its members many British and German officers as well as dignitaries like the Foreign Secretary, Sir Edward Grey, who had his own collection of wildfowl which he kept at his ancestral home, Fallodon Hall. Horrified that birdwatchers should be taking up arms against each other, the *Avicultural Magazine* said in an editorial dated September 1914 that it was 'calamitous and infamous that not only peace-loving nations should be forced into a stupendous war, but also that thousands of Germans who must hate and loathe it should have to be involved, and become our enemies'. Believing the Germans had been betrayed by the Kaiser, the society stated, 'the vileness of the plots of the Prussian War Party, with the inflated vanity of the Kaiser to back it up, is completely outside our experiences of and dealings with German bird lovers'. As an example, it cited the late Herr Carl Hagenbeck (1844–1913, he is credited with creating the modern zoo), describing him as 'a fine type of a Christian spirit, a great enthusiast for the wonderful collection of animals and birds which he made'. The magazine believed Hagenbeck, his sons and 'many many others whom we trust' would be shocked about the 'whole truth of the scandalous mode of German warfare'. Fearing their 'estrangement from England' and a 'great loss to their trade', it squarely blamed the conflict on 'the appalling upheaval brought about by their Kaiser and his war-party'.

The *Avicultural Magazine* in its editorial looked forward to both countries being friends again after the war but only when Germany was completely vanquished. 'We look forward to the day when, with these blood-thirsty and covetous invaders and their leader crushed down forever, we can once more resume friendly relations and correspondence with our bird-loving friends and acquaintances,' it wrote, adding, 'who will we trust no longer be units of the German Empire, but peaceful citizens of a better and a smaller country, able to pursue their various studies and trades in calmer and brighter years.'[3]

The declaration of war also proved a challenge for the ZSL. Each year it published the prestigious 'Zoological Record', a global index of scientific literature and names used in zoology. This relied on contributions being sent to it from around the world including many from Germany. However, the war now threatened to prevent the publication of its 1914 volume due to a lack of funds and contributors. To help the ZSL in its task, the BOU through its magazine *Ibis* urged all its readers to support them by subscribing to an advance copy.

For the RSPB the outbreak of war in 1914 was a particularly bitter disappointment because Parliament was just about to make the plumage bill law. The bill, to prevent the trade in feathers to adorn women's hats, had been reintroduced a year previously and was the culmination of years of campaigning on behalf of the society. It had passed its First and Second Readings in the House of Commons by an overwhelming majority of 297 to 15 and only required the report stage followed by the Third and final reading. The RSPB had had to fight at every stage 'after every possible method of resistance and obstruction had been tried by the handful of opponents'. Then, it reported in its autumn 1914 magazine, 'At the last moment came the storm-burst of War, overwhelming the civilization of a Continent.'

According to the society, 'Up to and even beyond the terrible and memorable Bank Holiday of August, 1914, it still seemed possible that the Bill might go through.' Extraordinarily it had even garnered the support of German ornithologists as a month before 'a Professor Schillings, of Berlin, had been in London, urging, as a naturalist, the importance of the British lead to Germany in this matter, and the need for the co-operation of the two nations'. Much of the exotic plumage trade then came through German ports with French buyers purchasing the plumes in order to supply London millinery shops. But the bill had not been passed and now there was no chance of further German co-operation, the society reflecting that the enemy at home's tactics of 'delay delay, delay, and yet again delay', had now been 'crowned by the German Emperor'. However, there was at least one silver lining 'It may be trusted that the appalling war upon man will at least shut down the plume market and lead even the most frivolous of women to understand that the day for twenty-guinea aigrettes and flaunting paradise-plumes is not now.'[4]

The outbreak of war also posed the society with a more immediate problem: a decline in the number of subscribers and a sudden reduction in its income. To help, it urged its readers to keep up payments 'in order that the work of the Society may be maintained and no step backward may be necessary'. With only a limited annual income and capital investment, 'a decrease in funds at the present time would not only starve effort in many directions where immediate action is needed, but would necessarily destroy to a large extent the effect of past labours and expenditure. It may also be remembered that the provision of work, and payment, whether for watchers or for printers, is a direct service to the country in the present crisis'. The society also noted that many of its 'Watchers', members who monitored birds on its behalf, had been redeployed as 'Town and Special Guards' to monitor any subversive activity by 'enemy aliens' or foreign nationals then living in Britain. For this work they were given special permission to use the field glasses the society provided them with for their new war work.

The RSPB also had a far more practical reason for bemoaning the outbreak of war: all its nest boxes were made in Germany, based on a design by Baron von Berlepsch (1850–1915). A renowned German ornithologist, landowner and industrialist, he was the father of the modern nest box, manufacturing them on a huge scale before the war. 'It is needless to say that the R.S.P.B. stock of Nesting-Boxes will not be replenished this autumn from Germany,' it wrote ruefully. Acutely embarrassed, it apologized to all its members who had ordered, or were proposing to order, 'tree-hole' boxes for next spring for the inevitable delay in meeting their requirements. Instead, it announced that it would create a new industry building 'British Boxes for British Birds'. 'The industry is one that should take good root on English soil,' it said confidently, 'and it is hoped that arrangements may be made for the supply of British-made Boxes on the Berlepsch pattern.'[5]

With the declaration of war, the RSPB reluctantly accepted that its Plumage Bill would not be given parliamentary time until the conflict was over, which it hoped would be by Christmas. However, its first priority was to replace its German nest boxes as quickly as possible to salvage its reputation. In the next issue of its magazine in the winter of 1914 it proudly announced it had made progress. 'The difficulties encountered by the Royal Society for the Protection of Birds in providing Nesting-Boxes on the Berlepsch principle, but British-made, have now been happily overcome,' it wrote, 'and two enterprising firms have laid down special machinery by which boxes equal in every respect to those formerly imported in Germany are being turned out.' While it admitted that the pattern devised by Baron von Berlepsch was undoubtedly 'most ingenious, strong, and attractive', it assured its readers that the society and the firms it had employed would 'show that England can meet and beat the German manufacturer'. It concluded all that was needed to establish this great new British business was 'the co-operation of bird-lovers and of those who value the economic services of birds'.[6]

To promote its new British boxes for British birds the RSPB carried an advert on the back page of its magazine promoting its new business:

NESTING-BOXES AND BIRD TABLES
'Tree-Hole' (Berlepsch principle) and Walden Boxes; Tables and Trays. All British Made, best designs, strong.
Send for Catalogue to the
R.S.P.B. 23, QUEEN ANNE'S GATE, S.W.

By the winter of 1914, bad news coming from the Western Front made it increasingly clear that the war was not going to be over by Christmas, the Germans proving to be much tougher adversaries than expected. The RSPB portrayed the reality of the troops' first Christmas at war when it quoted a *Times* story about a soldier befriending a robin on Christmas Day 1914:

For five days he had been surrounded by crashing bullets and bursting shells; he was exhausted for want of sleep, and smothered in dirt. And he writes: – 'Shall I ever forget this Christmas Day? My two hours ended at midnight, a bell rang in the ruined village, and instantly a great volley, preconcerted, from all our line – our way of heralding Christmas with a message of "Peace on earth, goodwill towards men."

Slowly dawn rose, and there was I, with rifle between two loopholes, the ground white with frost … feeding a tame Robin at my feet, the only Christmassy thing on this Christmas morn. On my left what remained of a once beautiful old church; I could see a lovely old oak-carved screen and pulpit, all shattered, every house ruined. A little flock of Chaffinches, two Bullfinches, and some Sparrows joined my Robin just at dawn. Suddenly I heard deep singing on my right, louder and louder – the stirring strains of the 'Marseillaise' [the French national anthem], wild and beautiful in the semi-darkness.[7]

The RSPB added its own patriotic postscript to the story, stating, 'It may be doubted whether any other nation could have furnished that picture of the soldier in the trenches, feeding the "Christmassy" Robin.'

Those troops not lucky enough to have their own Christmassy robin at least got the consolation of receiving the Princess Mary Christmas gift box. The box was the idea of King George V's 17-year-old daughter, Mary, who had launched an appeal in October 1914 seeking donations for a 'Soldiers and Sailors Fund'. The fund proved incredibly popular and soon raised well over its target, bringing in over £150,000 in just a few weeks. To give the troops at the front a treat at Christmas a small brass, embossed box was made, decorated with an image of Mary and filled with a portrait of her, a Christmas card from her royal parents, an ounce of tobacco, two yellow monogramed packets of cigarettes and a lighter.

Troops who didn't smoke, instead of the tobacco and cigarettes, received a packet of acid drops and a stationary kit consisting of a pencil, paper and envelopes. However, most troops at the front did smoke as it was one of the few pleasures still available to them in the trenches, the health risks then being largely unknown. Some smoked to steady their frayed nerves while others did it simply to while away the time. As a result, many became addicted to nicotine and ended up chain smokers, the only limitation being the availability of cigarettes at the front. So, the highlight of the week for many Tommies was Sunday morning when the cigarettes or 'fags' were doled out before the pastor gave his service, each soldier receiving between twenty and forty fags. The main brand issued to the troops was Woodbine although occasionally they got lucky and received superior brands like Goldflakes, Players or Red Hussars. If they were unlucky, they were were issued with Life Rays which were less popular. When the Life Rays were dished out, a soldier remarked:

> Then the older Tommies immediately get busy on the recruits, and trade these for Woodbines or Goldflakes. A recruit only has to be stuck once in this manner, and then he ceases to be a recruit. There is a reason. Tommy is a great cigarette smoker. He smokes under all conditions, except when unconscious or when he is reconnoitring in No Mans Land at night. Then, for obvious reasons he does not care to have a lighted cigarette in his mouth.[8]

Such was the demand for cigarettes and tobacco from soldiers serving abroad that regular 'Smokes for the Troops' fundraising campaigns were launched at home. Smoking was so popular that it soon ended up being the butt of many a dark joke. According to trench folklore many stretcher bearers were really cigarette bearers on the battlefield. On coming across a casualty, they would firstly ask, 'Want a fag?' before asking 'Where are you hit?' The Tommy would look up and answer, 'Yes. In the leg.'

The most famous distributor of cigarettes was the Reverend Geoffrey Studdert Kennedy (1883–1929), an army chaplain, more commonly known as 'Woodbine Willie'. He would distribute fags around the front-line trenches as part of his spiritual aid, in the process winning the Military Cross for bravery. He also wrote rhymes, one of his most memorable being, 'Quarters kids us it's the rations, And the dinners as we gets, But I know what keeps us smilin', It's the Woodbine cigarettes.'[9]

Woodbines were produced by the W. D. & H. O. Wills company who were the first firm to mass-produce cigarettes and pioneer cigarette cards. The cards were introduced in 1895 and by the outset of the war had become extremely popular, many people, especially children, collecting and swapping them. For their 1915 issue Wills decided to produce a set on British birds which they believed would appeal both to their home market and the troops in the trenches. With fifty to collect, the birds featured in the set ranged from common or garden ones like the starling, chaffinch and goldfinch to less common species like the red-backed shrike, nightingale and dipper. The cards not only proved useful for identification in the field, they also became highly collectable and most importantly provided a welcome distraction from the horrors of war. Each of the cards contained a drawing on the front of the bird with a short description of the species on the back including its length, nest and eggs. Most of the cards carried a simple report of the status of the bird with some interesting fact about its biology, the exception being the card on the humble house sparrow. This said 'The common Sparrow, with his quarrelsome habits and noisy chirrup, is one of the most familiar birds. In this country his numbers have increased rapidly while in America and Australia ruthless war has to be waged to keep him in check.'[10] The card did not add that by far the most ruthless war against the sparrow was being waged on home soil where it was being slaughtered in numbers akin to the troops serving on the Western Front. This would have been well known to the cigarette-card team at Wills but they clearly thought better of including it, perceiving that it would not be well received by the troops at the front, who generally had a very different relationship with the sparrows that shared their trenches, many taking great solace from their vivacious nature and seeing them as friends.

With the onset of spring in 1915, a profusion of bird reports from troops serving at the front started to appear in letters home and these in turn were picked up by local and national newspapers. Consequently, the RSPB, which up to then had only reported sporadically on the war, decided to introduce a new section to its magazine, *Bird Notes and News*, called 'Bird-Notes from the trenches.' At the beginning of the war the society had been concerned that the widespread fighting along such a long front would affect bird migration across the Channel. However, this had not been realized, birds sensibly steering clear of the fighting and migrating at a height that put them well out of range of the guns or doing so at night. The society commented with some relief, 'If events have not affected migration to this country in the manner anticipated by many ornithologists, still less expected were the many records of birds heard and seen in the war-area and even from the trenches.'

One of the more bizarre letters sent home was from Private R. H. Pickering of the Honourable Artillery Company to his family in Bedfont, near London, which was reported in the *Bucks Advertiser*. Telling his family that there had been 'signs of renewed activity' at the front, he wrote that the Germans had detonated a mine under his trench but luckily it had not collapsed: 'The other night the Huns exploded a mine under a trench to our immediate left and we thought we were going into the air as well, but nothing happened.' What he found even more amazing, though, was that a blackbird had built its nest inside his field gun. Pickering's field gun was the Ordnance QF (quick firing) 4.5-inch howitzer, which had first entered service in 1910. The gun was horse drawn and was operated by a crew of six. It had a rate of fire of four rounds per minute with a maximum range of about 6,000 metres, more than enough to pound the German trenches and rear lines, there usually being just 50 to 250 metres of no man's land separating the two sides. The 4.5-inch referred to the size of the shell and on firing the noise was, according to Pickering, 'deafening'.

To disguise them from the enemy the howitzers were often covered with branches and sticks so the blackbird had probably mistaken the gun for a hedge, albeit one that moved and made a deafening noise ever time the gun was fired. Pickering's blackbird had started to build the nest during a lull in the fighting, he commenting that they 'did not fire for about four days, during which time the nest was built and three eggs laid'. A blackbird can take up to two weeks to build a nest but it can be completed much more quickly, as Pickering found out, especially when the grass, straw and twigs would have been readily to hand on the gun. Once committed the female would have continued to build unless she felt threatened enough to abandon the nest. However, the noise of the gun clearly made no difference to the blackbird and she persevered with building her nest, much to Pickering's admiration. At the start of his letter, which was written over about a week, Pickering had counted three eggs. Despite the gun firing for the next three days, incredibly, he wrote, 'two more eggs have been laid' so that the blackbird had 'five eggs in the nest and the bird should start sitting soon, but I don't know how it can'. As a consequence of the blackbird's fortitude, she soon became adopted as the seventh member of the crew and Pickering commented, 'last night when the bird came back to her nest they were standing-to and getting the gun ready for action. The bird sat on a bough above and waited till they had finished. It hardly seems credible but the nest is there right enough.'[11]

Blackbirds were not the only birds building their nests with the troops according to a letter printed in *Keene's Bath Journal*. A soldier serving at the front wrote to his parents in Clifton, Bristol, that a couple of robins had built their nest in his trench. Describing them as 'venturesome couple', he commented that they had 'elected to build this year's nest in a dug-out, and have hatched five eggs'. The soldiers were so taken with the robins that they began to leave food out for them and after a couple of weeks they became tame enough to feed by hand. Clearly impressed with their loyalty, the soldier commented, 'They further show their sympathy with the Allies by fearlessly accepting food from the hand, and in other ways proving themselves very much at home – "obus [shell]" or "no obus".'[12]

Birds not only nested with the troops but also carried on with their lives right up to the front line as a letter printed in the *Daily Chronicle* testified. A Private C. T. Burgess of the Honourable Artillery Company wrote to his father, Alderman C. Burgess of Godalming Town Council in Surrey, that 'Just by the trenches we are occupying there is a wood, and although it is fairly riddled with shot and shell both day and night, you would be surprised how full of life it is. There are two or three nightingales, which sing most rippingly, at least one pheasant, one green woodpecker, one stoat, and also a tree-creeper, and, of course, the usual thrushes and blackbirds.' What made the whole experience all the more remarkable was that the wood was the subject of regular bombardment by the enemy, Burgess asking his father, 'Don't you think it rather strange that they should choose a place like that, as the noise from the shells that burst there is terrific, but it is very comforting to hear some of the old familiar woodland noises again.'[13]

For many ornithologists the highlight of their year is the dawn chorus which reaches its peak in the first week of May. The troops serving at the front were no exception, those on watch at dawn in the spring of 1915 having a ringside seat as a letter in the *Worksop Guardian* showed. Private J. Knight of the Canadian Highlanders was fortifying a trench he had captured the night before when dawn broke. He wrote, 'As morning was dawning, the Colonel thinking our position not a secure one, led us back to the trench we had captured. We commenced to make ourselves more secure by digging deeper and building the parapet in front. It was now almost dawn. As the morning broke through the darkness of the night, the birds in the wood beyond broke forth into song.' For Knight what happened next was a deeply spiritual experience, contrasting the beauty of God's creation with the carnage and ugliness of war:

> Everything was quiet, the men seemed to stop their digging and listened to the song of the Almighty's songsters. I stood up in the trench and looked across the battlefield of the night before. What a sight! Highlanders and Germans were lying all around, having paid the price of war. As I listened to that glorious song; looked at the tranquil scene in front; thought of the awful carnage of the night before; and as I looked around for familiar faces that I could not find, I thought, what an antithesis – on the one side peace and tranquillity, on the other war, bloodshed, and death.[14]

In the spring it was not just at dawn that birds sang but also in breaks in the bombardment. A private from the Cameron Highlanders who formerly worked for *The Times* was recovering from his injuries in a hospital at Neuve Chapelle and recorded his war in the paper:

On Wednesday, March 10, we were told to 'stand to' earlier than usual. Our aeroplanes were up very early, and punctually at 7.30 a.m. a terrific bombardment of our artillery commenced. It is impossible to explain what the noise was really like; the sensation was awful. The Germans immediately set up a violent rifle and maximum gun fire, so that we couldn't see the effect of our shelling very well. The bombardment lasted well on to midday; it wasn't quite so violent during the final stages. I have always relished the singing of a lark high in the air on a fine summer day, but it seemed a perfect heaven when during a slight pause in the shelling a lark could be heard singing merrily away, about 50 yards high.[15]

The issue of birds and shell fire was also addressed in a letter dated 30 April 1915 to *British Birds* magazine from Patrick A. Chubb of the 2nd King's Own Yorkshire Light Infantry who was serving with the BEF. Chubb had been reading articles in the papers about birds seen at the front so he thought the magazine might appreciate 'a few personal observations on the subject'. He had seen many birds flying about 'in front of our own and the French artillery during an artillery duel', including house sparrow, swallow, house martin, chaffinch, yellowhammer, skylark, willow wren, magpie, kestrel and wood pigeon. He particularly admired the house sparrow which continued to sit on its nest in devastated houses about a mile from the French trenches 'although the shells are continually knocking large holes in the roofs. So far, I have only seen one of these birds killed at all'. However, other species took cover during a bombardment when 'lyddite shells are flying about, all the birds seem to realize that the ground is the only safe place for them, and accordingly they seek cover in the lowest parts of the hedges'. Skylarks in particular had to be on their guard as they 'are continually up in the air, and are continually being mistaken at first sight for aeroplanes'.

Intriguingly Chubb also mentioned that birds had been used as a cover by spies and fifth columnists. In a village he could not name for security reasons Chubb had found three pairs of house martin nests under the eaves of two cottages. While all the surrounding villages had been pulverized by the German guns, village X had been left standing. The reason, Chubb convinced himself, was it harboured a nest of spies. He commented, 'I may add that this village has had about twenty shells fired over and on it each day for the last two days. In fact, it is only left standing because there are so many spies in it. We have caught three of them.' His regiment had also found a fifth columnist whose love of wood pigeons had given him away. Noting that the local people kept them as pets, Chubb had found the man hiding in an attic with six of the birds. On closer ornithological interrogation he turned out to be a 'German gentlemen [who] was found in an attic here with six of his pets, and a note-book, and he swore he was English [the pigeons were more than likely homing pigeons which could be used as messengers rather than as Chubb thought wood pigeons]'.[16]

As well as the common species troops were familiar with at home, to their surprise Tommies also discovered the nests of birds like nightingales and even golden orioles, both of which were rare in England. On 29 May, *The Spectator* published a letter from a young soldier based 'somewhere in France', to his mother:

I saw a flycatcher here this afternoon, pretty little chap ... I have only seen one bullfinch but heard several. This place is full of nightingales. I have got one nest within four or five yards, but it is in a blackthorn thicket ... I was so surprised the other day sitting in my room reading to hear a noise like a cat having its tail trodden on. I got my glasses (guessing it was a bird) and hunted the tree-tops outside the window carefully, and finally spotted a big bird nearly the size of a jackdaw, certainly as big as a jay, almost completely yellow, with long beak and some black on the wings and tail. I have heard it since but not seen it, and must put it down as a golden oriole. The bird was right on top of a tall beech tree, and remained about three minutes and flew off.'[17]

Reflecting on the letters that had been sent home, a Canon Vaughan writing in *The Outlook* on 24 April 1915, contended that the noise of even a heavy bombardment, deafening to human ears, is 'no more to birds than the rumbling of trains is to the pigeons and sparrows that nest among the girders of railway stations'. Birds it seems were indifferent to the noise of war but there were limits. One observer noted:

We have a favourite blackbird, who sits up in the tree above us, and answers when the men whistle to him, no matter how heavy the firing may be. I was amused to watch two old magpies the other day. They wanted to cross over from this side to the German lines, but every time they started to leave a row of poplars just below my shelter, there would be a crack from some rifle and back they would turn and perch again to chatter about it, until they had plucked up courage to make another try, and then the same thing would happen all over again.[18]

In its spring 1915 edition of *Bird Notes and News*, the RSPB returned to the vexed subject of its bird boxes, noting with great pride its new 'British Boxes for British Birds' design was more than a match for the German ones it had provided to its members before the war. 'It is satisfactory to know that the British-made Nesting-boxes, manufactured for the Society, have proved equal in every respect to those formerly imported from Germany,' it proudly told its readers. To make their point the society quoted one happy member, 'The Bird-box came on Saturday and was put up at once, and on Monday morning the Tits were busy with it, going in and out, and we find it most interesting.'

Despite their gung-ho attitude in print, the society had experienced real difficulties in constructing and delivering the boxes during wartime. Chief among them had been the dire shortage of wood, the War Office commandeering all timber supplies for the front. To add to the society's woes the exact measurements required for its 'tree-hole boxes appeared to be precisely the same as those needed to make trench posts'. This had proved a particular problem as the boxes could not be constructed from 'odds and ends'. To make matters worse the society had then faced a plethora of new challenges: 'Then the special machinery was hard to get, and tools equally so, because of the dearth of workmen and the holding up of goods on the railway,' it wrote, adding, 'and, finally, transit was made irregular, expensive, and complicated by the dislocation of all goods-train services and the temporary cessation of collection of goods by the usual carriers.' Eventually overcoming all these obstacles, the RSPB boasted it had set up a new British business in nest box production and would never again be reliant on German ingenuity. It concluded sanguinely, 'But all these troubles are merely side-products of the War. When the War is over another industry will have been added to British production, and Nesting-boxes will be among the thousand and one things for which German makers will never again pocket British money.'[19]

The society also continued its campaign for a ban on the plumage trade despite the lack of Parliamentary time, adapting its message to wartime by likening 'the feathered woman' to a collaborator who was supporting 'German barbarity'. Singling out the attempt on behalf of the industry to reinstate osprey and other wild birds' feathers to women's hats, it gave four reasons why no self-respecting woman would be seen dead with wild plumes on her head:

(1) that this trade has its roots, not only in German commercial profits, but in German barbarity; (2) that ostentatiously expensive ornaments are an offence and a disgrace when military needs and civilian misery call on all sides for help; (3) that no excuse can be made on the score of providing employment, since feathers give less of this than does any other form of trimming; (4) that the flaunting of these badges of cruelty and death in a world anguished with slaughter and suffering speaks little for the refinement or the taste of the wearer.[20]

The RSPB's campaign came at a time when feathers of a very different kind were being increasingly seen in society: white feathers. The so-called 'Order of the White Feather' had been founded by Vice-Admiral Charles Cooper Penrose-Fitzgerald (1841–1921) with the aim of getting women to use white feathers to publicly shame young men who had not joined the army. The idea was based on the old cockfighting belief that a cockerel with a white feather in its tail was a coward. The order was launched on 30 August 1914 in Folkstone, Kent, when Fitzgerald gave thirty women the duty of handing out white feathers to men in the town not in uniform. Fitzgerald was contemptuous of any man not fighting abroad for King and Country, referring to them as 'deaf or indifferent to their country's need'. By using women to white-feather 'cowards' in public he was determined to show them that they had 'a danger awaiting them far more terrible than anything they can meet in battle'. The *Chatham News* covered the launch and wrote an 'amusing, novel, and forceful method of obtaining recruits for Lord Kitchener's Army was demonstrated at Deal on Tuesday' when the town crier walked the streets and 'crying with the dignity of his ancient calling, gave forth the startling announcement: 'Oyez! Oyez!! Oyez!!! The White Feather Brigade! Ladies wanted to present the young men of Deal and Walmer ... the Order of the White Feather for shirking their duty in not coming forward to uphold the Union Jack of Old England! God save the King.'[21] With the help of the press his idea quickly took hold and began to sweep across England headed up by a small army of 'patriotic women'.[22]

Many women, barred from fighting, saw joining the White Feather Brigade as their patriotic duty, supporting their men fighting at the front by shaming those who refused to enlist. For some women though the campaign had ulterior motives and was used to redress other perceived and real grievances ranging from being spurned to the lack of gender equality and political representation. However, many notable pacifist feminists like Emmeline Pankhurst (1858–1928) and Virginia Woolf (1882–1941) were split on the issue, reflecting the rank-and-file members of organizations like the Women's International League of Peace and Freedom. One man given a white feather astutely asked why some women would shame men into joining the army while their pacifist sisters were campaigning with precisely the opposite aim of stopping the war.

The campaign, like the society's efforts to ban the plume trade, was highly controversial from the outset. Women would hand out feathers on buses and trams or in theatres and pubs to young men of military-service age based entirely on outward appearance, usually without knowing much about them. So not only did so-called cowards get white-feathered but so did men who had been excused on medical grounds, were on essential war work or worst of all, were home from the trenches on leave. As a result, 'On War Service' badges were soon issued to male civilians so that people could see they were engaged in important war work. These badges were intended to show that the holder was not shirking his duty to King and Country even though they were not in uniform, many being issued to munition workers or those labouring in dockyards. While badges certainly helped to prevent young men being white-feathered, people still found themselves targeted if they forgot their badge. To avoid any humiliation, they had to buy several badges to escape unwanted attention, needing one for every change of clothes or coat.

Other white feathers, instead of being handed out, were sent anonymously through the post such as one sent to William Weller, who was an architect in the city of Wolverhampton. A white feather and a letter were addressed to him courtesy of the 'Conservative Club,

Lichfield Street, Wolverhampton'. Weller, who was in his forties, had been excused from service on medical grounds and was also carrying out essential war work by building homes for steel industry workers. Despite this, a white feather was still sent to him together with an anonymous letter which included the line, 'Your gallant + protracted defence against the brutal attacks of the local tribunal has been brought to the notice of the Supreme Council of the Most Noble Order of The Trench Dodgers'. It was signed 'A. Chicken Heart, clerk to the council'.[23]

While many of the white feathers generally came from chickens, others would almost certainly have come from swans or more exotic birds like egrets which were then popular in the millinery trade. The result was that rightly or wrongly feathers soon became associated in the public's mind with cowardice, which no doubt helped and hindered the RSPB's campaign in almost equal measure. The society itself was unusually quiet on the subject, no doubt aware how controversial white-feathering was but also fearing that it would deflect from its wider campaign of banning all feathers in the plume trade. The introduction of conscription in March 1916 meant that white-feathering declined as a way of shaming men although some women continued with the practice targeting pacifists and other war 'shirkers'. Reviewing progress on banning the plume trade, the society wrote in its journal that year: 'Two and a half years ago the outbreak of war might have well suggested to any Government the desirability for suppressing useless extravagance and to any woman the decency of refraining from "murderous millinery" and the "white feather" of cruelty.'[24]

The spring 1915 edition of *Bird Notes and News* carried a lot of anecdotes and quirky stories from the front line. These included the sentinel ability of birds to detect large explosions and oncoming aircraft at great distance, often long before humans could detect them. It cited the example of pheasants displaying 'agitation ... at the time of the North Sea battle'. This was the Battle of Heligoland Bight, the first naval battle of the war fought on 28 August 1914. The battle took place in the North Sea when the British fleet, the largest in the world, ambushed the German one off their north-west coast at Heligoland Bight. Surprised, outnumbered and outgunned, the German's lost several ships. Despite the inequality of the fight, the battle was regarded as a great victory in Britain, where the returning ships were met by cheering crowds and the loud 'cock,

cock' call of the pheasant. *Bird Notes and News* also quoted the even more bizarre example of parrots being deployed by the French to detect oncoming aircraft. 'As to Parrots, they, it is said, work themselves into an intense state of excitement and screech loudly before human eyes discern an aeroplane in the sky.' This was backed up by the *Evening Standard*'s Paris correspondent who reported that a number of these birds had been posted on the Eiffel Tower and other stations 'in order to ascertain how far they may be useful in signalling the approach of aircraft'. As the RSPB pointed out the trouble was that no amount of training could make parrots distinguish between French and German aeroplanes.[25]

As the war progressed feeling towards German ornithologists among the ranks of Britain's bird organizations hardened. While at the the outset they were simply viewed as being on the wrong side, as the war dragged on, they became increasingly castigated as avian enemies of the state. Many organizations like the Avicultural Society banned them for the duration of the war while others sought to show their patriotic credentials by highlighting German 'barbarity'. To show the Germans in their true light, the RSPB reported on experiments that they had carried out on gulls before the war when they had removed part of their brain to test whether or not they could still fly. 'It is worth recalling that less than a year ago, at a great Aviation Congress at Dresden, a cultured Hamburg professor of aeronautics gave a demonstration with living Sea-gulls and Doves, to show that although a great part of the brain of these birds had been removed, they could still maintain their balance,' the society wrote. 'This experiment was supposed to demonstrate that aeroplanes could be invented which would keep stable in the air without attention from the airman. But the portentous German brain has not yet invented the equal of a Sea gull, even though one of his huge Zeppelins succeeded in the raid on King's Lynn, in killing a Canary in its cage.'[26]

In contrast to the cruelty of German experiments the British had, according to the RSPB, instead employed the brains of seagulls to help win the war. In the 1915 edition of its magazine, it reported on their ability to help find U-boats, stating:

> Following on these stories came an anecdote narrated by a bluejacket [seaman of a warship], who tells how a flock of Gulls following his warship in the North Sea for the usual supply of food, gave the alarm

of a submarine's presence by circling round about its periscope when no one on the ship had detected it. 'I assure you,' says the A.B. [able seaman], 'had it not been for the Sea-Gulls, we should have been in Davy Jones's locker [the bottom of the sea].'

Commenting on the veracity of the story *The Spectator* magazine speculated:

> One may indulge the fancy that the seamen accepted the warning as a reward for having fed the Gulls. Apart from the scraps which continually go overboard and cause the Gulls to follow any vessel, no doubt the seamen followed the ordinary British practice of sharing their food with any living creature that happened to come their way. Here was the reverse order of things from the curse which fell on the Ancient Mariner's ship after the killing of the Albatross.[27]

Despite the scepticism of *The Spectator*, the idea of using gulls to detect U-boats was given a lot of attention during the war, experiments being conducted at the very highest level of government. So serious was the U-boat threat deemed to Britain's survival that the Admiralty were willing to consider any proposal to neutralize it, from naval staff, scientists and even the public. As a result, even the most bird-brained of ideas were considered and some were actually investigated.

At the outbreak of war Britain was still completely reliant on its merchant shipping vessels to provide it with raw materials and food: in 1914 80 per cent of its wheat, 40 per cent of its meat and almost all its sugar was imported. John Jellicoe (1859–1935), Admiral the of the Fleet, was quick to recognize the threat that the U-boat posed, commenting, it was 'the most serious menace with which the empire has ever been faced.' An official Admiralty memorandum put it in stark terms: 'Of all the problems which the Admiralty have to consider, no doubt the most formidable and the most embarrassing is that raised by submarine attack upon merchant vessels. No conclusive answer has as yet been found to this form of warfare.'

The first attacks on merchant ships began in October 1914 and by February 1915 U-boats had sunk nineteen ships, totalling 43,000 tons. The need to come up with an answer to the U-boat menace grew steadily as supplies dwindled and the press became increasingly critical of the escalating losses. On 7 May 1915, the pressure increased considerably when the RMS *Lusitania* was torpedoed off the Irish coast with the loss of 1,198 lives, an act which outraged the public. To find an answer, in July 1915, Arthur Balfour, the First Lord of the Admiralty, launched the Board of Invention and Research (BIR). Its job was to evaluate the problem and find a solution before Britain was starved into defeat.

Britain's response to the U-boat threat up to that point had been to rely on mines and booms in the English Channel backed up by patrols in the North Sea but these measures had proved woefully ineffective. The patrols came under the command of the unconventional Admiral Sir Edward Fitzmaurice Inglefield (1861–1945), who despite being close to retirement age, had been appointed as president of the 'Motor Boat Committee' by the Admiralty. However, only one in ten of his motorboats was armed and only one in eighty-five had a radio, so from the outset the patrols had little chance of seeing any U-boats, let alone sinking them. Inglefield's truly bizarre answer was to put onboard a team of two swimmers, one with a black plastic bag, the other a hammer. On sighting a U-boat periscope, the swimmers would be put in the water, one swimming up to the periscope and putting the black bag over it while the other hit it with the hammer. His other not so bird-brained idea was to attempt to train gulls to defecate on periscopes, Poole harbour in Dorset becoming home to a bird bombing range consisting of a series of guano-covered dummy periscopes. However, on 9 June 1916, he was placed on the retired list nominally at his own request 'in order to make room for the promotion of younger officers who are rendering important services to the Empire in this war'.[28]

When it was launched the BIR had attracted widespread press attention, the challenge of defeating the U-boat clearly appealing to the inventive nature of the public. Consequently, the Admiralty was inundated, the BIR receiving over 37,500 ideas from the public in just over a year, of which about 14,000 related to submarines, anti-submarine measures and wireless telegraphy. In private many senior members of the Admiralty were contemptuous of the idea of involving the public and deeply sceptical of many of their ideas. This was no better illustrated than the three categories they used to classify the ideas they received: 'Proposals by Officers of the Fleet', 'Device and suggestions from the Admiralty', and rather scathingly 'Suggestions by arm-chair critics'. Among the latter was the proposal to investigate the use of gulls to detect U-boats which was championed this time by an eccentric Australian inventor called Thomas Mills. He had made his fortune prospecting for gold in Queensland in the 1860s and 1870s, returning to England in the 1880s. He fervently believed that if a submarine periscope could be detected at sea by gulls, then the U-boat could be destroyed before it had a chance to attack any shipping. To train the gulls to find the periscope, Mills's idea was that ships should tow a dummy one from which offal was discharged at regular intervals, gulls already having proved themselves to be very adept at following trawlers.[29]

When the idea was first mooted in 1915 the BIR simply ignored it but Mills, who believed passionately and wholeheartedly in his own idea, was annoyingly persistent, inundating the Admiralty with reports, telegrams and photographs. Eventually the Admiralty gave in and the following year it was finally referred up to Rear Admiral Duff, the Director of the Anti-Submarine Division. He was initially dismissive but asked Sir Charles Parsons of the Central Committee of the BIR to look into it, who in turn consulted with Dr Chalmers Mitchell, the secretary of the prestigious Zoological Society of London. They both agreed that the idea had some merit and so proposed to the Admiralty that a sea trial be carried out investigating the potential of using a dummy periscope to attract gulls.

At the next meeting of the BIR on 10 May 1917, chaired by the former Admiral of the Fleet Lord Fisher, it was minuted that 'In consequence of a suggestion made by the Board of Invention and Research to test the possibilities of attracting seagulls to the periscopes of submarines by ejecting food there from and thereby training them to follow and locate enemy submarines, the Admiralty have approved an experiment being made in [submarine] B3 and have asked BIR to provide a suitable food box for the purpose'. Consequently a Mr Carnegie was asked to build a dummy periscope which would discharge food to attract gulls, the eminent ornithologist and naturalist William Henry Hudson advising on the composition of the offal. At the meeting the idea of using pigeons and hawks was also discussed but it was dismissed as impractical, gulls being seen as having the most potential. The programme was placed under the overall supervision of Richard Kearton (1862–1928), one half of the Kearton brothers who were renowned wildlife photographers. He thought the idea could be made to work but shortly before trials began difficulties arose using the submarine B3 in the experiments and on 30 August 1917 the secretary to the BIR announced that the trials had been abandoned. No official reason was ever given but it was probably due to the contemptuous attitude of Captain Ryan who was in charge of the B3, he epitomizing the 'uncooperativeness of naval officers in business they considered the sole province of the Royal Navy'.[30] Certainly Ryan thought the idea a distraction from proper war work and complained in writing to the Commander-in-Chief of the Grand Fleet, Admiral Sir David Beatty (1871–1936). The letter stated, 'That the training of seagulls would interfere seriously with this work [B3 was working on hydrophones], and that the advantages that might be gained are so extremely doubtful, that it would be inadvisable for B.3. to be detailed for this purpose.'

Mills, who had not been involved in the experiment, had previously written to the BIR on 27 February 1917 with his own idea which was to 'Have a small float containing a dummy periscope; the float to contain a quantity of rough food, say dog or cat's flesh or any other food which will float on the water. The machine to discharge small quantities every few minutes so the birds will see the food floating on the sea'. According to him, using this method birds could be trained in two weeks to 'fly around the periscope or over the wake of a submarine'. However, he was informed in a curt reply that similar proposals had already been tried and rejected. Never someone to take no for an answer, Mills instead built his own machine called 'The Sea Gull Decoy' and again approached the BIR with it, stating it was 'small and torpedo-like, weighing about 20 lbs, costing about £5 apart from the float, and able when under tow to discharge small pieces of "tape food" in various quantities and thicknesses, at distances of up to a mile, and either near the surface or up to 100 ft below'. However, he was again rejected by the BIR and the embittered Mills instead patented the idea and started his own sea trials at Exmouth with his 'No 1 machine'. Here, he told the *Exmouth Journal* on 23 February 1918, 'I have found that by towing the dummy 200 or 300 yards behind the boat and making it show its periscope, it attracts birds. I then make it dive, and the gulls will follow it while it is under the water.' In the absence of support from the Admiralty, he then sent details of his machine, including photographs, to MPs and even the Australian premier. The limited response he received left him even more dejected as did a final approach to the BIR on 6 March 1918 to which he received a terse reply. In September Mills finally left Exmouth still believing earnestly that the Admiralty had missed out on a war-winning idea.

The credibility of the BIR had also been damaged by the affair, its willingness to experiment with gulls and other animals like sealions being an anathema to many in the deeply conservative Admiralty and at the end of 1917 it was wound up. In the meantime, convoys had proved their worth in protecting merchant vessels from U-boats and, as a result, from mid-1917 their success in sinking British shipping had declined markedly. Mills was left to vent his spleen with the Admiralty in a book which he wrote in 1919 called *The Fateful Sea-gull* (the full title well reflecting Mills's obsessive character: *The Fateful Sea-gull: Reminiscences, Including an Account of Gold Mining Experiences in Australia and of the Author's Scheme for Training Sea-gulls to Locate German Submarines in World War I*). In it he wrote:

> I fully believe the British Empire would have gone ahead if the Authorities had carried out my invention for the training of sea-gulls in a proper manner in February 1917 ... I have had many hardships in my life, especially about fifty years ago in exploring and working, and even being stuck up by floods without food, but I never felt that as much as I have the rebuffs and insults experienced during the past two years, prior to the signing of the Armistice.[31]

Chapter 4

Birds at the Front

By the autumn of 1915 birdwatching on the Western Front had become firmly established as a favourite pastime among the soldiers, even indifferent troops finding that taking an interest in the birdlife around the trenches helped to while away the long hours spent keeping watch. The RSPB continued to report on sightings from the front line in its magazine, doing a regular roundup of reports that had been sent in to it or appeared elsewhere. These included not just sightings from the trenches and their environs but also from the surrounding buildings and towns which had been destroyed after finding themselves in the firing range of the enemy.

The society had received a letter from a Captain R. Crawshay who had written from his brigade headquarters in France about the great joy that the return of swallows had brought to the Allied troops the previous spring. However, on arriving back, the swallows had found that many of the buildings which they had previously occupied had been reduced to rubble. This had initially puzzled the birds who had flown round and round in search of their former nesting sites before discovering nearby 'a small hut constructed for military use'. Ever resourceful, the swallows had then decided to locate their new nests in the hut, much to the pleasure of the Belgian officer using it. Crawshay reported that this had been particularly welcome as 'Belgians retain the old belief that Swallows bring happiness to the house which gives them shelter'. More importantly, since the swallows had returned not a single German shell had landed on the hut, the soldiers believing the birds brought good luck. Delighted at his new housemates, the Belgian officer had said to Crawshay, '*Les verrons-nous dans les abris l'année prochaine, Dieu seul sait? Quoi qu'il en soit, nous exprimons le souhait que ces abris peuvent être conservés jusqu'à la reconstruction, jusqu'à la résurrection de nos maisons détruites. Les hirondelles, et nos paysans aussi, pourront y rester quand nous sera à la poursuite des Barbares.*' ('Will we see them in the shelters next year,

God only knows? Anyway, we express the wish that these shelters can be preserved until reconstruction, until the resurrection of our destroyed homes. The swallows, and our peasants too, will be able to stay there when we will be in pursuit of the Barbarians.)'[1]

Sadly, other birds were not quite so adaptable when the buildings they had nested in were destroyed, Crawshay reporting: 'I have often reflected on this very matter of the Swallows in the field of war. Barn Owls, also, cannot but be greatly affected in districts where towns are destroyed and even cathedrals and churches reduced to ruins.' The devastation had particularly affected ground-nesting species, he pointing out, 'Harriers are apt to come in for a hot time when gun positions are located in low bottoms which form favourite hawking grounds for these birds, as I have remarked in the section where I now am. Partridges I sometimes see scared by bursting shells.'

In its coverage of the war the RSPB also contrasted the British love of wild birds with the indifference of its allies, citing an example of how a soldier had helped to liberate a caged wild bird from the 'ignorance' of its French owners. According to the society, an artillery soldier billeted in a French home had found to his horror a young owl in a cage, which had 'fallen from its nest in the belfry tower, and been condemned to a slow death by its ignorant owner'. Pleading for the bird to be given to him, the soldier had then attached the cage to the local church wall. Returning the next day to his delight he found the owlet had recovered after its parents had fed it 'three mice and two sparrows'. The soldier had the great satisfaction of seeing it released before receiving his marching orders, the RSPB stating that his story threw 'into vivid relief, amid the horrors of battle, the tenderness of heart of British heroes'.

The society also continued to campaign vigorously on the plume trade and its connection to 'German barbarity', drawing on the strong sense of British patriotism during wartime to shame women into giving up a love of feathers in their hats. In another hard-hitting article it kept up the pressure on the government and women at home by accusing them of wearing 'Hun-headgear' stating that 'Women have accepted as many falsehoods on this subject as even the Germans could supply but the feathered headgear remains the Hun-headgear, typifying slaughter of the helpless and harmless'. The letter section of its magazine also continued to be popular, its content reflecting the fact that for the first time, bombs were falling not just on the battlefield but also on the home front. In particular, towns and cities had been targeted, courtesy of a huge German aluminium bird which had descended from the skies at night.

In the first month of the war Germany had formed the 'Ostend Carrier Pigeon Detachment', a cover name for a secret Zeppelin airship unit to be used for bombing English ports, towns and cities. On the night of 19/20 January 1915, the first successful raid by a Zeppelin airship took place, the original target of Humberside being abandoned because of high winds, bombs instead being dropped on Great Yarmouth, Sheringham and King's Lynn. Named after its inventor, the German Count Ferdinand von Zeppelin (1838–1917), voyages on Zeppelins had been extremely popular before the war when well-heeled tourists had flown around the world in airships boasting every type of luxury.

The Zeppelin's unique design feature was its rigid metal, cylindrical framework covered in fabric, the airship being filled with hydrogen and propelled by two powerful Daimler-Benz engines. The framework was made of duralumin, a combination of aluminium, copper and other metals (its exact content was kept a secret). Its primary use during the war was as a reconnaissance vessel, but as the people on the coast of East Anglia had found out to their cost, it could also be used for bombing raids. At the beginning of the conflict the German high command had high hopes that Zeppelins could be used to bomb the British into submission, the Kaiser having given the go-ahead for raids to begin on 7 January 1915.

By the beginning of June 1915 over ten raids had taken place on British soil by Zeppelins. The airship was feared and hated by the British public who christened them 'baby killers' because they flew unseen at night. On the evening of 5/6 June, naval Zeppelin L9, commanded by Kapitänleutnant Heinrich Mathy, set out with the aim of attacking London but, due to strong winds pushing his airship off course, Mathy instead decided to bomb Hull. The raid began shortly before midnight, the giant airship coming in over the King George V dock where it caused panic. In total thirteen high-explosive and thirty-nine incendiary bombs were dropped that night, destroying about forty houses and shops. By the end of the night twenty-six people had been killed and forty injured.

Lucky to not be included on the list was a 10-year-old girl who got wind of the Zeppelin's approach thanks to the house martins outside her bedroom window. 'Early Sunday morning, June 6th, a great shock was felt in this district. I woke up and felt the house shake. I thought it was a Zeppelin,' she wrote in the RSPB's magazine. 'It disturbed my birds, for the noise they made kept me awake, and they seemed unable to settle down, flying around about the rest of the morning. I could see their shadows on my blind.' Another 9-year-old boy, also writing in the RSPB's Bird-And-Tree essay competition, highlighted the sentinel ability of moorhens to also detect Zeppelins, a skill that had given his family enough time to take cover. 'When a Zeppelin came over Beechamwell [in Norfolk] all the Waterhens called out "Crr-ook! Crr-ook!",' he wrote 'and my mother looked out and saw them all flying.'[2]

While many birds were able to detect the approach of Zeppelins, there was one recorded notable exception. On the night of 25/26 September 1916 Zeppelin L21, commanded by Oberleutnant-zur-See Kurt Frankenburg, appeared above the small Lancashire town of Bacup. Flying over, he dropped twelve incendiary bombs causing minor damage to the town and one fatality: a song thrush. The bird was killed outside the Emmanuel Holcombe Church of England Primary School, an act which so upset the children that it was preserved for posterity by a taxidermist. Displayed in a glass case, it has been stored at the school ever since. On the case is inscribed: 'The Thrush, Being the only fatality in the raid of World War 1.' Unfortunately, the death toll did not end there and the Zeppelin went on to fly over Bolton, dropping more bombs and this time killing thirteen people. Unlike birds, people lacked the sentinel ability to sense the approach of airships and suffered accordingly. In all, during the course of the war, there would be over fifty raids by Zeppelins killing over 500 people, the RSPB commenting 'It says something for ... children that they thus calmly observe the effect of Zeppelins on their birds without a word as to any alarm of their own.'

As the war entered its second year, the society felt the increasing need to justify its existence in wartime, no doubt with an eye on its income but also aware that many of its subscribers were away fighting. In a long and rambling editorial in its autumn 1915 magazine, the RSPB sought to do this by stating: 'A year and more ago, when the horrors of War descended upon Europe, it was supposed by some persons that the Royal Society for the Protection of Birds was one of those institutions which, however excellent in time of peace, would not weather the storm. The Society is an institution of humanity and civilization, and humanity and civilization were ceasing to count.'³ The cause of the society's soul-searching had been critical letters to the press about its role, one correspondent stating that birds must 'take a back seat. They must get along as best they could while man was at death-grips with man'.

In response to the criticism the society felt the need to produce a long list of its many achievements, boasting:

> Throughout the most terrible twelve months of history, the work of the Society has been pursued steadily, quietly, unfalteringly. Preservation of rare species, safeguarding of migrants at the lighthouses, efforts to secure and extend legal protection against the bird collector and the bird catcher, the educational campaign in the schools and out of the schools, protests against the skin-and-feather traffic, have one and all been continued.

However, keenly aware that its best argument was to make the connection between its work at home and the struggle abroad, it also stated:

> To those responsible for the work it has not seemed desirable to turn a blind eye to the barbarous pole-trap because men were receiving barbarous treatment at German hands; to tolerate the 'osprey' badge of callousness on a woman's head because she might be patronizing a concert for the Belgians. It should encourage the teaching of children about the birds of their country when old Bird-and-Tree Cadets and other bird-students in the fighting line write of the poignant joy of memory that has come to them with the song of a Skylark or a Blackbird.

The society in wartime was a subject that it returned to in its winter 1915 magazine, again dedicating another long editorial to its work, this time about the value of its educational activities and its desire to foster a new generation of children inspired by conservation. It wrote:

> thousands of children are learning half-unconsciously to think and notice for themselves, and are having eyes and minds trained to observe accurately, to discriminate intelligently, and, in time, to

judge. With this new interest and new knowledge, they can as adults never go back to the haphazard persecution, the ignorant destruction, or the purely sentimental protection of former days.

With the onset of the second winter of war, bird sightings at the front became rarer but even more important for morale as soldiers tried to survive the wet and cold as well as the enemy. The conditions were appalling, trenches becoming flooded and turning into a muddy quagmire. Despite the dire conditions, bird reports continued to be sent back to Britain, not just from the Western Front but from all the theatres of war. On 2 January 1916, Sergeant Bernard W. Gill, of the Royal Army Medical Corps, wrote to *The Observer* newspaper about the birds of Gallipoli.

The Gallipoli campaign, the brainchild of the First Lord of the Admiralty, Winston Churchill, had started on 17 February 1915 with the aim of capturing the Dardanelles straits that provided a supply route to Russia. It had been a disaster for the Allies, the Turks inflicting huge losses on the invaders. By the time that Gill wrote to *The Observer*, the Allies were on the verge of evacuating with approximately a quarter of a million dead on both sides. Given Gill's predicament, it is quite miraculous that he found the time to write, let alone record the birds he saw there. He had 'a habit of observation, acquired and cultivated among peaceful fields and hedgerows, a real blessing in time of war, a true relaxation from wounds and weariness, and the dull monotony of a long, protracted campaign [the campaign while protracted was anything but dull, however, Gill would have been very aware of the censor when writing it].'

The most ubiquitous bird that Gill had found was also one of the species most regularly recorded on the Western Front: the skylark. He commented 'By far the commonest bird out here is a Skylark, larger in size, but with a less varied range of notes than the caroller of English skies, yet he gives out a sweet, wild warble at dawn, standing on a hillock with crest erect in the jaunty, Lark-like way.'[4] Gill took a particular delight in the skylark's song but had never got to examine one closely until he found a wounded bird near his station, writing:

> One morning a Lark, as I drew near, instead of rising, ran under the lee of a small bush. I had no difficulty in catching the bird, and found a slight wound on the left wing, which made flight impossible.

The ground thereabouts is exposed to shrapnel fire, and possibly the wing had been grazed by a bullet. More than once I have seen a shrapnel-shell burst among a flock of birds, and a casualty now and then seems inevitable. Although unable to fly, the wounded bird was well fed, and lay in my hand unresisting. When I put it down it made off at a great pace towards the cover of some scrub-oak.

A couple of days later Gill came across the same bird, which had been rescued by one of his staff, in a very unexpected place.

Two days later my duties led me to visit an orderly's dug-out, and my attention was drawn to a biscuit-tin in a corner; the lid was pierced with holes, and from within came an impatient tapping. My Lark a prisoner! It had taken kindly to Army rations, and fed heartily on biscuit crumbs made moist with water. In a few days the wing was healed, and the bird released.

Commenting on the rest of the birdlife, Gill thought his piece of Turkey very like England, where:

Magpies fly from tree to tree in flocks of five or six; Whinchats scold from the tops of juniper-bushes; Pied Wagtails run lightly at the margins of the creeks, and the Redbreast flits across your path as you walk among the low scrub. It seemed like home yesterday, when, just after seeing a Robin, I lighted upon a daisy. It flowered alone, gold-eyed, crimson-tipped, in a little clearing among the alien growths of prickly-leaved dwarfed oak and juniper.

One bird that Gill was particularly pleased to see but could not identify he christened a 'Firetail'. He described it in his article, stating: 'One bird we often see – a bird that is not to be met with in England. It is long, brown and slender, with the build of a Warbler – much like a Whitethroat, in fact; and when it flies its tail-feathers glow out bright orange. We call them "Firetails". The Firetail is, of course, the Redstart' (Gill was mistaken in that the Redstart does occur in England but is generally confined to the north and west with the greatest concentration in Wales. It is likely that Gill lived in a part of the country where it did not occur). In the next issue of *Bird Notes and News* Gill was corrected about his identification. The editor wrote:

> With regard to the little warbler noted by a soldier-ornithologist in Gallipoli, to which the name of 'Firetail' had been given, and which was identified by correspondents of *The Observer* with the Redstart ... probably, almost certainly, refers to the Grey-backed Warbler (*Agrobates familiaris*), the Eastern form of the Rufous Warbler (*A. galactodes*) [now the rufous-tailed scrub robin].

While bird reports were sent in from all the theatres of war, the majority still came from France and Belgium where birdwatching had become a great source of solace and distraction in the face of ever-increasing fatalities. On 2 March 1916, *The Times* carried an article entitled 'Birds at the Front', about a year spent birdwatching in the north of France, by an officer X 'whose name it is not permitted to give but who is related to one of the RSPB Vice-Presidents'. Initially believing that the deafening sound of war would drive away all the birds, contrary to his expectations officer X had been pleased to discover many new species:

> A summer and winter spent at the front, and at the back of the front, have proved to me that the north of France is no birdless region. The noise and bustle of war do not drive away the birds, even from the trenches, and I can remember no nesting season which introduced more birds unknown to me than last summer. Sitting still is a common military manoeuvre, and one can watch birds common in England as well as in France, and others which seldom cross the Channel.[5]

Much to his delight in the summer this had included a number of new species of warbler, officer X stating, 'The only English warblers I did not see were the Dartford and the Wood Warbler, but Nightingales, Blackcaps, Garden Warblers, Sedge, Reed, Grasshopper Warblers all duly came, and with them three Warblers new to me – the Marsh, the Icterine, and the Great Reed Warbler.' The continual bombardment did, however, take a toll on their nesting success. 'The Blackcaps and Garden Warblers had had their first nest blown sideways by shells, and the latter never tried to nest again but the Blackcaps rebuilt within 10 ft. of their old nest, though the three eggs the lady laid were as white as a wood pigeon's,' he recorded. 'The cock did quite his share of incubation, and neither bird moved when they were shelled, nor did the Reed Warblers even raise their heads out of their nest when there was firing.'

Officer X, like many others serving at the front, especially relished finding nests, any search for them among the war-torn landscape often proving to be quite a challenge. 'The Icterine's nest, which I discovered after a search, was very beautiful, rather bulky, deep, and rounded on the outside surface, tied, I think, to a lilac bush about 5 ft. from the ground,' he excitedly wrote, adding, 'the eggs were covered with cherry-coloured spots.' Yet some birds seemed to be almost immune to the noise of shelling, notably the nightingale. 'On May 13, at 3 a.m., in the garden of my chateau I heard a Nightingale begin to sing,' the officer recorded. 'Half an hour afterwards German shells were rained upon the garden incessantly throughout the day. The bird sang without a pause where the shells fell thickest until 12 p.m. and survived, for next morning he started again as cheerily as ever.'

For soldiers who had their own birdwatching 'patch' at home, discovering new species abroad to add to their life list was a real bonus and top of many soldiers' lists was the golden oriole, famed as much for its exotic call as its striking yellow and black plumage. However, it was a call which left officer X unimpressed, although he much admired the bird. 'The Oriole's whistle has a very human sound, rich and full, but his repertoire is meagre. He starts with a splendid note, which can be heard 400 yards off, but it is all over after half-a-dozen bars,' he wrote sniffily. 'The call note is loud and screechy; I can take off both it and the whistle passably. Orioles are amusing, active birds, full of life and sound, and the oak woods of Flanders and the Pas de Calais support a fair stock of them.'

The officer, like many other ornithologists serving in the army, had his favourite birds much like he had his favourite troops and wrote as glowingly about them. 'One of the commonest birds about the trenches is the Crested Lark, a tame cheeky little creature who sings his pleasant trilly song even in January,' he wrote. 'Round Vermelles and Loos he seems to be commoner than anywhere else. I like him immensely, but not quite so much as his cousin the Wood Lark, whom I have not met in Northern France.' He had searched repeatedly for the nest of his second favourite lark on several occasions coming 'within an ace of finding a

Crested Lark's nest'. Success had finally been achieved unexpectedly when he was 'standing-to' during the Second Battle of Ypres. 'It looked more like that of a Skylark than a Woodlark, and was not so neat or so deep as that little bird makes hers,' he wrote fondly. Among the birds of prey, officer X had also seen were 'quite a number Hen Harriers and Buzzards, and I once saw a Peregrine'. He concluded, 'A naturalist who keeps his eyes and ears open will see on the Western Front practically all the birds he would expect in a southern English county, together with those which I have mentioned, and others which may have escaped me.'

Another report from the front by a Lieutenant Colonel Tweedie was published in the March 1916 edition of the *Avicultural Magazine*. Based in Flanders, Tweedie had seen 'the autumn pass and the winter take its place' and despite being within easy shelling range of the 'Bosch lines', he had found a 'fair show' of birds in the neighbourhood. Billeted close to a chateau with a moat and a small ornamental lake in the grounds, he had kept a close eye on the birds there, noting that 'never a day passes without shells of all descriptions flying backwards and forwards'. The bombardment had killed most of the big fish in the lake but the moorhens had continued to feed 'in a field adjoining the lake; they paid not the slightest attention to the shelling. A kingfisher haunts the lake and takes his toll of the small fish'. Commenting on the birds he had seen Tweedie said:

> I have seen some sparrow hawks and a couple of kestrels and one large hawk flying fast and high. I could not distinguish the species. Flocks of chaffinches were all over the place a couple of months ago, but now there are only a few, and the same with wagtails. I saw none but the pied wagtail and one yellow wagtail. Small flocks of larks are in the bare fields, and there are a few blackbirds and thrushes. They sing whenever the sun shines, but this exercise is unlikely to strain their vocal cords as the sun very seldom shows himself. Only once have I seen any redwings, and very occasionally a fieldfare. We have had no cold weather so far, but constant rain and damp, and some gales. There are a few robins, but they do not seem to be so friendly and tame as they are at home [he was obviously not hand-feeding them].[6]

When demolishing an outhouse Tweedie had come across a 'curious little animal hibernating in a straw nest'. Unsure what it was he appealed to readers of the *Avicultural Magazine* to help him identify it, providing a description of it in comparison to the ubiquitous rats in his trench. 'It is about the size of a small rat, colour on back rather darker than an ordinary rat; underneath a dirty white; tail long and hairy but not bushy with a distinct tuft with a grey tip; grey patches on the cheeks; black eyes and rounded ears, larger than a rat's.' After disturbing it he fed the curious little animal some shortbread and moved it to more 'comfortable quarters' in an adjacent hay loft. To thank him for his troubles it had tried to bite him before resuming 'its rudely interrupted winter slumbers'. Despite this Tweedie was quite taken by the creature commenting, 'I hope to bring it home if we both survive.' The mystery of the creature's identity was solved by the editor who added a post note to the article: 'perhaps the oak dormouse – Ed.'

One of the biggest curses of living in the trenches was the other mammal in Tweedie's life: the rat. Attracted by the scraps of food that littered the trenches as well the decomposing bodies of dead soldiers, both brown and in some areas black rats multiplied to plague proportions. Gorged on food left in discarded empty tins and rotting flesh, larger than life rats which knew no fear of man soon became the stuff of legend, even if many of the stories were exaggerated. One soldier wrote: 'The rats were huge. They were so big they would eat a wounded man if he couldn't defend himself.' Some rats became very bold and would even attempt to snatch food from the pockets of sleeping men. Dead bodies in particular attracted them, they reportedly going for eyes first before burrowing their way right into the corpse. One soldier described in macabre detail finding dead bodies while on patrol: 'I saw some rats running from under the dead mens' greatcoats, enormous rats, fat with human flesh. My heart pounded as we edged towards one of the bodies. His helmet had rolled off. The man displayed a grimacing face, stripped of flesh; the skull bare, the eyes devoured and from the yawning mouth leapt a rat.'

The rats in turn attracted a number of predators, notably owls who were very effective at keeping their numbers down as a letter sent to *The Times* by Captain Tailby testified:

When I was up in the trenches recently, I saw numerous Owls; they used to flap about among the trenches at night, quite regardless of shells and snipers, getting a fine harvest of rats and mice, with which the trenches literally swarm. They were the big brown Owls [tawny owls]. They always disappeared two hours before dawn; I never could make out where to, but I suppose to woods behind the lines.

Word soon spread about the effectiveness of owls as rat catchers, many regiments purchasing their own eagle owl from a zoo or breeder back home to rid the trenches of rats. These birds were assigned to soldiers with experience of falconry who trained them to catch rats in confined spaces, the owls soon becoming regimental pets.

Rats became such a problem that in 1915 the British Army appointed an Official Rat Catcher on the Western Front. Philip Gosse (1879–1959) was born in Kensington within a stone's throw of the Natural History Museum. His father was Sir Edmund Gosse, a poet and author, and his grandfather, Philip Henry Gosse, was a famous marine naturalist. Gosse studied medicine at St Bartholomew's Hospital in London and then became a general practitioner, setting up a practice in Beaulieu in the New Forest before joining the Royal Army Medical Corps in 1914. A keen ornithologist, Gosse was billeted at the village of Steenvoorde in northern France. One day confined to his bed with a severe cold, the door was suddenly flung open and in walked a senior officer. In his biography, *A Naturalist Goes to War*, published in 1934, he recalled their conversation:

'Are you Captain P. H. G. Gosse?'

'Yes,' I admitted, though wondering whatever it was about.

'Well,' continued the staff officer, 'am I right in understanding you know all about rats?'

Now that, I thought, is a strange question to be asked by a total stranger, still more so when you are lying in bed. I wondered what was at the back of it, and whether it might lead to some nice quiet job, or if I was to be court-martialled for a pastime so unbecoming an officer and a gentleman as skinning mice. Like everybody else who had been in the line for any length of time, excepting those rare and to-be-envied blood-lust soldiers who enjoyed the War, I was all for a safe and cushy post if such was offered me.

But this odd question, 'You know all about rats?' No … I wanted to learn a little more before giving a definite answer. So, to gain time I replied, 'Well, I know a good deal about birds.'

'That's excellent,' said he. 'You are appointed Rat Officer to the Second Army, and will report forthwith to the Director of Medical Services to the Second Army at Hazebrouck.' Whereupon without waiting for any further observations from me or bidding me farewell or even expressing any interest in my bad cold, the fierce one right-about turned and marched out of the room.[7]

Gosse's job was to travel around the trenches lecturing the officers and their men about the need for good sanitation and how to use rat traps, he making and demonstrating a variety of his own designs. At first, he found it was a hard slog, his audiences largely being unappreciative, the only subjects lower on their list 'being flies and parasites, the experts on which were familiarly referred to as O.C. [Officer Commanding] Maggots and O.C. Flies'. However, after a while his lectures began to be better received and by early 1917, they had become quite popular, particularly his table of macabre exhibits, Gosse having captured and stuffed a wide range of animals to be found in Flanders from birds to beetles and rats to bats. 'In fact, my lecture became in time to be looked upon as a sort of drawing-room entertainment,' he wrote proudly, 'and I went about from place to place giving performances much in the way conjurers and ventriloquists do, who give refined entertainments at children's Christmas parties.'

As a result of their popularity, his lectures on rats were added to the 'schools' soldiers were required to attend along with 'sniping, bombing and musketry' as well as the 'academies' on 'bayonet fighting, trench mortars, poison gas and the construction of latrines and incinerators'. After the lecture was over there would be questions, Gosse finding it a 'pleasant surprise to find out how keen these soldiers were on natural history. At first, I feared they would be bored with anecdotes about birds and beasts, but the majority seemed very interested.'

By far the most popular part of the session was when right at the end Gosse produced 'Darkie's Rat'. This had been trapped at a popular *estaminent* (café) 'ruled over by a big, tousled Flemish hoyden called 'Darkie'. So, Goose had christened the rat Darkie after the madame owner who was 'not without good looks of a sort' and a great favourite among the soldiers, both for her food and her favours. Unflatteringly to her figure, Gosse described it as a 'colossus of a buck rat' which after being killed he stuffed with cotton wool until it assumed 'surprising and alarming' proportions. Gosse would then produce his 'super-rat' at the end of his lecture just like a conjurer would pull out a rabbit from his hat. According to Gosse this was a popular 'crowning touch, and never failed to bring the lecture to a pleasant if boisterous conclusion'. However, on one occasion Darkie was greeted with such loud clapping and cheering that the soldiers failed to notice at the door to the lecture a glowering general. Upon seeing him, the audience's laughter suddenly petered out and the room went deathly silent, the general making it clear he was not expecting 'frivolity at military lectures'.

Even Gosse's unbridled enthusiasm for wildlife met its match with Captain Scrivener, the Town Major and Area Commandant, whom he was billeted with, a man he described as having 'limited interests'. Finding him not interested in books, Gosse asked him about wild birds and 'was pleased to learn that birds were a particular passion of his. But on going more deeply into the subject I found that his interest in birds was entirely confined to one species, the pheasant'. His interest in them was their 'whole-scale slaughter', in the process Gosse stating sarcastically that the English countryside would then be reduced to a place full of 'woods and coppices provided by an all-wise deity to harbour vast numbers of pheasants for Scrivener and his city friends to shoot on Saturday.'

By the summer of 1916, birdwatching had become so popular that it competed on a par as a pastime with smoking, writing letters, cards, draughts, chess, gambling, sports and shooting rats. When not at the front in the trenches preparing for battle, soldiers were sent to the rear for leisure and relaxation, essential to provide a break from the overwhelming stress of combat. Typically, troops spent four to six days in the trenches at the front before moving back and spending an equal number of days in secondary and reserve trenches. This system of rotation, along with occasional leave to England, gave the troops ample opportunity to birdwatch if their shell-shocked eyes and ears permitted it.

A piece in *The Times* dated 10 May 1916, by an anonymous officer who was previously a gamekeeper, recorded the birdlife in the grounds of a deserted, bombed-out French chateau. The note spoke volumes about his prejudices, he finding 'spinneys filled with warblers, and almost every thicket holding its Nightingale or Blackcap, Blackbirds, Thrushes, Wrens and Robins even more plentiful than in an English park, despite an Irish abundance of Magpies and Jays enough to break a gamekeeper's heart'. Vermin even thrived in the ruins so that:

> Every house that is blown to bits by shell-fire provides an endless choice of fascinating nesting-places for sparrows among the chinks of the ruined walls; and never did Starlings have such opportunity for unmolested housekeeping as in the remains of these poor battered churches. As for the guns, they are to the birds, presumably, no more than thunder, and when a shell falls near it is only some new, if startling, natural phenomenon.

It was not just at the front and in no man's land that serving ornithologists recorded birds but also at sea on the world's oceans. On 31 May 1916, the Battle of Jutland took place off the North Sea coast of Denmark's Jutland Peninsula. The clash between the battleships of the Royal Navy's Grand Fleet and the Imperial German Navy's High Seas Fleet was the major naval engagement of the war. Using the battleship *Hipper* as bait the German High Seas Fleet had set a trap to destroy part of the numerically superior Royal Navy and break their naval blockade of Germany. The Royal Navy under Admiral Earl John Jellicoe (1859–1935) had a fleet of over 100 ships, the Germans just under a hundred. During the ensuing battle the British lost fourteen ships and the Germans eleven with both sides suffering thousands of casualties. Among the British ships destroyed that day was HMS *Queen Mary*, a battlecruiser commanded by Harry Pennell (1882–1916) who had made a name for himself serving on Robert Falcon Scott's British Antarctic Expedition between 1910 and 1913. A keen supporter of the RSPB, their obituary of him stated, 'Commander Harry Pennell, R.N., who went down in the *Queen Mary*, in the Naval Battle, was a keen bird-student and a supporter of the Society, taking special interest in the work of the Watchers Committee.'[8]

While the Royal Navy had its fair share of birders on board, it couldn't compete with the army whose static soldiers had the unenviable advantage of being able to comprehensively survey their local patch, albeit often from a trench. On 10 June 1916, *The Times* carried an article from a 'correspondent' entitled 'Birds of a French Wood' about the many species found there including the bird which most soldiers wanted to see, the exotic golden oriole. However, it was a bird far more often heard than seen, its fluting song usually delivered unseen from high in the treetops. For some soldiers dreaming of escaping to warmer lands, its foreign-sounding call even conjured up images of tropical islands. Hearing it floating above the noise of war, *The Times* correspondent wrote:

> The Orioles are of course the chief joy of the wood. They are always in the same small section. One has only to go there and stand still for a while, and sooner or later the beautiful flute-like liquid call comes ringing from somewhere out of the green world above. Then a brilliant meteor of yellow and black flashes through a gap between the tree-tops, and the liquid whistle which sounded on the left hand is now on the right. Then it is behind one, then in front; and from somewhere inside the circle of sound one hears the harsh wheezing answer of the hen bird. The note of the hen Oriole is as ill-matched to her lord's as is the croak of the hen Nightingale.

The golden oriole was typical of many of the rarer birds in the field which often only gave away their presence through their song. For many soldiers on guard duty, confined to their trench or working behind the lines, trying to actually see birds in battle was often fraught with danger so instead they had to fall back on their ability to identify bird songs and calls. Bird song was at its loudest at dawn which was often the time when the first artillery barrage opened up so troops near a wood were often treated to a crescendo of competing sounds at first light. In the case of birds like the nightingale, famed for its astonishingly rich repertoire and volume, this meant it often went head-to-head with the guns behind the lines – and won: the nightingale's song is so loud because it is able to produce over 1,000 different sounds, compared with just 340 made by skylarks, about 100 by blackbirds and one by a howitzer.

So as the sun rose over the wood a chorus of birds often competed in the volume stakes with a barrage of guns. When it came to which commanded the most attention, W. Waldegrave Little, an officer serving with the Royal Army Medical Corps (RAMC), thought there was no contest, writing in *Bird Notes and News*:

There was an article in *The Times* recently on 'Birds at the Front' ... discuss[ing] the reasons why the birds take so little notice of gun fire and bursting of shells, saying they seem to treat it like thunder, as a loud noise which does them no harm. It must be so. Last spring it was discussed in *The Times* whether the demon of war would drive the birds away, and I agreed with the writer that it would not. It was interesting that I heard the first Nightingale while in my bed on the tailboard of a motor lorry, in a cornfield, while I lay listening to monster shells bursting in a town eight miles back from the firing-line. This year it was in a roofless village and close to a noisy field gun that I heard the first Nightingale; but they are nothing like as common in this part of France as they were in Belgium last year.[9]

While most soldier 'birders' could identify some songs, other species heard at the front would have been unfamiliar or new to them, even experienced birders having to refresh their knowledge and retune their ears at the start of spring. Waldegrave Little was no exception and decided to use the pages of the RSPB's magazine to appeal for help. Clearly a man with a deadpan sense of humour, he wrote tongue firmly in cheek:

Three birds still baffle me. One that hides in the fields and says 'Wit-wit-it'; one that pipes in the trees with fluty notes like a Blackbird just beginning, and says 'Oriol-ole' nothing more. I think I saw it once, about the size of a Cuckoo. The other is the one that calls at night like a big frog [his ornithological challenge would be taken up by another officer, F. Goodyear, in the next issue].

Humorous asides apart for Waldegrave Little, like so many troops serving at the front, the time he spent studying birds was a welcome distraction from the boredom and danger associated with trench warfare, even if he didn't appreciate the French landscape. When posted on rota behind the line he wrote, 'I get plenty of opportunities of seeing the country, having continually to walk from one village to another, and my nature studies are a great relaxation from a life that would otherwise be very monotonous. I cannot say I like this perpetual hedgeless landscape, with all the villages completely hidden by trees.'

Over time certain birds developed the ability to not only compete with the noise of war but also to mimic it, sometimes with humorous results. A particularly accomplished mimic was the starling which was common throughout the front. Soldiers noted they were especially astute imitators of sounds that had a whistle but their vocalizations could also include whizzes, rattles and pops (the reason starlings do this is still the subject of research but scientists believe it is a complex ploy used to identify their location, deceive or keep rivals at bay and impress potential mates). An artillery officer, writing in *The Spectator*, said, 'The Starlings out here have acquired the trick of giving three shrill taxi whistles, in imitation of the call for enemy aeroplanes. It is great fun to see everyone diving for cover; I was nearly taken in myself the other day.'

Yet for many unfortunate soldiers bird song was not just background noise but the last sound they heard in this life when lying mortally wounded in no man's land. One of the most common birds on the battlefield was the skylark, whose beautiful song is produced on the wing and could often be heard even above the noise of battle. Their importance can be gauged by the frequency with which they appeared in the diary entries and letters soldiers sent back home from the front, skylarks being immortalized by men like John William Streets (1886–1916) who wrote a hauntingly beautiful poem called 'A Lark Above the Trenches':

> Hushed is the shriek of hurtling shells: and hark!
> Somewhere within that bit of soft blue sky –
> Grand in his loneliness, his ecstasy,
> His lyric wild and free – carols a lark.
>
> I in the trench, he lost in heaven afar,
> I dream of Love, its ecstasy he sings;
> Doth lure my soul to love till like a star
> It flashes into Life: O tireless wings
>
> That beat love's message into melody –
> A song that touches in this place remote
> Gladness supreme in its undying note
> And stirs to life the soul of memory –
> 'Tis strange that while you're beating into life
> Men here below and plunged in sanguine strife![10]

The eldest of twelve children, Streets started work as a miner at the age of 14 and educated himself in his spare time, poetry becoming his passion. A sergeant in the Sheffield City Battalion, the so-called Sheffield Pals, he was killed on 1 July 1916, the first day of the Battle of the Somme. His poems were posthumously published the next year under the ironic title 'The Undying Splendour'.

As birdwatching grew in popularity so did the demand for field guides so soldiers could identify birds they had seen in the field. To distribute the guides the RSPB teamed up with two charities operating huts at the front: the Church Army and the Young Men's Christian Association (YMCA), who worked alongside the Royal Army Medical Corps and the Red Cross in hospitals and convalescent camps treating the troops. While the Red Cross concentrated on relief work with refugees and prisoners of war, the YMCA focused on the welfare of the serving soldiers. Despite being a 'men's association', the YMCA decided at the outbreak of the conflict that it needed to appeal to women volunteers to help treat the wounded. So, in the month following the declaration of war, the YMCA Women's Auxiliary was formed and soon 250 social centres or 'huts' for troops were operating at the front. By 1916 the total number of huts had grown to 1,500 which were located in training camps, garrisons, transit towns, railways stations and even bombed-out buildings. Huts were also set up in tents and dugouts in the trenches, each providing an opportunity to escape the boredom and horrors of the war. The huts provided hot drinks and refreshments, some of the larger ones also providing meals, showers, games and even a library. The RSPB ensured that each hut was well stocked with books on birds, including identification guides, leaflets and copies of its journal, *Bird Notes and News*.

One of the most important jobs the YMCA did was to help relatives visit their loved ones if they were wounded or dying in one of the hospitals at the front. By the end of the war over 40,000 women wearing the YMCA's red triangle had volunteered in the huts, many taking great risks to help the men in their care. They included a young driver called Betty Stevenson, who commented:

> Our motorcars met every boat at Boulogne and at Havre, and automatically the relatives of men dangerously wounded were handed over to us and we motored them to their destination, wherever it

might be. Another job for the drivers was to take visiting relatives to funerals, a distressing job for everyone involved. The YMCA also provided each relative with a photograph of the grave to take home.

On 30 May 1918, Betty was driven to her own funeral in her motorcar after she was killed by an enemy plane while serving as a member of the Women's Auxiliary just after her twenty-first birthday.[11]

Many ornithologists serving in the trenches continued to be members of bird organizations at home, one of the most prestigious being the British Ornithologists' Union (BOU). Founded in 1858, the BOU is one of the world's oldest ornithological organizations and in 1916 boasted an international membership stretching across the world including some of the most venerable names in ornithology. However, like many organizations of the time, it was a men-only club, members wishing to join having to be proposed and voted on at its annual general meeting. The BOU published its journal *Ibis* quarterly, containing papers at the forefront of ornithological research and it also maintained the British List, the definitive list of birds which had been seen in Britain.

Like many organizations the war took its toll on the BOU, many of its members going off to fight, while at home it had seen a reduction in both its membership and income. According to its minutes the number of members serving abroad in 1916 included nine in the Navy, a hundred and thirteen in France, seven in Egypt and Gallipoli, eight in India, three in East and South Africa, together with thirty-seven serving on the home front. Of these five had already been killed in action or died from illness and one was a prisoner of war in Germany. With the list of those enlisting or dying in action lengthening all the time, the BOU found itself having to take some tough decisions to ensure its own survival.

The BOU's 1916 AGM took place on 8 March at the offices of the Zoological Society of London.[12] Mr Henry Munt stood in for the president, Colonel Robert George Wardlaw-Ramsay (1852–1921), and thirty-nine members were present. Munt was eccentric even by BOU standards and was known as the 'white egg collector' because he only collected white or unpatterned eggs (his collection still resides with the Natural History Museum in Tring and is unique in that it is the only collection not catalogued in the museum's register). The secretary opened the meeting by stating, 'The Committee regrets that owing to the very heavy extraordinary expenditure during 1914–15 they have to report a further grave decrease in the funds of the Union.' Despite reducing the cost of its *Ibis* magazine, the BOU still registered an overall debt of '£268 1s. 6d', the result of existing publication commitments together with another £150 one-off debt to cover the heavy cost of producing an index to the *Ibis* covering the years 1895–1912. After outlining the union's dire financial position, the committee with regret stated that a number of members had died since the last meeting, many of whom had been killed in the war, including Lord Brabourne, Cecil MacMillan Dyer, Gerald Legge, Dr Charles Stonham, Major Whitehead and Richard Bowen Woosnam (for their obituaries see the Ornithological Roll of Honour). Membership figures for the union were then given, showing it had declined from 433 'ordinary members' in 1914 to 420 in 1916. With no sign of the end of the war, it was clear that the union was going to have to find new ways of boosting its flagging membership. After electing a further fifteen 'gentlemen' the vexed subject of whether or not to admit women was raised. This immediately provoked controversy, one member highlighting the tactics of the women's suffragette movement before the war and a heated debate ensued. It was finally decided that a vote should be taken and on the recommendation of the committee, it was proposed 'That ladies be admitted to Ordinary Membership of the B. O. U.'. However, the motion was spoken against by several prominent members, one then moving an amendment 'That the question of ladies becoming Ordinary Members of the B. O. U. be held over until after the War', effectively kicking the matter into the long grass. Following further impassioned debate led by Lionel Walter Rothschild (1868–1937), the banking magnate and zoologist, the amendment was first put to the meeting and lost, ten voting in favour and twenty against. The original motion to admit ladies was then put and declared carried with twenty votes in favour and fifteen against. Over fifty years after its creation women were finally to be admitted to the BOU.

The admission of women to the BOU was a small but significant step in women's historic struggle for equality. Just after war had been declared the women's suffragette movement suspended hostilities in its campaign for the vote, although it remained split over its support for the war. When it came to birds it was women who had founded the Royal Society for the Protection of Birds back in 1889; in March 1917 the Women's Army

Auxiliary Corps was formed in response to the shortage of workers and the conscription of men a year earlier. Although women could not fight, they served in a wide variety of roles on the front line from doctors to ambulance drivers and on the home front from tram drivers to munition workers. Like the BOU, the War Office had found out the hard way that women were indispensable for winning the war.

Chapter 5

Birds and Enemy Aliens

As the war progressed some eccentric ornithologists wrote to the RSPB with their observations, the organization flattered enough to publish their sometimes off-the-wall reports. A good example was a Mr F. Goodyear who was an officer serving with the Royal Engineers in Flanders and, despite being an amateur ornithologist, clearly fancied himself as an authority on birds in the field. The war had been the first time that Goodyear had been lucky enough to see golden orioles and the bird had made a lasting impression on him. Writing in the autumn 1916 edition of the RSPB's magazine, he stated:

> Golden Orioles were quite new to me, and they have impressed me with their tropical habits – the elusiveness of their call, its mellowness, their amazingly brilliant flight, high up from tree to tree – they seem made for the deep shadows of a far sunnier land than Flanders during these last few weeks. I find that the bright colour of the male is not without protective value when brilliant sunshine falls through a broken canopy of leaves[1].

Goodyear also vouched for how common the nightingale was at the front, writing about the pleasure it had given him:

> As for the Nightingales, during May I lived in a chateau where about six pairs were nesting in the grounds. One was frequently singing within a few feet of our window and I seldom went in or out without catching glimpses of their chestnut tails as they whisked into a clump of bushes or the lower boughs of a tree. They were a perpetual delight.

Goodyear's flowery observations on orioles and nightingales were just a pretext for his real reason for writing: he liked solving ornithological mysteries. Despite his limited knowledge, Goodyear couldn't resist having a go at identifying the three birds that had baffled Waldegrave Little, the officer in the RAMC, in the previous issue. Waldegrave Little had written, tongue firmly in cheek, that he couldn't identify a bird saying 'Oriol-ole', one producing a frog noise at night and another with a 'Wit-wit-it' call. At first Goodyear was unable to decide whether or not to take him seriously. 'When he says he can't identify the "Oriol-ole", I think he's joking,' Goodyear complained. 'His syllabization of the note gives the show away: though it is not the size of a Cuckoo, of course.' Goodyear also solemnly pointed out that even he had at first failed to identify the orioles call, a French ornithologist friend telling him it was made by 'yellow magpies'. Mystified, they had looked up the word magpie in a an English–French pocket dictionary, the entry stating 'Magpie (ornith) – Pie'. On seeing the word 'ornith' his friend had pointed to it excitedly. 'Then it suddenly dawned on me,' the serious Goodyear wrote: 'ornith — oriole: and a day or two later I was able to verify my inference in person.'

Goodyear was even more determined to also solve the mystery of the birds that made a frog noise at night and the 'Wit-wit-it' call. So, he pondered, 'As for the bird that calls at night like a big frog, isn't it a frog? This is a tremendous country for frogs [the poor Goodyear clearly failed to get the in-joke. As most experienced ornithologists knew, Waldegrave Little was referring to a nightjar whose churring song is often likened to natterjack toads calling].' As to the bird which had made the 'Wit-wit-it' call, the stumped Goodyear exclaimed, 'I would sell my tired soul to get a sight of that bird. I have pages of notes on it.' He went on earnestly, 'My own version of the cry is "Whitt-wit-whitt", which is pretty nearly the same as his. It runs in the crops and ditches. The note is given with great violence, so that you can hear it a long way off. Sometimes I have thought it was a sort of frog, I wish somebody could throw some light upon it.' Goodyear finished by posing his own ornithological question: 'Is the Blue-headed Wagtail an inhabitant of these parts?' he inquired, adding, 'I think I have seen it, but without adequate books of reference cannot be sure.' He signed off, 'I am not in the firing line, but thoroughly agree with Mr Little that the habit of noting birds, etc., affords a great relaxation out here.' At this point the RSPB's editor felt the need to step in and save Goodyear's soul as well as his own sanity, stating in square brackets: '[The "Wit-wit-wit" bird is the Quail, whose call is generally rendered

"Wet-my-lips". Mr. Goodyear was probably right as to the Blue-headed Wagtail.— Ed. B. N. & N.]' Sadly, like so many other ornithological correspondents, Goodyear was later killed, the editor mourning his loss in the winter 1916 issue.

It was not just eccentric writers who provided the society with sometimes questionable copy but also its own staff. In the autumn 1916 edition of its magazine, the RSPB put forward the idea of turning cemeteries into bird sanctuaries by managing them for nature, essentially not cutting them during the summer and putting up bird boxes. While the idea was undoubtedly beneficial for birds, the timing of the piece was not very sensitive with hundreds of young soldiers dying each day at the front. However, the society did at least have the tact to report that the idea was an American one, stating:

> It is interesting to know that the idea is being widely adopted in the United States; and a charming leaflet on the subject, by Mr Gilbert Pearson [1873–1943, founder of National Audubon Society], has been issued by the Audubon Association. At present Omaha, Neb[raska], claims to possess the largest of such sanctuaries. It contains 320 acres, and forty nesting-boxes and two bird-baths have been installed.

After the war over 4,000 cemeteries were created to bury the dead, the majority being located in France and Belgium. They are maintained by the Commonwealth War Graves Commission and are immaculately kept, the grass being closely mown. For many of the ornithologists who died in action the idea of turning their cemeteries into a living bird reserve by managing them for nature would have appealed. One soldier by the name of Alexander Gillespie had a similar but even more audacious idea: to turn all of no man's land from the Belgian coast to the Swiss border into a *'Via Sacra'* or 'Sacred Way' for nature (for his extraordinary idea see the Roll of Honour).

Despite having no final resting place from the fury and noise of war, birds proved very adept at adapting to their new surroundings. One soldier to record just how the remarkable they were at living in a war zone was H. Thoburn Clarke who was with the Royal Field Artillery where he was responsible for a horse-drawn gun. He had already recorded a blackbird 'raising a brood of four among the sandbags only about four feet from the muzzle of his gun' and a 'pair of hedge-sparrows, whose nest site was the hub of a broken wheel which was continually under fire, feeding their nestlings with complete disregard of dropping shrapnel and bursting shells'. Trudging around the front line, Thoburn Clarke recorded in detail the lives of the swallows, house martins and swifts he saw in his diary, including the dates they arrived, fledged and left. On 7 October 1916, he used this information to publish an article in *Country Life* magazine called 'Swallows at the Front' about the hirundines and swifts who had made his battery their home.[2]

Thoburn Clarke recorded his first swallow of the year on Easter Sunday, alerted by his air-scout who was looking out for hostile aircraft. He noted the bird was 'hawking about over the guns catching insects in the most natural manner in the world'. Amazed that it took no notice of the noise, he watched the swallow flying overhead with the aeroplanes which were 'looking like somewhat larger birds against the perfectly blue sky'. Later that day a service was held just behind the lines to commemorate the dead and Thoburn Clarke watched the swallows skimming backwards and forwards as the chaplain gave prayers. It was, he thought, 'a message from our dear homeland' and described it as 'a scene to live in one's memory for ever'. The next day he recorded that swallows and house martins arrived in force but the war had devastated the buildings and barns in which they had previously nested. Writing that this 'did not trouble them in the least', at one ruined house he noticed them 'flying joyously in and out of a great shell hole, and later on I saw several pairs of Martins hurriedly nest building on the walls of a drawing-room, the ceiling of which had been swept away with the exception of a handsomely moulded cornice.'

As his horse-drawn gun moved between positions, Thoburn Clarke watched them gather mud from the dry and dusty roads, noting they appeared to devote 'all the early part of the morning to nest building, the rest of the day to collecting food and resting'. On one occasion the Germans shelled his position for an hour and a half and Thoburn Clarke had to retreat into a cellar. On coming out, he found that shells had demolished the building above him but 'the Swallows apparently did not care, for they were not in the least perturbed by the noise of the shelling, and continued feeding their young ones as if nothing had happened. Before the day was over, they were using the shell hole as a convenient entrance through which to pass backwards and forwards with food for their young'.

Recording the number of young fledged in each nest, Thoburn Clarke found they made a pretty picture sitting together on a rafter so that 'one regretted that a camera was forbidden at the front. I should have dearly loved to snap the row of white-throated heads peeping down at us'. He was particularly taken how tame the birds seemed to be given the devastation and noise around them, noting that on one occasion a pair 'calmly appropriated the rack on which we hung our jackets. Needless to say, we resigned the rack to them'.

At dusk on the evening of 26 August 1916, Thoburn Clarke saw thousands of swifts migrating overhead and, homesick, could not 'help wondering whether they had come from England'. On 4 September, he recorded large flocks of swallows 'hanging thick as beads on the telephone wires along the communication trenches. I did not see the final act of the migration, for as usual we were moved on, and our next position did not happen to be near a river, which, I think, is always the Swallows' gathering place when collecting for their flight'. He concluded that:

The idea that gun-fire would chase away the birds has been quite exploded [sic] ... Personally, I think the Swallows and Martins prefer the ruins. The vast quantity of insects which the life on the battlefield encourages provides them with plenty of food and accounts for the fact that Swallows and Martins are far more plentiful than they were during pre-war days.

One incident in particular stuck in his mind and showed how insouciant swallows could be:

During one of the battles on the Somme the Germans shelled a small wood. One shell struck the trunk of a tree in which a large number of Martins and Swallows were perching. The tree slowly bowed, and the birds went up with the cloud of smoke as it fell. It was only when the birds scattered that one realized that they were not bits of shrapnel, yet, after flying about for a few minutes, they settled down on another tree, preened their plumage and twittered as if nothing unusual had happened. No doubt, having been hatched and reared amid the surroundings of battle, they would think it strange if the incessant clash and clang were silent, and the country once more assumed its ancient aspect of peace and calm. Certainly they would miss the vast quantities of insects which the battle has attracted, and which must be an ever abiding joy to the insect-eating birds.

Another soldier to write about the birds he found at the trenches was the famous author and satirist, Lance Sergeant Hector Hugh Munro, whose nom de plume was 'Saki'. On 14 October 1916, he wrote an article called 'Birds on the Western Front' for the *Weekly Westminster* magazine. It was a particularly poignant piece because it would be his last as just a month later, on 14 November, Munro would be killed by a sniper. Best known for his short stories which contrasted the banality and hypocrisy of Edwardian society with the life and death struggles of nature, at the age of 45 he was too old to be fighting at the front but being a patriot had volunteered anyway. Typical of his dark, waspish sense of humour was a carol he composed for Christmas in the trenches:

> While shepherds watched their flocks by night
> All seated on the ground
> A high-explosive shell came down
> And mutton rained around.

When it came to ornithology, the birds of prey attracted to the rats and mice in the trenches particularly interested Munro, he commenting:

> .... there has been a partial mobilization of Owls, particularly Barn Owls, following in the wake of the mice and making laudable efforts to thin out their numbers ... The Buzzard, that earnest seeker after mice, does not seem to be taking any war risks, at least I have never seen one out here, but Kestrels hover about all day in the hottest parts of the line, not in the least disconcerted apparently when a promising mouse-area suddenly rises in the air in a cascade of black or yellow earth. Sparrowhawks are fairly numerous, and a mile or two back from the firing line I saw a pair of Hawks that I took to be Red-legged Falcons circling over the tops of an oak copse.[3]

The interest and enthusiasm birds generated on the Western Front was in marked contrast to the attitude taken by gamekeepers on the home front. While many had been sent to war in France, some of those at home in the absence of any controls or monitoring had declared war on wildlife, particularly what they considered 'vermin'. It was an issue that the RSPB was campaigning hard on, stating in its autumn editorial, 'it is the gamekeeper who is mainly responsible for the disappearance of so many of our once common birds of prey and for reducing the numbers of other species which we can ill afford to lose'. Munro was also highly critical of gamekeepers and used his article to contrast the partridges he found back home on shooting estates with those he saw on the battlefield. 'The English gamekeeper, whose knowledge of wildlife usually runs on limited and perverted lines,' he wrote, 'has evolved a sort of religion as to the nervous debility of even the hardiest game birds.' Gently mocking them, he continued, 'according to his beliefs a terrier trotting across a field in which a Partridge is nesting, or a mouse-hawking Kestrel hovering over the hedge, is sufficient cause to drive the distracted bird off its eggs and send it whirring into the next county.' In contrast he noted:

> The Partridge of the war zone shows no signs of such sensitive nerves. The rattle and rumble of transport, the constant coming and going of bodies of troops, the incessant rattle of musketry and deafening explosions of artillery, the night-long flare and flicker of star-shells, have not sufficed to scare the local birds away from their chosen feeding grounds, and to all appearances they have not been deterred from raising their broods.

The partridge of the war zone was, he believed, a lesson that a lot of gung-ho gamekeepers could learn from. Clearly aware of the war on birds, especially the sparrow, going on at home, he declared, 'Gamekeepers who are serving with the colours might seize the opportunity to indulge in a little useful nature study.'

The most touching of Munro's stories concerned a chaffinch which lived in the 'corner of a stricken wood', which he commented, 'has had a name made for it[self] in history, but shall be nameless here.' Writing about the moment that the wood was devastated by exploding shells, he described the 'lyddite and shrapnel and machine-gun fire' which 'swept and raked and bespattered that devoted spot' as though 'the artillery of an entire Division had suddenly concentrated on it'. In the mayhem he had watched a female chaffinch, 'a wee hen', who 'flitted wistfully to and fro, amid splintered and falling branches that had never a green bough left on them'. As the small bird wandered among the wounded, Munro wondered 'why anything having wings and no pressing reason for remaining should have chosen to stay in such a place'. He concluded that the chaffinch must have a nest nearby and young 'whom it was too scared to feed, too loyal to desert'. Later on, he saw a small flock of chaffinches 'blundering' into the wood in search of food but 'unlike the solitary hen-bird, they made no secret of their desire to get away as fast as their dazed wits would let them'. It was a lifesaving move which sadly Munro failed to apply to his own predicament (for his obituary see the Ornithological Roll of Honour).

Birds were not just monitored by ornithologists on the ground but also in the air. As well as aerial combat, officers in the Royal Flying Corps and the French Flying Corps flew regular reconnaissance missions over enemy lines. Early in the war these were low-level flights with pilots reporting verbally on enemy lines when they got back to base but as the war progressed planes started carrying a full-time photographer. By 1916 radio had been developed so that pilots were in constant touch with their bases. Pilots flying missions soon started seeing birds and those who were ornithologists took great pleasure in recording the species and the height they were flying at, particularly during migration. On 11 November 1916, a French pilot who was a member of the RSPB published some of his notes in the *Pall Mall Gazette*:

> Swallows seem to prefer an altitude of 2,000 ft, whereas Wild Duck fly usually at fully 5,000 ft. They are remarkable, also, for the marvellous uniformity with which they follow their leader. The turns and twists are taken with such simultaneity that a flock appears to turn and wheel automatically, so extraordinarily together do they move. When climbing they fly at about sixty-five miles an hour, and are good for seventy once they have got their height and have spread out to let themselves go. Last March [we] met some Plovers at 6,500 ft., which is the highest at which [we have] seen a company of birds.[4]

In December 1916, a new ornithologist joined the Royal Flying Corps who was to make an exceptional contribution to conservation. Collingwood 'Cherry' Ingram was born in 1880 within a stone's throw of the Natural History Museum in London. On Monday, 11 December 1916, at the age of 36, he reported for duty as a compass officer at the Aircraft Repair Section of No. 1 Aircraft Depot on the old racecourse in St-Omer, northern France. One of his first acts was to record the behaviour of crested larks in his diary which 'strutted about in pairs between the aeroplane sheds and around the mess and canteen tents'.[5] Four days earlier he had set sail for France on the same day that the new coalition government had been sworn in, headed up by David Lloyd George (1863–1945) as Prime Minister.

Ingram's parents were Sir William Ingram and Mary Eliza Collingwood Stirling who were both independently wealthy. His grandfather was Herbert Ingram, the founder of *The Illustrated London News*, the world's first weekly illustrated magazine and a hugely popular title. After Herbert's death in 1860, the business was taken over by his father William who was also a Liberal politician and sat in the House of Commons representing Boston from 1878 to 1895. Both Collingwood's parents were very eccentric nature lovers, who kept a small private zoo and a menagerie of pets at home. Their love of nature extended to them sharing their house with an exotic range of animals and wild birds, blackbirds reportedly nesting in the dining room and sparrows sleeping in the sleeves of Mary's nightgown. During the nesting season Mary hand-fed them with mealworms and gave the sparrows locks of her own hair and ribbons from her dress to build their nests.

From the age of 10 Ingram spent his days searching for wild birds and sketching them in his diary. By the age of 15 he had produced a hand-illustrated book of the birds of Britain. His father had used his wealth to finance collecting expeditions to Australia and Papua New Guinea and one of Ingram's first jobs was cataloguing the specimens brought back at the Natural History Museum. In 1906, he married Florence Laing and, reflecting his interests, they went on honeymoon to Japan so Ingram could locate the rare White's thrush. When war broke out, he was working on an illustrated book on the birds of France and was commissioned in to the Kent Cyclist Battalion (KCB) with the temporary rank of captain.

Ingram cycled off to war not just with his gun and bicycle but also his sketchpad and binoculars.

After training at Romney Marsh, where he was in 'ornithological heaven', in 1916 the KCB was redeployed and Ingram was transferred to the Admiralty where he learnt how to set and monitor compasses. After training, his captaincy was confirmed and he was seconded to the newly formed Royal Flying Corps. Next to enemy planes and the cold, the biggest challenge facing most pilots was navigation and Ingram's specialist knowledge on compasses was much in demand. Travelling between bases in northern France, he made sure his sketchbook and binoculars were always at hand to record the birds he found along the way. Ingram's love of birds not only made a major contribution to ornithology but also helped him make sense of the slaughter he saw in the air, the average lifespan of a pilot in 1916 being measured in days.

While visiting the aerodromes, Ingram sought out pilots known to be interested in ornithology such as Charles Portal (1893–1971) who would go on to become Marshal of the Royal Air Force during the Second World War. Together they produced detailed notes on the heights that different birds flew, Ingram summarizing their research in a short paper published in 1919 in *Ibis*. (After the war Collingwood focused more on horticulture than ornithology, becoming a world authority on Japanese cherries. Despite this, he remained a member of the BOU for a record 81 years. His war diaries were finally published in full a century after the start of the war, in 2014. They contain a wealth of ornithological notes, highly detailed pencil sketches and reflections on the war and appropriately enough were given the title *Wings over the Western Front*.)

The start of the year 1917 saw the war enter a decisive new phase when Germany declared unrestricted submarine warfare with the aim of starving Britain into defeat. This was followed in April by the United States entering the war on the side of the Allies, although American troops did not arrive at the front in numbers until June. At home anti-German sentiment reached new heights with rioting, assaults on suspected Germans and the looting of stores owned by people with German-sounding names. Before the war ornithologists in Britain and Germany had worked closely together and organizations like the RSPB and the Avicultural Society had counted many Germans among their members. However, when war broke out British bird organizations soon showed their true colours, especially after the sinking of the *Lusitania* in 1915, severing links with former German colleagues and instead reporting on 'German barbarity'. Reflecting the zeitgeist, a note in the RSPB's spring 1917 edition of its magazine read:

> One of the daily papers, apparently at a loss how to fill its columns, reports that certain German prisoners are 'happy in their captivity' and so 'fond of birds and animals' that they have gone in for keeping rabbits to give variety to their menu and have a number of caged Robins in their camp. This is precisely the way in which Germans might be expected to exhibit their 'fondness'; but why they should be permitted by the authorities to further outrage a heaven they have sufficiently offended, by keeping English Robins in captivity is more than the normal Englishmen can understand.[6]

The continual reporting from the front particularly impacted on the lives of Germans and other 'enemy aliens' living in Britain such as William Teschemaker. He was a highly experienced aviculturist whose articles on breeding and rearing birds had regularly appeared in the pages of the *Avicultural Magazine* before the war. Although he was a naturalized British citizen, Teschemaker had a distinctly German surname (originating from the German word 'tasche' or 'bag', referring to a maker of bags). He lived in Ringmore, Teignmouth and had been a member of the Avicultural Society since 1904. Following the outbreak of war, he had experienced at first hand the rise in nationalist feeling, many people taunting and abusing him because of his German surname.

Teschemaker's sister, Constance, also lived in Teignmouth and had experienced similar prejudice. To prove her loyalty to King and Country she had volunteered with the Voluntary Aid Detachment of the British Red Cross where she packed supplies, knitted garments for the troops at the front and also served on a hospital committee.[7] Her brother, however, decided to make his stand in a very different way by penning an article in the February 1917 edition of the *Avicultural Magazine* with the highly controversial title, 'The Influence of German Aviculture'. Given the times, it was a brave, if naive, move that would severely strain the faith of his editor and end in a jingoistic war of words with a rival publication.

The editor of the *Avicultural Magazine* was Hubert Delaval Astley (1860–1925). He was a bird illustrator, author and also the rector of St Peter and St Paul Church in Ellesborough in Buckinghamshire. Astley had graduated from Oxford University with a Master of Arts, was a Fellow of the Zoological Society of London and a long-standing member of the BOU. He had asked Teschemaker to write the article, sympathizing with his view that aviculture should be above nationalism, politics and war. However, he seriously underestimated the impact that an article about the achievements of German aviculture would create during wartime when so many ornithologists were serving and dying at the front.

Teschemaker started his piece by justifying why he had chosen such a controversial subject, writing 'So long a time has elapsed since I last contributed to the Magazine that it may perhaps be advisable to explain why I have accepted the Editor's invitation to write something, and, in particular, why I have selected the above subject [The Influence of German Aviculture].' Feeling strongly about his treatment, he had both a private and a public reason for publishing it. His private reason was to address the surge in anti-German sentiment he had experienced, his public one being to elevate aviculture above the war. Teschemaker wrote 'I wish to show our members that I have not forgotten them (as I hope they have not completely forgotten me), and I always set before myself the possibility of raising aviculture from the very restricted sphere of influence, which it at present occupies, to a plane of greater dignity and wider outlook.' To find common ground with his readers he looked ahead to a shared future after the war was over, stating:

> No doubt one takes a risk or two in writing of German aviculture at a time when we are at war with Germany, but the psychological moment must not be lost. The old order of things is passing and there is a promise – or at least a possibility – of a new world and new ideals; so we will take the risk and hope for the best.[8]

In the article Teschemaker put German aviculture into a historic context, showing the contribution it had made over centuries to the science of rearing and breeding birds. To encourage members to think beyond the present war he postulated about the values he believed that both British and German aviculturists shared:

> My postulate is that aviculture is based on certain instincts and sympathies, which are common to the aviculturists of all nations, and is therefore above and apart from all considerations of race or nationality. I claim that we should regard the aviculturists of all nations in war time as being fellow-sufferers united by a common misfortune; for, however excellent the objects of any war may be, it is bound to be destructive of the best interests of aviculture.

Teschemaker also used his article to protest against ornithologists who sought to use the war to promote division. 'My protest is against those (if any) who would try to thrust this terrible war into the quiet realms of aviculture. We should not only regard them, I think, as disturbers of the peace, but as seeking to destroy the cosmopolitan character of aviculture and its potential function as a link to draw all nations more closely together after the war.' He went on to state that he believed peace would only come when nations talked to one another and did not settle their differences by war. 'One result of this conflict, which we can all foresee, will be racial animosities more bitter and more enduring than that inspired in the French by the loss of Alsace-Lorraine [ceded by France to Germany after the Franco-German War in 1871, its occupation by Germany was bitterly disputed by the French].' He added, 'There will be no real peace in the world until those animosities have been extinguished by effluxion of time and by the intercourse of nations.'

Teschemaker then tackled the rise of what he considered to be the wrong type of patriotism, stating, 'We have heard a great deal during the last decade in this country of that type of patriotism which has produced a certain national self-complacency, which, when put to the test in the keen struggle for existence, has not been always justified by results.' Instead he believed patriotism should be used to improve nations so they could learn from each other, writing, 'Another form of patriotism, less popular but, we think, more profitable, is to point out what other nations are doing and to compare it with that which we are doing, and to thus attempt to discover our relatively strong and relatively weak points. It is this latter method which we shall pursue today.' The remainder of the article, spread over four pages, went on to trace the history of German aviculture, its contribution to the science and the differences with its

British counterpart. He finished by stating that the second part of the article was to follow, his editor Astley adding at the end 'to be continued'.

Following publication, the response to Teschemaker's article was swift and scathing. A deluge of letters flooded into the office of the Avicultural Society complaining about an article featuring the accomplishments of German aviculture at a time when so many members and British soldiers were dying at the front (this inference is borne out by events, no letters being included in the magazine). Fearing an even greater backlash and the intervention of the War Office, Astley lost his nerve and pulled the second part of the article, instead asking Teschemaker to write about nightingales, a subject he hoped would be far less controversial. Suitably chastened, Teschemaker wrote in the May 1917 edition:

> Our Editor having asked me to postpone the completion of my recent article, in view of his wish to secure some 'copy' to accompany two most excellent photographs of our greatest song bird, I have as a matter of course acceded to his request. He has not confided to me the particular object he had in view, but the moment is certainly appropriate, for 'spring is y-cumen in', and the Nightingale is presumably just reaching our shores.

Teschemaker's ordeal was, however, far from over for following publication he got into an argument with the editor of the rival *British Birds* magazine, the learned and very patriotic Harry Forbes Witherby (1873-1943). The two men while having a common interest in birds couldn't have been more different: Teschemaker was a German immigrant while Witherby was a lieutenant in the Royal Navy Volunteer Reserve who would later be called up and awarded the MBE (Member of the Order of the British Empire) while serving as an intelligence officer in Dunkirk. Witherby accused Teschemaker in his article on nightingales of besmirching a late ornithological friend who had died the previous year, Thomas Hudson Nelson (1856–1916), Teschemaker describing him as being an 'incorrigible egg collector'. Witherby's letter waspishly concluded:

> if I may be allowed to say so, I think to put such an uncorroborated story into print when the man concerned is no longer here to defend himself is, to say the least, unfair. I note that the article was written

to fill space, but would it not be more fitting to lessen the number of pages rather than to publish what some consider an aspersion on a friend now dead.

However, reading between the lines, Witherby's other motivation was clear: Teschemaker was a German who had dared to tarnish the reputation of a dead English ornithologist during wartime and needed to be put in his place.

Responding to the criticism in another follow-up letter published in the magazine, Teschemaker tried to defend himself, writing:

For the past twenty years I have done my best for the cause of our vanishing birds, and I shall continue to do so until the end of the chapter. I have always endeavoured to avoid giving offence, but there seems to be a very sensitive spot in most ornithologists – can it be their consciences? It is important for us all to remember that our life-work lives after us, and that we must so build that the house we leave remains strong and firm. If we have devoted our lives to the destruction of birdlife, posterity will not forget the fact.

But Witherby refused to let the matter rest and wrote a further letter rebuking Teschemaker which was also published in the *Avicultural Magazine*. Astley now moved to draw a line under the argument, using his position as editor to have the last word, adding in brackets to Witherby '[We fear we do not agree. The article was not written to fill space, and advice is certainly tendered as to our Magazine being reduced in compass. The remark as to filling up space is surely intended for sarcasm. – Ed.]' However, the society took a different view fearing the damage caused to the reputation of the *Avicultural Magazine*. As a result Teschemaker was quietly dropped as a contributor and Astley resigned as its editor in October 1917. Xenophobia had triumphed over aviculture, faith and humanity.

In the spring of 1917, birds on the Western Front continued to provide solace, inspiration and hope in the face of long periods of boredom and the terrifying fear of 'going over the top' which hung over every soldier. One was Captain Antony Buxton (1881–1970) who served with the Essex Yeomanry and had been awarded the Distinguished Service Order for bravery the year before. Like many officers of his generation, Buxton had been educated at Harrow and Cambridge University where he had become famous for being involved in the infamous Dreadnought hoax in 1910. This was a practical joke played by his student friend Horace de Vere Cole, future brother-in-law to the Prime Minister Neville Chamberlain (1869–1940), who had tricked the Royal Navy into believing he was the king of Abyssinia. Buxton, who was part of Cole's entourage, had applied heavy black makeup for the prank, the navy treating them like royalty and giving the entourage a tour of their flagship battleship HMS *Dreadnought*. When the visit was revealed to be a hoax, the Admiralty became a laughing stock and were furious.

Buxton, as well as being a practical joker, was also a keen ornithologist who regularly wrote to *The Times* about the birds he saw at the front. Occasionally birds which were rare or absent at home turned up on the battlefield, much to the joy of Buxton who was in charge of organizing a continual watch on no man's land. One unexpected bird was the exotic-looking hoopoe which has a pinkish body, striking black and white wings and a long, black, down-curved bill. However, it was the pink crest on its head, which the hoopoe erects when excited, which first alerted Buxton to its presence on the battlefield. Although hoopoes do not not breed in Britain, Buxton knew they turned up on passage in small numbers, particularly in spring. On arriving at the Somme, he was amazed to see how common they were, some even hopping around in front of his trench. Writing, in *The Times* on 10 January 1917, Buxton excitedly reported on their presence together with an even rarer bird found in Britain:

> I found the valley of that now famous river the Ancre full of Hoopoes, and of a mysterious silent bird which flitted from reed bed to reed bed on one of the marshy ponds so common in the valley, the haunt of great and small Reed Warblers. The reeds were too thick to get a sight of this bird except when flying, and then only for a moment, but, after several days of watching, I got my telescope on to a pair apparently courting in the air over the centre of the pond. They were what I had suspected them to be. Little Bitterns, and if only I had had a boat, I think I could have found the nest.

Buxton when not fighting at the front became particularly obsessed with another bird which was common on the Somme but very rare in

Britain, the Montagu harrier. It was named after the English army officer George Montagu (1753–1815) who wrote the pioneering *Ornithological Dictionary* in 1802, widely considered to be the first accurate book on the status of Britain's birds. Buxton would watch the harriers hunting on the Somme battlefield and over no man's land for hours on end with his telescope and became determined to find their nest. So, on being sent to the rear trenches for rest, Buxton set himself up by a marsh and dedicated three evenings to finding it:

> On the first evening I saw two cocks, met in the air by two hens, and undoubtedly the latter were fed by their husbands ... on the second evening, with a friend, I distinctly saw through the telescope the cock come over the place where I believed the hen to be sitting and thrust out its claw, in which was something – I believe a lizard.[9]

Buxton was then treated to the most amazing and spectacular piece of harrier behaviour, the food pass. 'In a moment she was up and circling towards him. When just below and downwind of him, she turned a back somersault, while he dropped his prey through the air for 6ft. or 10ft. from his hand into hers. It was done without effort on the part of either, and looked the easiest thing in the world.'

On the third evening Buxton finally located the nest and walking to within ten yards of it, noted the female harrier 'rose in fright and noisy rage from her nest of four eggs in the grass, and while we looked at them she never ceased her cries, and circled continuously above us'. However, Buxton was less than impressed with the eggs which reminded him of Easter eggs and an unhappy episode from his childhood. 'The nest of flattened blades of grass and uninteresting-looking eggs had an artificial appearance; they reminded me of a clutch of Easter eggs I was once unfortunate enough to find in a haycock at a children's party, to the undoing of my stomach, for they were bad,' he wrote, adding 'There are plenty of such nests to be seen at the proper season in confectioners' shop windows.' More helpfully Buxton also found out that the female birds were punctually fed at the same time each day, noting that his hen was 'fed at 5.25 to a minute on each of the three evenings, and I would advise anyone in search of a nest to post himself, with a good glass, at 5.15 at an advantageous spot not too near where he believes the nest to be. I say not too near, because the cock is much more shy, though less bad-tempered, than the hen.' Suddenly remembering that the reason Montagu's harriers were so rare in Britain was because of egg collectors he pronounced, 'Heaven grant that no egg clutcher benefits by this advice!'

Unlike many ornithologists fighting at the front, Buxton survived the war and went on to become the Deputy Lieutenant of Essex in 1920 and the High Sheriff of Norfolk in 1945. He married Mary Philomena (née Constable Maxwell) in 1926 and they had a son and three daughters together. He continued writing and became an author, writing about sport, fishing and birds for a variety of newspapers. Among his publications were the *Fisherman Naturalist* in 1946, the *Travelling Naturalist* in 1948 and the merrily named *Happy Year – The Days of a Fisherman Naturalist* which was published in 1950.

By the summer of 1917 bird reports had become a staple part of all British newspapers and magazines including the satirical magazine *Punch*. Despite having a reputation for poking fun at the British establishment, especially the upper middle classes from which nearly all officers were drawn, on the outbreak of war, *Punch* did its patriotic duty, helping to maintain morale at the front. On 18 July 1917 it published 'What the Kingfisher knew' by the writer Madeline M. Oyler:

The wind ruffled the grey water of the stream under the old stone bridge.

'Ssshhh, ssshhh,' whispered the young willows, 'what will become of us? what will they make of us? Ssshhh, ssshhh.' But no one replied, chiefly because no one knew, excepting the kingfisher, and he was away on a fishing expedition.

Then one day the woodcutters came and the sound of their axes rang out over the meadows by the quiet stream. A great many of the older willows were laid low that day, and the young trees bent and whispered among themselves, 'Ssshhh, ssshhh, what will become of them? what will they make of them? Ssshhh, ssshhh.' This time the kingfisher answered them, for he was just back from a fishing expedition.

'They will make them into cricket-bats,' he said; 'that is what willow-trees are used for.' And he sat and preened his gay little body in the sun.

A portrait of Sir Edward Grey by the painter James Guthrie. Foreign Secretary from 1905-1916, Grey worked tirelessly to preserve the peace but ended up convincing the House of Commons to go to war, famously commenting on 3 August 1914: 'The lamps are going out all over Europe; we shall not see them lit again in our lifetime.' Birds were his hinterland and the lasting love of his life. (*Author's collection*)

The most famous picture of Sir Edward Grey shows him in his finest tweed sporting jacket and deerstalker hat with a robin on his head. Over his lifetime he built up an impressive collection of ducks from Britain and around the world. Blind in his final years, he could no longer see his beloved birds but the song that he had learnt at The Cottage came into its own giving him peace and pleasure in his old age. (*Edward Grey Institute*)

The medallion to Sir Edward Grey outside the Foreign Office. Grey summed up all that birds meant to him when he said at a Royal Society for the Protection of Birds (RSPB) conference: 'The love of birds and pleasure of seeing and listening to them is in the long run a happier thing than personal success.' (*Author's Collection*)

In 1914 it was not just Germany whom the Government declared war on but also the humble house sparrow. Farmers falsely accused it of destroying Britain's dwindling grain supplies so the Board of Agriculture resurrected Rat and Sparrow Clubs to oversee its slaughter. They were opposed from the outset by the RSPB who, after a long battle, emerged victorious, becoming the powerful voice for conservation we know today. (*Iva Villi*)

Wills cigarette card of the house sparrow. The company issued a set on British Birds in 1915 and collecting them proved to be popular at home and at the front. Unlike the slaughter of sparrows in Britain, the troops in France had a very different relationship with the birds that shared their trenches, many taking great solace from their vivacious nature and seeing them as friends. (*Author's collection*)

The British Expeditionary Force sent to France in 1914 has often been described as the 'Best British Army Ever Sent to War'. It was also the 'Best Birdwatching Army Ever Sent to War' for among its ranks were hundreds of amateur and professional birdwatchers. Many were officers but among all the ranks were birders who swapped their local patch for the battlefield. (*Media Drum World*)

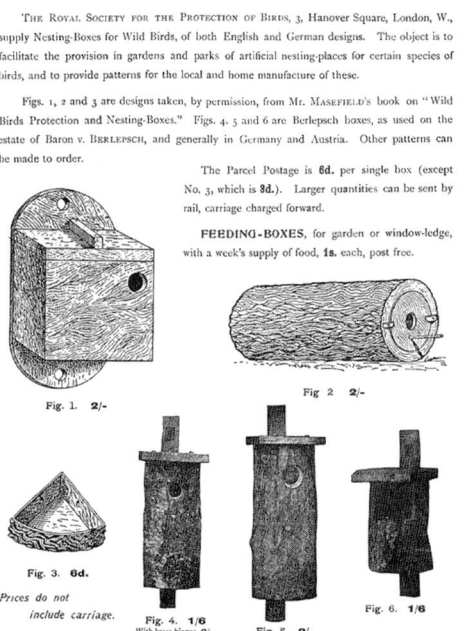

At the start of the war all the RSPB's 'tree-hole' nest boxes were made in Germany, based on a design by Baron von Berlepsch. Acutely embarrassed, it apologised to all its members and announced that it would create a new industry building 'British Boxes for British Birds'. (*RSPB*)

The red letter bird for troops serving at the front was the golden oriole. A soldier, F. Goodyear, serving with the Royal Engineers wrote, 'Golden Orioles were quite new to me, and they have impressed me with their tropical habits — the elusiveness of their call, its mellowness, their amazingly brilliant flight, high up from tree to tree — they seem made for the deep shadows of a far sunnier land than Flanders.' (*Wikipedia*)

The song of the skylark was not only background noise but the last sound many soldiers heard in this life as they lay mortally wounded in no man's land. The birds were immortalised in a hauntingly beautiful poem called 'A Lark Above the Trenches' by John William Streets: 'Hushed is the shriek of hurtling shells: and hark! Somewhere within that bit of soft blue sky; Grand in his loneliness, his ecstasy; His lyric wild and free – carols a lark.' (*Pixabay*)

Some birds seemed to be almost immune to the noise of shelling, notably the nightingale. 'On May 13, at 3 a.m., in the garden of my chateau I heard a Nightingale begin to sing,' an officer recorded. 'Half an hour afterwards German shells were rained upon the garden incessantly throughout the day. The bird sang without a pause where the shells fell thickest until 12 p.m. and survived, for next morning he started again as cheerily as ever.' (*Pixabay*)

Suddenly producing a large white feather, she jabbed it into his waistcoat. And in another tone, fierce and scornful, she added: . . . "You coward! Why don't you enlist?"

White feathers from chickens, ducks, swans and exotic birds like egrets were used by women to publicly shame young men who had not signed up, members forming the so called White Feather Brigade. Controversially many men were mistakenly labelled as cowards or war shirkers when they were exempt on medical grounds or doing essential war work. (*Collier's, 1914*)

DEFENCE OF THE REALM
Regulation 21A.

SHOOTING HOMING PIGEONS.

Killing, Wounding or Molesting Homing Pigeons is punishable under the Defence of the Realm Regulations by **SIX MONTHS IMPRISONMENT OR £100 FINE.**

The Public are reminded that Homing Pigeons are doing valuable work for the Government, and are requested to assist in the suppression of the shooting of these birds.

£5 REWARD

will be paid by the **NATIONAL HOMING UNION** for information leading to the conviction of any person **SHOOTING HOMING PIGEONS** the property of its Members.

Information should be given to the Police, Military Post, or to the Secretary of the Union, C. C. PLACKETT, 14, EAST PARADE, LEEDS.

Homing pigeons made a major contribution to winning the war by delivering vital messages under fire. However, they kept being shot by farmers for pigeon pie, so the Defence of the Realm Act 1914 was quickly amended making it illegal to shoot them, anyone caught doing so being liable to six months' imprisonment or a fine of £100. (*Author's collection*)

The most famous pigeon of the war was Cher Ami (or Dear Friend), who had been lent by the British to the US Army Signal Corps and saved the lives of nearly 200 men in the 77th Infantry Division when they became trapped behind enemy lines on 3 October 1918. General John Pershing, commander of the American Expeditionary Force, said, 'There isn't anything the United States can do too much for this bird.' (*Smithsonian Institute*)

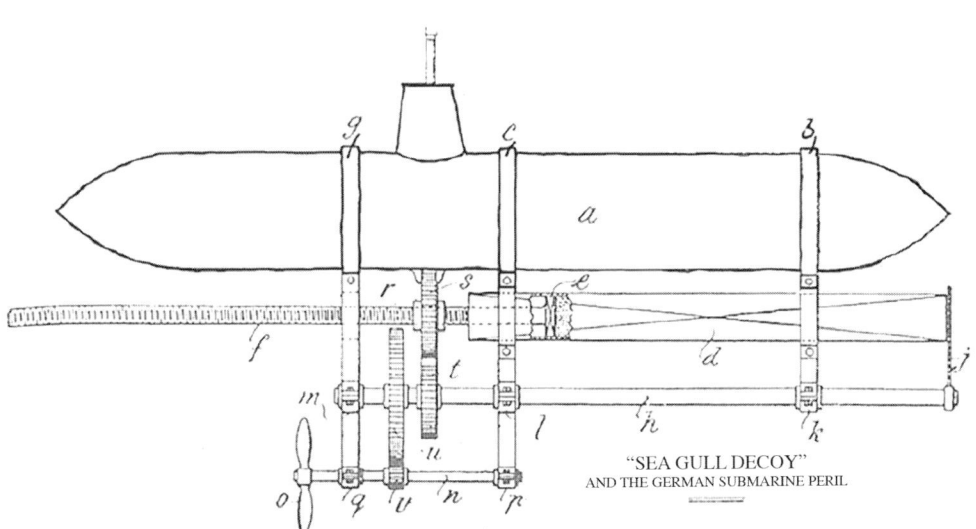

"SEA GULL DECOY" AND THE GERMAN SUBMARINE PERIL

According to the Admiralty the U-boat was the 'most serious menace with which the Empire has ever been faced'. The use of sea gulls to detect them was championed by an eccentric Australian inventor called Thomas Mills using his 'Sea Gull Decoy'. To train the gulls to find the periscope, Mills's idea was that ships should tow a dummy one from which offal was discharged at regular intervals. (*The Fateful Sea-Gull*)

In the first major action of the war, the Battle of Mons, Lieutenant Colonel Aymer Edward Maxwell was killed. He dedicated his life to the study of game birds, rapidly becoming an expert on grouse, pheasants and wildfowl shooting. His youngest son Gavin was born in July 1914, just two months before he left for France and would grow up to become one of the most famous naturalists of his era, writing *Ring of Bright Water* in 1960. (*Imperial War Museums*)

On 8 November 1914 Staffordshire lost one of its most promising ornithologists with the death of Francis Algernon Monckton, a lieutenant in the 1st Battalion Scots Guards. In a letter dated 22 October 1914 from St. Nazaire, at the mouth of the Loire, where he was quartered before going to the front, he described the species he found there including those on migration. His younger brother and cousin were also killed in the war. (*Imperial War Museums*)

Lieutenant Lewis Neil Griffith Ramsay, of the 4th Battalion Gordon Highlanders, was killed in action on 21 March 1915 aged 25 when he was shot by a sniper while repairing a trench. At Aberdeen University he had taken part in the first organised bird-ringing scheme in Britain with an ornithologist friend Arthur Davidson, who would also be killed during the war, and another undergraduate, Arthur Landsborough Thomson. (*Imperial War Museums*)

On 21 April 1915 Private Maxwell Green was killed instantly when he was shot in the head in the trenches at Ypres, aged 19. On Green's body was found an article he had been writing about the birds he had seen in Flanders for publication in the *Selborne Society Magazine*. His article was left unfinished but published posthumously, the editor stating, 'It is with melancholy pleasure that we print the letter above, together with the notes which accompanied it.' (*Imperial War Museums*)

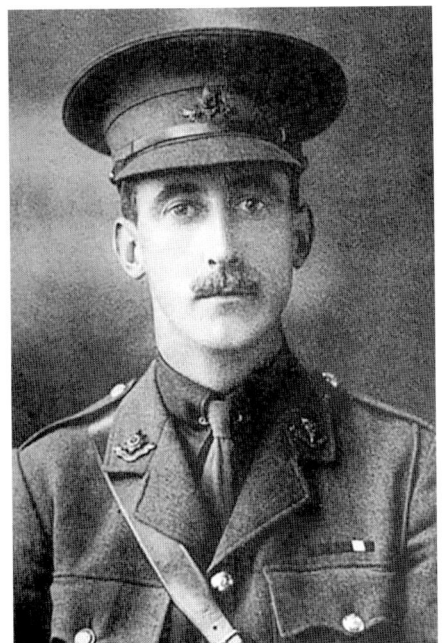

Second Lieutenant Richard Bowen Woosnam was killed while gallantly leading his men in an attack on the Turkish trenches on 4 June 1915 during the Gallipoli campaign. Woosnam was a brilliant field naturalist, explorer and game warden who was a member of the British Ornithologists' Union and was awarded the prestigious silver medal by the Zoological Society of London. Woosnam's name lives on in the large number of birds and other animals named after him from cisticolas to vipers. (*Imperial War Museums*)

Alexander Douglas Gillespie, serving with the Argyll and Sutherland Highlanders, was killed on 25 September 1915, aged 26. Gillespie wrote many letters home about daily life including the birds he saw at the front which were published posthumously in 1916 with the title *Letters from Flanders*. His dream was to transform no man's land into a 'Via Sacra' – a sacred pathway for nature – stretching 450 miles from the Belgian coast at Nieuwpoort to the Swiss border near Basel. (*Winchester College*)

Frontispiece for *Notes of an East Coast Naturalist* by Frank Southgate called 'Spring. Shovellers and bearded tit'. While serving with the 24th Battalion Royal Fusiliers, he was killed on 23 February 1916. Southgate was a member of the prestigious Royal Society of British Artists and specialised in Norfolk landscape scenes and birds, particularly waterfowl, waders and game birds. (*Wikipedia*)

On 8 March 1916 an Anglo-Indian force tried to relieve the town of Kut but were repelled. Lieutenant Colonel Herbert Hastings Harington, who commanded the 62nd Punjabis, was killed in the action. Attached to the Burmese Police for over twenty years, he carried out a detailed inventory of the country's birds which was published in 1909. His name lives on in a number of species named after him. (*Malvern College*)

Within the space of one week two birding brothers were killed. Lieutenant Hugh Vaughan Charlton (inset) fell on 24 June 1916 just after having received a promotion. A week later his brother Captain John Macfarlane Charlton (bottom) was killed on 1 July 1916 which was his birthday, having just been recommended for the Military Cross. Both brothers were artists and keen birders, Hugh was 32 years old when he died, his younger brother John was 25. (*Northumberland Archives*)

On 1 July 1916 the British and French launched the Somme Offensive on the Western Front. Eleven days later as the battle raged over 200 miles away Lieutenant Colonel Boyd Robert Horsburgh died from his wounds at his home in Surrey. An eccentric aviculturist, in 1912 he published his seminal work, *The Game Birds and Water-Fowl of South Africa*. (*Wikipedia*)

On 11 September 1916 Captain John Cyril Crowley was killed giving covering fire to a raiding party attacking Nasiriyah, a city on the river Euphrates. Crowley was an accomplished amateur photographer, who used his images to stop birds being killed by 'sportsmen who shoot'. Instead he promoted photography as a way to engage and interest them in conservation. (*Keble College*)

Lord Lucas was shot down flying over German lines on 3 November 1916, bringing an end to a life that read like an adventure story in *Boy's Own* magazine. As a *Times* journalist he had his leg amputated below the knee in the Boer War. Undeterred by his disability, he went on to become a captain in the Hampshire Yeomanry, a member of the Cabinet and finally a pilot. A keen ringer, his ornithological claim to fame was helping to bring back the marsh harrier as a breeding bird to Britain. (*Private collection*)

On the night of 14 November 1916, the satirical writer Hector Hugh Munro was killed while serving with Royal Fusiliers at the age of 45. Under the nom de plume 'Saki', his short stories were hugely popular, contrasting the banality and hypocrisy of Edwardian society with the life and death struggles of nature. His last article was 'Birds on the Western Front' which he sent to the *Weekly Westminster* a month before he died. (*Wikipedia*)

On 4 January 1917 the famous big game hunter Captain Frederick Courteney Selous, of the 25th Battalion Royal Fusiliers, was killed in action at the ripe old age of 65. He was one of the most celebrated adventurers of his era, counting President Roosevelt and the magnate Cecil Rhodes as personal friends. A prolific collector, he donated over 5,000 animal and plant specimens to the Natural History Museum in London. A bronze bust of him was unveiled there on 10 June 1920 by Sir Edward Grey where it still stands in the Main Hall (*Author's collection*)

Captain John Dighton Grafton-Wignall was killed in action fighting with the 82nd Punjabis on 26 January 1917. His obituary in *British Birds* read, 'he had that perfect sight which enabled him to "pick up" a sitting Woodcock or a clutch of shingle-laid eggs...or at rest some bird a great way off. A rare combination, and one to be envied...his loss is irreparable : ornithology, has lost a very accurate, first-rate and indefatigable observer.' (*Author's collection*)

The poet Edward Thomas was killed in action soon after arriving in France on Easter Monday, 9 April 1917. Thomas wrote over 140 poems in just two years, including some of the finest poems of the early twentieth century, excelling as a master of the short poem. Throughout his poetry birds feature as a reoccurring subject, Thomas using them to explore themes from sorrow to spirituality. His book *Poems* was published posthumously in 1917 and he is commemorated in Poets' Corner in Westminster Abbey. (*Wikipedia*)

On Easter Monday 1917 the artist Henry Edward Otto Murray-Dixon was killed. Tutored by the world famous wildlife watercolour artist Archibald Thorburn, he designed the RSPB's Christmas cards during the war. Otto Murray-Dixon's two designs, a dove to illustrate a 'Bird of Good Omen' and a kestrel to accompany the poem 'Into Battle', were both very popular. The picture *Hooded crows on French corn stack* was completed three days before he was mortally wounded by a splinter from a shell, dying the next day. (*Imperial War Museums*)

Edwin Epharim Riseley of the 9th Battalion of the Rifle Brigade was killed on 1 August 1917. Before being called up he was Head Librarian at the prestigious Linnean Society of London. The previous incumbent, a German by the name of August Wilhelm Kappel, had been unceremoniously sacked by the Society as an 'enemy alien' based on very flimsy and probably fabricated evidence. (*Linnean Society*)

Captain Leonard Gray of the Essex Territorial Regiment died in hospital on 31 July 1917 at Alexandria in Egypt from heart failure and typhoid contracted during the Palestine campaign. A solicitor and keen ornithologist from childhood, he bequeathed his extensive egg collection to Chelmsford Museum. A month after Gray's death his practice was renamed in his honour and continues to operate to this day in Chelmsford. (*Andrew J. Begent*)

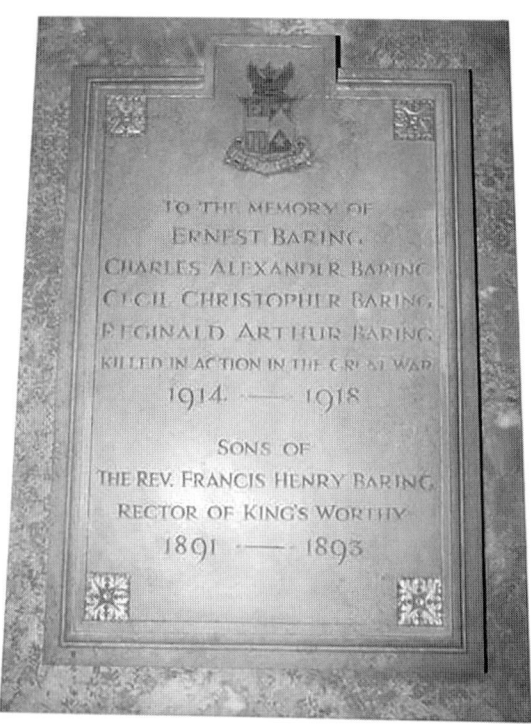

Cecil Christopher Baring, a second lieutenant in the 8th Battalion of the Queen's Own (Royal West Kent Regiment), was killed on 21 March 1918. In 1914 he won the RSPB's Silver Medal and in the autumn of 1916 sent in a remarkable bird diary from the front line in France which was published in the society's magazine. It included a night patrol in no man's land where he ran into a flock of redshank which fortunately did not alarm call otherwise 'we should have had a dozen Hun lights at us'. One of seven children, three of his brothers were also killed in action. (*Author's Collection*)

On 14 October 1918 Lieutenant John Bateson was killed near Passchendaele. Only 20 years old, he had already been singled out as a 'naturalist of exceptional promise' having been awarded Charterhouse School's 'Poole Prize in Natural History' in 1914, 1915, and 1917, a remarkable record. For his bravery attempting to rescue wounded comrades under fire, he was posthumously awarded the Military Cross. (*Charterhouse School*)

Birds and Enemy Aliens

'Sss-shameful! Sss-shameful!' whispered the young willow-trees. 'To cut and maim and carve us up just for men and boys to play with. Sss-shame! Sss-shame! If they only used us for tools to work with or for swords to fight with, we shouldn't mind; but just for sport! Sss-shame! Sss-shame!' And they trembled and whispered among themselves on the edge of the silver stream.

But although the kingfisher happened to have a very little body he had a very big mind, and he explained to the young willow-trees that, even if cricket might be only a game, yet it trained boys and men for the Battle of Life. But the willow-trees were young and of course they thought they knew best, so they went on whispering among themselves, 'Sss-shame! sss-shame!'

After the War began the kingfisher used to bring back what news he could gather on his fishing expeditions. 'They are cutting down the oaks in the lower spinney,' he told them one day. I expect they will be used for building ships.' And he preened his little dazzling body in the sun.

'I wish they would use us for building ships,' whispered the willows. 'I wish they would let us die for our country. All our brave men and boys have gone to fight; they do not even need us for cricket-bats now,' they sighed sadly. 'I wish they were back and wanting us to play games with.'

And then one day, when the young willow-trees had grown older and more wise, the woodmen came again to the quiet stream.

'What have they come for? What will they do with us?' whispered the willow-trees as they shivered and trembled on the reedy margin of the stream. The kingfisher was preening his small many-hued body in the sun.

'I'll find out,' he said, and flashed away like a fragment of rainbow gone astray. Almost by the time the first stroke of the axe rang out over the sleeping meadows he was back again.

'You are going to die for your country,' he told them. 'They are using willows to make new limbs for our brave soldiers and sailors who have lost their own; they are using willows to make new limbs for our brave sailors and soldiers.' Up and down the stream he darted, spreading the wonderful news; and so the willow-trees were comforted.

'Ssshhh, ssshhh,' they whispered. 'Ssshhh! ssshhh! for our brave soldiers and sailors, for our dear sailors and soldiers – ssshhh, ssshhh.'[10]

By mid-1917 a steady stream of soldiers from the war were returning to Britain with missing limbs, many lacking legs, others arms and some both (nearly a quarter of a million British soldiers had a leg or arm amputated as a result of war wounds – of these nearly 70 per cent lost a leg, just over a quarter an arm, and nearly 3 per cent lost both legs or arms). The early artificial leg limbs were crude and made, as *Punch* magazine reported, of willow because this was found to be the most pliable wood to model. To create the limb a willow and leather basket was constructed into which the stump of the upper leg could be fitted. On the bottom of the basket was attached a long piece of wood, terminating in a rubber ferrule or cap. Each limb was bespoke and was made by cabinetmakers who were too old to enlist and as the war progressed they experimented with newer and lighter materials.

A number of hospitals soon opened specializing in amputees, including in 1915 the Queen Mary Convalescent Auxiliary Hospital, based in Roehampton, and in 1916 the Princess Louise Scottish Hospital for Limbless Sailors and Soldiers, based in Erskine. Both hospitals employed men with physical disabilities to make prosthetic limbs, learning their trade from craftspeople. As a result, production increased dramatically and as the war progressed metal was used instead of willow and attached to the body using a range of leather straps and laces. Prosthetic arms were also produced although they were more difficult to make than legs. They were attached to the arm using a complicated series of leather straps and laces, which often made the limb heavy and difficult to manoeuvre. Only after the war were artificial legs and arms designed which allowed real manoeuvrability, these being mass manufactured from metal to standardized sizes.

As the war progressed injured servicemen from all the theatres of war returned to Britain to convalesce including from Macedonia in the Balkans. The theatre there, also known as the Salonica Front, was established after the Allies had failed to stop the invasion of Serbia by German, Austro-Hungarian and Bulgarian forces in the autumn of 1915. By 1917 the front line was static and stretched from Albania in the west to the mouth of the River Struma in Greece in the east. Here a multinational Allied force under French command faced the Bulgarian Army who were supported by German, Austro-Hungarian and Turkish units. In April an Allied offensive was launched but it failed, resulting in a return to static trench warfare. Living conditions for soldiers on both sides was unrelentingly harsh, with freezing conditions and deep snow in winter and long periods of drought in summer when malaria caused more casualties than the fighting.

One compensation for the harsh conditions was the birds, a soldier commenting in the *Balkan News*:

> What a paradise for the student of natural history is this apparently so desolate expanse of plain and mountain, but especially for the observer of birds! Every change in the wind brings us the trumpeting of vast hordes of Greylag Geese echeloning in flight against the morning sky. The variety of wild fowl approaches the teeming swarms of the Danube marshes, and but for the ceaseless depredations of the numerous Eagles, Buzzards, Falcons, and Harriers, observation would yield even better results.

Those observations included species not seen in Britain like weaver birds as well as arguably Europe's most colourful bird, the bee-eater. Breeding in colonies, their kaleidoscope of colours were a welcome break from the monotony of khaki life in the trenches, as a soldier known only as 'ICB' testified in *The Scotsman*:

> On a branch a foot or two above the stream, the weaver bird builds its nest, which is made of the blossom of a species of willow and has the texture of thick, closely woven felt. By July the nests of the bee-eater can be seen, or at least the holes in the banks of streams in which the nests are built. These birds are about the size of a starling, but when flying high in the air their flight is so light and graceful that they might easily be mistaken for swallows. The bill is black, but the head of a fine bronze colour; the body green and blue, and the wings light brown, tipped with green.[11]

Other soldiers serving in the Balkans were surprised at how common and tame some of the birds were. An unnamed officer in the Royal Army Medical Corps wrote on 14 July:

The Kestrels are nesting in the roofs of the houses in nearly every village. They compete for sites with the Jackdaws. Squabbles are common between the two species, but on the whole relations are friendly. I have seen a pair of Kestrels, a pair of Turtledoves, and a couple of pairs of Jackdaws sitting amicably on the same roof. The birds are astonishingly tame. Though most of the houses are only one storey and so low that, sitting on my horse, my head may reach above the eaves, the birds will allow me to watch them from a distance of only a few yards. The number of Kestrels is surprising. It is common to see ten or a dozen pairs in one village.

Despite exotic birds being a fascination for troops in the Balkans, it was the species who reminded soldiers of home which really pulled at their heart strings. Chief among these was the nightingale as J. C. Richardson, a member of the Mounted Military Police, wrote in *The Times* on 28 July 1917:

The *Balkan News* to-day (June 22) prints an article, or portions of it, of yours on 'English Woods and Shakespeare'. And in the course of it the writer says in May-time the poet had often heard the 'nightingale's complaining note'. And so have we out here heard 'the nightingale's complaining note', but more often his joyful notes, under conditions which are worth recording. You will have a terrific tearing and roaring noise of artillery and shot in the dead of night; then there will be a temporary cessation of the duel, with great quietness, when, lo! and behold, and hear! Hearken to his song! Out come the nightingales, right about the guns, perched sometimes only a few yards from them in some bushes, in a ravine where the guns are hidden. And another kind of love music is introduced into our ears and souls, which does us good. Think? It makes you think – and beautiful thoughts come along to relieve you from the devilment of war and the men who cause it ... I was down at Salonika with some heavy gun men on leave a few days ago, coming from various positions. I brought up this subject, and got from them confirmation, with admiration, of the doings and wonderful songs of these nightingales under the noses of our guns.[12]

For ornithologists in the trenches the end of August was a tough time because many of the migrant birds which had sustained their interest over the summer started to leave for their wintering grounds in far sunnier and peaceful lands. Not only did the birds' departure make the soldiers long for home, it also signalled the beginning of the autumn and with it the rains which would turn their trenches into a quagmire. However, before they left, young birds often provided a parting finale, especially swallows as a letter home from a soldier published in the *Notts Guardian* published on 18 Aug 1917 showed:

It has been a vile week, quite in keeping with our usual luck when starting a 'push' – cold, windy, and wet. But I have had some enjoyment in watching the young swallows and martins. The second and last broods are out now practising and getting strong for their long trip south which is fast approaching. One set of five baby swallows have taken possession of a loop of telephone wire hanging between two battered pear trees just outside my store [situated behind the trenches, stores provided for all the soldiers' needs at the front including food, toiletries and clothing]. The progress they have made in less than a week is wonderful. Last Tuesday I noticed them out for the first time battling against the wind and flying about a dozen yards at a time. The earlier attempts were very weak, and they were blown from tree to tree. One little creature was actually blown inside my store.

All day they seemed to be going through gymnastic exercises, and at the end of the day they were able to sit securely on the swaying wire. This henceforth was their favourite perch, and five little funny things they looked all bunched together like balls. When the parent came, immediately a wholesale squeaking started and a rapid fluttering of wings and tails. The mouths opened to such an extent that the heads were lost behind the yellow gapes. It was quite marvellous to notice how each one was fed in turn without the parent perching once. For two whole days this mode of feeding continued, with every minute or two a short flight round.

The third day the mother fluttered about two yards above them. It was the funniest thing imaginable. There, on the wire, were five agitated little things with gaping mouths, working their wings and tails to keep their balance, demanding to be fed, and the tantalizing mother refusing to approach. At last, one little hero fluttered up and took its food in the air, which method was henceforth adopted. The fourth day they had reached the stage of flying off to meet the breadwinner, even as far as ten yards away, and it was most amusing to watch the number of false starts for an adult bird that wouldn't own them. I was looking forward to today's performance, but it was cancelled 'owing to the exigencies of the service', for a bad signaller had arrived early this morning and had taken away the line, so that my little friends were missing.

But I lift my cap to them, for they gave me great pleasure during a most miserable week.

Among the many birders serving at the front were some who had already made a name for themselves in ornithological circles. Oliver Pike (1877–1963) was born in London and by the outbreak of war had already established himself as a leading pioneer in wildlife photography and filmmaking. Pike obtained his first camera at the tender age of 13 and by 1900 had published his first book, called *In Birdland with Field Glass and Camera*. His first film, also called *In Birdland*, soon followed and was shown at the Palace Theatre, London, in August 1907. It was the first British wildlife film to be screened to a fee-paying audience and it proved to be hugely popular during its six-week run. He later went on to make many other films including *St Kilda, Its People and Birds* in 1908 and *Cliff Climbing: The Egg Harvest of Flamborough Head*, released in the same year. In 1910 Pike became director of photography for the prestigious Pathé Frères, one of the world's leading film production companies. Here in 1910, he made *Glimpses of Bird Life*, a wildlife film years ahead of its time which helped to establish him as a world leader in his field.

In June 1914, Pike married Anne Primrose Chapman and two years later was called up, joining the Royal Flying Corps in France where he was put in charge of a workshop specializing in aerial photography. In May 1917, he wrote the first of a series of letters home describing the birds he saw at the front. Exploring a local town, he had come across a ruined cathedral which was home to jackdaws, pigeons and screaming swifts. 'It was a weird sight to stand below on a vast heap of debris and charred wood, and to find that this once fine cathedral was now the home of numerous birds,' he wrote. 'I went from there to another church, a much smaller one, and just the four walls were left standing, with big shell-holes for windows. The actual windows, of course, were blown to fragments.'[13]

Looking through one of the ruined windows he saw a thrush sitting on a branch, singing its whistled, flute like song:

> The setting sun was throwing a beam of light on to him, and the notes of his beautiful song rang through these sad ruins. Everywhere there was wreckage – the altar, organ, and once fine paintings on the walls were all simply blown to oblivion, and the only bright things in that desolate scene were that green branch framed by a shell-broken window, and that loud, pure song. I have listened to the music of the Thrush in some strange places, but never have I heard it under more tragic circumstances.

For Pike it was a poignant and deeply spiritual moment. 'What a whole world of tragedy could be written about that fine building since the last "Evensong" was heard there,' he mused, 'The destruction left behind by the Huns is awful – it is all so needless and wanton, and priceless buildings are just a heap of broken rubble.'

Following his squadron moving to a new location in France, Pike wrote another letter dated 19 July 1917. In it he took great pride in listing the species he had seen around the aerodrome, which included a kestrel, little owls, barn owls, skylarks, garden warblers, yellowhammers and a harrier, but what really impressed him was the wealth of wild flowers which bloomed on the battlefield. 'Some of the fields hereabouts, which a few months ago were the scenes of desperate battles and were running red with the blood of brave men, are now a mass of scarlet poppies; in other places thistles cover the ground, but everywhere there is a mass of white clover.'

Despite the botanical beauty seeing the destruction wrought on the towns and villages at the front brought Pike close to despair:

> It is a terrible and almost heartbreaking sight to look upon these once beautiful villages, with their farms, pretty red-tiled cottages, and little churches, smashed to a heap of broken rubble. You can

have no idea of what this destruction is unless you look upon it. Here and there you come across little things which remind you of the once happy days; perhaps it is the broken toy of a little child, or a wrecked pram, bits of broken pottery, a smashed piano, but one and all are battered almost beyond recognition.

Yet despite the destruction all around him, the deeply religious Pike literally saw Christ rising from the ashes of war. 'There is one strange thing that I have noticed, and it is a thing that might make some men think long and deeply,' he wrote. 'In a small village which I have seen, the whole place, from the chateau to the humblest dwelling, is battered to a mass of brick dust, yet the crucifix – a half-sized image of Christ on the Cross, is standing intact! There is not a mark on the image, and the cross itself has just a scratch on it caused by a piece of shrapnel.' At another cathedral it was the Virgin Mary who had been saved: 'In a large cathedral which I visited there was a large stone image of the Virgin Mary; although great shells had burst all around, and the surrounding walls were peppered with pieces of shell, this was not damaged in any way.' Yet it was again the image of Christ who had miraculously escaped unscathed which left him truly awestruck:

> In the same cathedral there was a small wooden image, about 18 inches long, of the Child Christ, lying on a heap of smashed masonry 20 feet high; this image had been blasted half across the cathedral, not once but many times, and had been exposed to the explosion of hundreds of the largest shells, yet it was practically undamaged. But, strangest thing of all, when we saw it there was lying by the side of it – almost touching it – a large German shell, and this had failed to explode.

For Pike religion and birds were what gave him hope and got him through the war. Nearly 40 years old when he was called up (just under the oldest age for conscription which was 41), like every other soldier he had been given a copy of the Bible with his kit. Growing up, Pike had attended Sunday School at his local church so like many other soldiers of his generation his outlook was deeply rooted in Christianity. In the Royal Flying Corps, the job of providing spiritual guidance to Pike and all those in his squadron fell to the chaplain who often used the cockpit of an aircraft as a pulpit (over 5,000 chaplains served during the war, most receiving little or no training). For some airmen the senseless slaughter they witnessed every day made them question or reject the existence of God but for others like Pike religion transcended war, even if he couldn't explain why it did:

> There is a certain village which was held by the Huns, and we shelled it. When I say that, I mean it was done properly, in the real British way. The whole place was churned up, the village was buried under a mass of earth and stones, it was turned over and re-turned until it looked like a jumbled mass of earth shaken up by a hundred earthquakes; and yet through all this the village crucifix stood intact! Can you explain it? Can anyone?

In Pike's eyes though it was not just man who was synonymous with Christ but also birds, their presence in ruined cathedrals and on the battlefield proving that faith would always triumph over war. 'On the top of the battered walls of a great cathedral I saw a pair of Kestrels had made their nest, and I could hear the young calling and saw the parents bringing food to them,' he wrote. 'It is strange how the birds are quite unconcerned by gunfire; they seem to stick to their old haunts, and it takes a tremendous lot to dislodge them.' He also believed the nightingale exhibited the same grit, he noting that they 'sing continuously through a night of bombardment; guns were in the wood, and shells were bursting there and machine-gun bullets were whistling through, but the Nightingale stuck it, and continued his battle-song.'

Birds' stoicism in the face of the enemy confirmed for Pike the invulnerability of nature, none more so than a female whitethroat he found who had built her tiny nest above his trench. 'I have stood by a Whitethroat's nest, with the largest Hun shells bursting near, and the very air seemed to be filled with a terrifying, tearing crash, followed by a long, echoing roar,' he wrote, adding:

> yet the little bird remained there quite unconcerned by the awful noise and vibration. If you went too near she just tumbled out into the trench beneath and pretended she had a broken wing, and if you

tried to pick her up she led you a nice dance over bully beef tins, rolls of wire and other oddments at the bottom of the trench, until you had been led about 50 yards away; then she jumped up and asked you how you liked being 'had'!

She was, he concluded admirably, 'a plucky little bird, and reared four young'.

Pike was demobilized in 1919 with the rank of captain. In 1907 he had been awarded Fellowship of the Royal Photographic Society and from 1924 to 1948 served on their council, afterwards being made an Honorary Fellow. During his remarkable career he produced 25 books, over 50 films and marketed his own portable 'Birdland' camera, a ¼-plate reflex camera which proved to be very popular with nature photographers in comparison to the heavy and cumbersome models then in use. His obituary in *British Birds* said 'Many bird photographers and ornithologists must owe their original interest to Oliver Pike's books and lectures and, although he had not been very active in recent years, his work will long be remembered.'

Chapter 6

The First Flying Corps

On 31 July 1917, the Battle of Passchendaele or the Third Battle of Ypres began, an Allied offensive which sought to break through the German lines by capturing a ridge near the ruined village of Passchendaele. Over the next three months over 300,000 British soldiers would be killed or injured in the attack before the ridge was captured. In common with previous battles of the war, many of the casualties were found to be suffering from 'shell shock'. The term had first been coined two years earlier by the English psychologist Charles Samuel Myers (1873–1946) who used it to describe the combat stress soldiers suffered on the battlefield (today known as post-traumatic stress disorder, over the course of the war it has been estimated that 20 per cent of those fighting suffered from the condition). The symptoms of shell shock ranged from fatigue, helplessness and panic to tics, trembling and stammers. The worst cases suffered from nightmares and impaired sight and hearing to such an extent that the soldiers were unable to sleep, walk or talk.

By the time of Passchendaele, the British Army was coming down hard on soldiers showing signs of psychological rather than physical injury, putting many cases down to a 'lack of moral fibre', a euphemism for cowardice. Despite this on the first day of the battle so many soldiers from 11th Borders, a Pals battalion known as 'the Lonsdales', were suffering from shell shock that they refused to go over the top. As punishment they were paraded in front of their colleagues and told by their divisional commander, 'You have failed in your duty and you have brought disgrace not only on yourselves but also on the battalion to which you belong' (despite the unit that day suffering from one of the highest casualty rates in the British Army). Other individuals caught refusing to go over the top, especially officers who were supposed to be setting an example to their men, if convicted at a court martial, were shot.

As a result of the sheer number of men displaying shell shock, the term was banned as a diagnosis by the British Army and the number of cases during the Battle of Passchendaele was censored by the War Office. Instead, the Director General of Medical Services announced that men suffering from the condition would be classified as having 'nervousness' and those showing symptoms should 'under no circumstances be recorded as a battle casualty'.

One of the most famous soldiers to suffer from shell shock was the war poet Siegfried Sassoon (1886–1967) who wrote the poem 'Survivors' while recovering from the condition in Craiglockhart War Hospital near Edinburgh, in October 1917.

> No doubt they'll soon get well; the shock and strain
> Have caused their stammering, disconnected talk.
> Of course they're 'longing to go out again,' –
> These boys with old, scared faces, learning to walk.
> They'll soon forget their haunted nights; their cowed
> Subjection to the ghosts of friends who died, –
> Their dreams that drip with murder; and they'll be proud
> Of glorious war that shatter'd all their pride ...
> Men who went out to battle, grim and glad;
> Children, with eyes that hate you, broken and mad.

Another unnamed soldier at the front writing in *The Scotsman* newspaper wondered whether it was possible that birds also suffered from shell shock:

> A day or two ago a shell burst not very far away, and afterwards I saw two Starlings roaming listlessly over the ground, every now and then staggering as if weak and unsteady on their legs. I caught one quite easily, but could see nothing wrong with it. It lay perfectly still in my hand looking at me with glazed, lustreless eyes. I caught the other and placed both in an old box to see what would happen. They settled down contentedly enough, but the next morning they had recovered sufficiently to protest vigorously against their imprisonment. When liberated they both flew off apparently none the worse for their experience.[1]

Unlike birds, the soldiers took far longer to recover from the condition, many taking months or even years to recover in hospitals, some never recovering at all. By the end of the war over 80,000 men had passed through British Army medical facilities suffering from shell shock.

The slaughter of men on the battlefield was also reflected in the number of birds which were shot, injured or maimed. Although birds showed an almost superhuman stoicism to carry on, even coping with shell shock, those that were caught in the line of fire or simply happened to be in the wrong place at the wrong time stood little chance. In particular many were killed during artillery bombardments and gas attacks, the same soldier who had written about birds suffering shell shock in *The Scotsman*, commenting:

I have sometimes found dead birds at rare intervals, but I have never seen a bird struck by a shell until yesterday. I was watching a flock of gulls circling at a little distance in front of our position. Suddenly I heard the whine of a 9-inch shell, and, to my astonishment one of the gulls appeared to dissolve into a cloud of feathers that floated about in the air. A minute later the shell burst. Apparently, the shell left nothing of the gull's body. That vanished, for only the feathers came drifting down.

The soldier also found birds who had died due to the pressure wave resulting from a blast but were quite uninjured, writing:

Strange to say, a few hours later I was examining the hole made by either a 10 or 11 inch shell, and to my surprise found a poor little sparrow lying dead at the bottom of the hole. It was quite uninjured, and had probably been flying over when the shell burst, and the blast had killed it. It was rather interesting to see on one day such evidences of the destruction of birds by shell-fire.

A few ornithologists serving on the front line had a lucky escape from the fate that befell so many. One was Philip Gosse, the War Office's official rat catcher. On 11 September 1917, he had just recorded migrating wheatears at Lederzeele in his diary when he was sent back to act as medical officer to his old battalion, the 9th Yorkshires. On enquiring about their welfare he was shocked to find that of the officers he had known at the start of the war all bar two had been killed. On arriving at his depleted battalion, he had no sooner started seeing to their medical needs than the battalion received orders to go back again to 'the bloody Salient'. As Gosse was travelling towards the front a motor dispatch rider handed his colonel an envelope who on reading it, 'handed it to me with the words, "Lucky devil". The dispatch was an order for Captain P. H. G. Gosse to proceed to England and then to the East [India].' His first response was profound thankfulness followed quickly by guilt at his second lucky escape. Writing in his diary he noted:

> I could not keep back the reflection that although I had been for over two years in or about the fighting line, I had, owing to the rat campaign, spent some six months in safety and comfort, while the rest of the ambulance had been in the thick of it ... That last night, by way of farewell to France, the town was heavily bombed; the next morning I went on board a steamer and set for England.[2]

The night before he left Gosse had heard the haunting cry of wild curlews flying over in the moonlight sky amongst 'the crash of exploding bombs, the roar of low flying German planes and the barking of our anti-aircraft guns'. The effect of aircraft on birds at the front was still the subject of debate, the RSPB discussing it an editorial, 'Birdlife and War's Alarums', in its winter 1917 magazine. Speculating what effect planes had on birds, it gave an example of jackdaws at St Omer from the bulletin of the *Ligue Française pour la Protection des Oiseaux* (the French League for the Protection of Birds). On seeing an enemy aircraft, the jackdaws had left their church steeples and attacked it, striking the plane with their beaks 'as if to drive away these enormous unknown birds'. However, other correspondents said that aircraft were simply ignored, Captain Shipton of the Royal Army Medical Corps serving in Palestine stating that 'Herons, Redshanks, Bitterns, Spoonbills, Sandpipers, betrayed no concern'. The society reflected that birds are generally not afraid of 'large objects on land or sea, until they learn by bitter experience that such objects are dangerous'. The exception was the large Zeppelin airships which struck fear into birds, especially hirundines, pheasants and poultry. However, it concluded that on the whole, 'From the actual field of war the records are continually of fearlessness or heedlessness on the part of birds, even amid the thunder of guns and bursting of shells.'[3]

Birds were, in the view of many soldiers, almost bombproof, the RSPB praising the 'Swallows and Starlings and Sparrows nesting amid ruins not yet free from shell-fire, and of Larks and Nightingales singing serenely in the pauses of artillery bombardment'. Its French equivalent, the *Ligue Française pour la Protection des Oiseaux*, agreed, stating, 'How greatly must our young soldiers of the front lines feel themselves upheld and sustained on the eve of an attack when they see flying all about them these gracious little birds, symbolic of the tenacity, the courage, and the hope of France!' The society concluded that the real tragedy of birdlife in the war was 'not on the battle-ground itself, but on the familiar homeland; not in shell or shock or poison-gas, but in the hideous destruction of trees and woods and every sort of cover in the progress of war'. The society particularly mourned the loss of 'Britain's glorious old woods' which were being sacrificed 'to national necessity, perhaps to a greed anxious to make something out of pressing wants; perhaps to a perverted sense of patriotism in placing all that is beautiful under the Juggernaut of war'. The juggernaut of war required vast quantities of timber to construct and maintain the thousands of miles of trenches along the Western Front (it has been estimated that over 35,000 miles of trenches were dug between the belligerent nations). The lack of it at home in England was a huge logistical challenge for the War Office, the Prime Minister, David Lloyd George memorably commenting that he was more afraid of losing the war due to a lack of timber than a lack of food. Timber was required to make posts, planks and stakes for the construction of trenches, fortifications, shelters and tunnels as well as at home for uses from railway sleepers to pit props in coal mines. At the outbreak of war Britain had so little forest cover that it was totally reliant on imports, over 95 percent of its timber being shipped from abroad. German submarines soon took their toll on Britain's trade routes, a situation made worse by the escalation of the U-boat campaign in 1917 which destroyed many supply ships carrying timber.

The government's answer was to clear fell more forests at home, especially in Scotland where there was more forest cover. To replace many of the foresters who had left to join up, lumberjacks and their families were recruited from across the British Empire, many of them going to work in the forests of Scotland. To clear woods in England the authorities didn't have enough manpower so they again turned to women, introducing Lumber Jills as part of the Women's Timber Service. They came to serve King and Country from as far afield as Newfoundland and Canada and soon became an integral part of the war effort. Many Lumber Jills were middle-class women who often lived and worked on site, most working-class women already being employed in the munition factories or on the land as part of the Women's Land Army. Lumber Jills identified any remaining woods which could be commandeered for the war effort, felling the trees by axe or using a two-woman timber saw. It was lonely, hard and exhausting work which, while boosting timber production, proved devastating for Britain's beleaguered woodland birds. In response to many of the country's remaining ancient woods being clear felled, the society angrily blamed the government 'for lack of national foresight in planting and providing perennial supplies of timber by scientific and systematic forestry'.

It was not just Britain's forestry cover that was denuded. The woods of northern France were also decimated by timber-hungry sappers from the Royal Engineers and while France was an ally, the scale of the damage caused real resentment. A French forestry report in April 1918 stated:

> Felling [by the British] is not always carried out with the care it requires ... Operations start before the forestry directorate or the owner has had time to mark out the reserve areas ... Quantities entered into felling records used to calculate the compensation for the owners of the forests sometimes fall short of the reality ... Prices paid are, in some cases, lower than normal.

Soon thousands of people were employed by the army to cut down French forests, the British using prisoners of war as lumberjacks but also Chinese labourers under a bilateral agreement signed with China (starting in late 1916, China began shipping out thousands of labourers to Britain, France and Russia to help with the war effort. They cut down forests, built trenches, repaired tanks, assembled shells and transported supplies and munitions. On 4 August 1917, China declared war on Germany and the Austro-Hungarian Empire although Chinese troops did not take part in the conflict).

At the end of the war Britain had less than 5 per cent forestry cover left but some hard lessons had been learnt, in 1919 the government passing the Forestry Act which established the Forestry Commission. Its job was to plant forests and woodlands so that Britain would never again be so reliant on imports, in the process creating thousands of jobs for demobilized servicemen. However, like the recovery in Britain's timber supplies, it would take decades before many woods and forests once again echoed to the song of birds.

The winter of 1917 marked the fourth Christmas that Britain had been at war. For its Christmas card the RSPB commissioned the famous artist Archibald Thorburn (1860–1935) to design it. The Scot was arguably the finest artist of his generation, inheriting his skill from his father who was a miniature painter to Queen Victoria. Before the war Thorburn regularly exhibited at the Royal Academy where he also taught and from 1915/16 he illustrated a four-volume seminal work called simply *British Birds*. Thorburn had also illustrated the RSPB's first Christmas card in 1899 and each one subsequently but at the outbreak of war had gifted the opportunity to one of his most promising students called Henry Edward Otto Murray-Dixon (1885–1917). The commission was Otto Murray-Dixon's big break and he subsequently designed the society's 1914/15 and its 1915/16 cards to great critical acclaim. In 1915 he was commissioned as a second lieutenant with the Seaforth Highlanders where he continued to paint and draw the birds he saw at the front. Otto Murray-Dixon was killed in the Battle of Vimy Ridge on Easter Monday 1917 aged 31, his death being marked by a moving obituary in *Bird Notes and News* which stated:

> Members of the society and others familiar with the society's greeting-cards will feel more than ordinary sorrow at the news of the death on the western front of Mr H. E. O. Murray-Dixon, whose pictures of the white Doves on the card of 1914, and of the Kestrel, in illustration of the Honourable Julian Grenfell's noble lines, on that of 1915, were so much admired [for his obituary see the Ornithological Roll of Honour].[4]

Thorburn was devastated by the death of his pupil so when the RSPB asked him to design the card that year, he did it with Otto Murray-Dixon very much in mind and drew 'A Robin in Khaki – behind the lines in France'. Thorburn chose the robin because of the legend that it had acquired its red breast when plucking the crown of thorns from

Christ's brow on the cross, his death and resurrection being celebrated by Christians every Easter. Reflecting the religious nature of the card, it was available with two separate insets written by the naturalist Aubyn Trevor-Battye (1855–1922). The first celebrated how the Robin got its red breast:

> It comes in legend down the centuries
> That when the World's Redeemer hung to die,
> A little pitying bird flew up to move
> The Crown of Agony.
>
> All snow-white was its breast! but even as
> In gentle flutterings it vainly tried
> To lift the torture of the piercing thorn,
> That wounded breast was dyed.
>
> This is the story of the Redbreast.
> It brings our loved the England that they know,
> And sings from this or that small wooden cross.
> Set in a drift of snow.

and the second mourned the ever-increasing roll call of the dead including Otto Murray-Dixon:

> Sleep, after faith unbroken,
> Sleep, after service done;
> Safely home at close of day
> And setting of the sun.
>
> Sleep, with the bugle calling
> Reveille to the day;
> The fighting and the weariness
> Have passed for thee away.
>
> Bells are a-peal in England,
> Under a village spire;
> There is holly, there are children,
> And the singing of the choir;

And hearts are beating proudly.
Although the eyes may weep;
They know thy gallant story,
Sleep, boy, untroubled, sleep.

No mention? See, on waking!
No medal? Let it be –
A King shall meet thee, bringing
His shining Star for thee.

Immediately after Christmas there was a heavy snowfall on the Western Front accompanied by freezing temperatures and by early January the countryside was under a blanket of white. Collingwood Ingram serving with his squadron neat St Omer noted that due to the hard weather many of the birds were so hungry that they had lost all fear of man. On Sunday, 6 January 1918, he recorded in his diary: 'The crested larks and chaffinches are especially fearless and come up to the very doors of the huts. The little top-knot of the former gives it a quaint, perky appearance and enables it to express its emotions – either fear or contentment, according to whether the crest is lowered or raised.'

The arrival of spring in 1918 heralded not only a great influx of migrant birds but also a massive new German offensive. In December the Russians had officially withdrawn from the war following the revolution there the previous month. Although the Americans had entered the war on the side of the Allies in April 1917, they had still not yet arrived on the Western Front in strength. So, with their forces no longer needed on the Eastern Front, on 21 March 1918, the Germans launched a final all-out push to split the British and Commonwealth armies from the French and drive them back to the sea.

Among those to fall in the offensive was the Jewish poet and artist Isaac Rosenberg (1890–1918) who was killed on 1 April 1918. Sent with the King's Own Royal Lancaster Regiment to the Western Front in 1916, he continued to write poetry while serving in the trenches. Among his poems was 'Returning, We Hear the Larks' which he wrote in February 1917 and probably recalls his time in the 40th Infantry Division, a works battalion (notable for its 'bantam' recruits who were below regulation height) patrolling the Hindenburg Line. In it he contrasts the terror involved in returning from a night patrol in no man's land with the angelic song of the lark which greets the day, 'showering' the returning soldiers in music:

> Sombre the night is.
> And though we have our lives, we know
> What sinister threat lurks there.
> Dragging these anguished limbs, we only know
> This poison-blasted track opens on our camp –
> On a little safe sleep.
> But hark! joy – joy – strange joy.
> Lo! heights of night ringing with unseen larks.
> Music showering our upturned list'ning faces.
> Death could drop from the dark
> As easily as song –
> But song only dropped,
> Like a blind man's dreams on the sand
> By dangerous tides,
> Like a girl's dark hair for she dreams no ruin lies there,
> Or her kisses where a serpent hides.[5]

In a tragic case of life imitating art, just over a year after writing the poem Rosenberg was killed at dawn after a night patrol. His death was one of thousands across the front as the British fell back, Field Marshal Haig (1861–1928) imploring every man to do his duty, on 11 April delivering his famous 'backs to the wall speech' in which he urged every soldier to 'fight on to the end'. Despite the severity of the fighting the line held and by the early summer over 300,000 American troops were reinforcing the hard-pressed Allied troops. The tide of war was finally turning, decisively, in their favour.

At the height of the German offensive the summer migrants had begun to arrive back on the Western Front, providing much needed consolation from the fighting. Like at home the bird that many soldiers particularly looked forward to seeing was the first swallow. The spring edition of the RSPB magazine featured Fleet Surgeon C. Marsh Beadnell who had made a visit to the trenches and took great joy in a swallow which flew up and down the line all day long despite the constant bombardment.

He wrote in the *Journal of the Royal Naval Medical Service*, 'In one of the observation posts I visited there was a nest inside the officer's dug-out and the parent birds would fly in and out and even perch on the table while the officer was eating his meals.'[6] However, the joy didn't last as like so many of the men defending the line it was later killed, the officer seeing it fly about fifty yards in front of a 4.5-inch howitzer just as it was fired, the bird dying instantly in the blast.

Like the swallow the German advance was eventually stopped in its tracks and between the spring and autumn of 1918 the Allies switched from headlong retreat to full-scale attack. In October there was a mutiny in the German Navy based at Kiel, dissatisfaction with the German generals and Kaiser soon spreading throughout the country. The departure on 26 October 1918 of Eric Ludendorff (1865–1937), General of the German Army, did little to quell the rebellion and on 10 November the Kaiser fled to Holland. A day later, on the 11 November, an armistice was signed ending the bloodiest war in Britain's history. After four years of fighting and over forty million casualties, the war to end all wars was finally over. The ornithologist Collingwood Ingram who was serving with the Royal Flying Corps, recorded the historic moment in his diary:

Monday, 11 November, St-André
Hostilities have ceased and the flags are flying in the streets. Owing to a steady drizzling rain, not many people were in the streets of Hesdin this afternoon and the majority of those were too-merry to mind much what kind of weather it was. I saw a great grey shrike this afternoon while riding.[7]

A great grey shrike was a grimly appropriate bird to mark the occasion. The largest of the European shrikes, its scientific or Latin name of *Lanius excubitor* literally translates as 'sentinel butcher'. The name refers to the bird's twin habits of impaling its victims on thorns and keeping watch from an elevated position for its prey, a macabre metaphor for the trenches. Its colour was also symbolic, *Feldgrau* or field grey being the official colour of German military uniforms. In northern England its old name of Wereangel or Wierangel was derived from the German *Warkangel* or *Wurchangel* meaning 'suffocating or choking angel'. Its other German folk name was also apposite, *Nünmörder* or *Neuntöter* meaning the murderer or killer of nine (this being the number of prey items the bird had been known to store on thorns). If ever there was a bird which symbolized the bloody conflict of the Great War it was the great grey shrike.

In anticipation of the armistice grand celebrations had taken place in London on 9 November 1918 at the annual Lord Mayor's Show. Hope had built up over the weekend that a peace treaty between the Allies and Germany was imminent and so the show was to all intents and purposes a lavish victory celebration. Thousands came to see the parade which despite the hardships at home and at the front had continued throughout the war. The 1918 procession at two miles long was the longest on record and a precursor of the unbridled victory celebrations which were to come two days later. Among the exhibits in the procession were British tanks, guns and trench mortars accompanied by detachments of the British Army, other Commonwealth forces and Americans. Thirteen captured German and Austrian guns were on show together with volunteers from each of the services, cadets and women corps as well as lorries on which women munition workers showed how they made shells, fuses and bombs. Overhead an airship and a range of aircraft accompanied the procession which was enjoyed by thousands of people crammed into Trafalgar Square and along The Mall.

Like previous shows pride of place went to the Lord Mayor, a title appointed by King John over 700 years previously, and his ornate state coach, itself then over 150 years old. However, for the first time a bird also featured in the show: the homing pigeon. A travelling pigeon loft was carried in the procession by the Royal Air Force, pigeons also having featured at the 'Savoy Fair' show earlier that year in London where they had been inspected by the Duchess of Portland, president of both the fair and the RSPB. The society celebrated their contribution in an editorial called, 'The First Flying Corps' in the winter 1918 edition of *Bird Notes and News*. It was a clever title which played on the success of the celebrated Royal Flying Corps who had by the end of the war merged with the Royal Naval Air Service to become the Royal Air Force. In 'The First Flying Corps' the RSPB wrote:

> Before the traditional Dove of Peace definitely settles on the tree-tops of a world so long submerged in war, and while British gratitude to the three services of King and Country is still burning brightly,

it is not too much to ask for some recognition of the war-work of the birds, that feathered Flying Corps which still transcends the marvels of aeroplane and airship, and but for the existence of which it is hardly probable man's thoughts would ever have conceived of aerial flight ... [in particular] the splendid achievements of the Carrier-Pigeon, the most essential and most renowned of the battle's feathered soldiers.[8]

The pigeon had played a crucial part in winning the war, over 100,000 birds being bred for use by the armed services, each carrying a vital message in an alloy container attached to its leg. The homing pigeon had first proved its worth as a messenger during the siege of Paris in 1870 but at the outset of war in 1914, the government had taken a very different view of the bird, ordering the destruction or internment of all unregistered pigeons along the coast, fearing they would be used by enemy spies. Instead permits had been issued by the police to fanciers who agreed to breed birds for the forces. Following this pigeons had been successfully used at the front during the Second Battle of Ypres in May 1915 and in the defence of Verdun in February 1916, the army employing them to send messages over short distances when communication cables had been cut and it was too dangerous to use a runner. As result there had been a change of mind about their value and later that year a pigeon service had been officially set up for the three armed forces under the auspices of Captain (later Lieutenant Colonel) Alfred H. Osman of the Intelligence Corps. Osman was one of the leading authorities on the bird, in 1898 abandoning his career as a lawyer's clerk to establish the weekly *Racing Pigeon* magazine. Under his leadership the pigeon service became an essential avian adjunct to the army, navy and air force.

Pigeons were first deployed on minesweepers and trawlers without wireless communication patrolling the North Sea in 1914. Many lives were saved by them returning to their lofts near the coast after a ship hit a mine. They also brought news of approaching Zeppelins and U-boat attacks. However, a problem soon arose in that homing pigeons heading for their lofts were being shot by farmers. Claiming to mistake them for wood pigeons, many precious birds ended up in pigeon pie, much to the chagrin of the navy. As result the Defence of the Realm Act 1914 was quickly amended making it illegal to shoot homing pigeons, anyone caught doing so being liable to six months in prison or a hefty fine of £100. A reward of £5 was also offered by the National Homing Union for anyone providing information that led to a conviction. Signs were soon put up all over the country quoting the new regulations and stating, 'The Public are reminded that Homing Pigeons are doing valuable work for the Government and are requested to assist in the suppression of the shooting of these birds.' The Natural History Museum in London also did its bit, putting up a display complete with stuffed birds in the central hall to help people tell the difference between stock doves, rock doves, wood and homing pigeons.

Following their protection, stories concerning the bravery of carrier pigeons soon abounded, the RSPB in its editorial reporting a touching story about a Canadian flight commander called R. Leckie, who held the Distinguished Service Order for bravery. Citing a letter home which was published by an American paper, the RSPB recounted his ordeal:

> After an engagement with hostile aircraft over the North Sea he came down, his seaplane riddled with shrapnel, over fifty miles from land, and then had to act as rescuer and host to the crew of an aeroplane, wrecked by engine failure. Six men were then adrift in a doomed machine, with no food and little water. The Commander had four pigeons; one was released at once, a second on the next day, a third on the third day. All failed to reach home, perishing over the waste of waters. The fourth, set free in a fog, hungry and thirsty, struggled over the fifty miles of sea without a landmark and without a rest. He could not reach his loft, but fluttered down in a coastguard station, and there fell dead from exhaustion. But his message was delivered, and six men were saved.[9]

An even more celebrated rescue took place in the North Sea on 15 August 1917 when an armed naval smack (Q-ship) called *Nelson* came under fire from a German U-boat. The skipper was Thomas Crisp, a fisherman from Lowestoft who had joined the Royal Naval Reserve in 1916 and was serving on the ship with his son. He had previously been awarded the Distinguished Service Cross for sinking two U-boats despite being heavily outgunned. However, Crisp was not to be so lucky a third time, the U-boat scoring several hits before the *Nelson*'s gun could be brought into action. The fourth shot holed the smack and blew both Crisp's legs off, but despite his injury the skipper managing to dispose of confidential papers and fire the ship's gun. Before dying in his son's arms, he was also able to let off a homing pigeon called Red Cock who successfully reached his loft in Lowestoft alerting the authorities, the six remaining crew members eventually being rescued. For his bravery Thomas Crisp was posthumously awarded the Victoria Cross and the rescue was raised in the House of Commons in an emotional speech by the Prime Minister David Lloyd George. When Red Cock died, his body was mounted and added to a display about Crisp at Lowestoft town hall, the bird later being moved to the Natural History Museum[10].

As well as the Western Front, pigeon services were also established in all the other theatres of war including Mesopotamia, Egypt and Salonika. The most famous pigeon of the war was called Cher Ami or 'Dear Friend'; she had been lent by the British to the US Army Signal Corps and saved the lives of nearly 200 men in the 'Lost Battalion' of the 77th Infantry Division when they became trapped behind enemy lines on 4 October 1918. Cher Ami was the third pigeon to be released, the other two having been killed, and when she finally arrived back at her loft headquarters it was discovered she had been shot through the breast, blinded in one eye, and had a leg hanging on only by a tendon. Army medics worked tirelessly to save her life but they were unable to save her leg, instead fitting her with a specially carved wooden one. Due to her bravery Cher Ami became the hero of the division and the bird was awarded the Croix de Guerre, one of France's highest military honours, for gallantry in the field. General John Pershing, commander of the American Expeditionary Force, said, 'There isn't anything the United States can do too much for this bird.' When she passed away eight months later from her war wounds her body was enshrined at the Smithsonian Institute and later added to the Racing Pigeon Hall of Fame.

If the pigeons themselves were incredibly brave, the job of looking after them, while deemed essential war work, was generally considered to be a 'cushy' number. Philip Gosse, the famous rat catcher of the Western Front, in his book *A Naturalist Goes to War*, recited an amusing incident he witnessed on the front line:

> It was sometimes quite pathetic to see how much the men liked following again their old peacetime callings. Once while I was

acting as a temporary medical officer to a battalion, an order arrived from Divisional Headquarters instructing the commanding-officer to make enquiries whether there were in his battalion any men with first-hand knowledge of the care of carrier-pigeons, because several experts were required to take charge of some mobile pigeon lofts which were being sent out. The news soon spread and caused much excitement. The battalion had been recruited in a Yorkshire town where pigeon fancying and pigeon racing were popular hobbies and sports. Here, it seemed, was a chance to get a 'cushy' job well away from the line, near some comfortable estaminet, with no officer, still no more R.S.M. [Regimental Sergeant Major] and no parades, indeed, it seemed to hold out the realization of the golden dreams of almost every infantry soldier. At noon the battalion paraded, the order was read out and any man who knew about the care of carrier-pigeons and how to fly them was instructed at the word 'Advance' to take two steps forward. When the order rang out ... 'Advance' ... the whole battalion moved two paces forward and halted. The adjutant had a difficult task before him, to select the two or three required, when confronted by some four-hundred carrier-pigeon experts from which to choose.[11]

By the end of the war, there were over 22,000 pigeons, 150 mobile lofts and 400 personnel serving in the British Army Carrier Pigeon Service. Their value to the army was well summed up by the aptly named Major General Fowler, Chief of Signals, who wrote:

If it became necessary immediately to discard every line and method of communications used on the front, except one, and if it were left to me to select that one method, I should unhesitatingly choose pigeons. When the battle rages and everything gives way to barrage and machine gun fire, to say nothing of gas attacks and bombings, it is to the pigeon that we go for succour.[12]

The RSPB's editorial in the winter of 1918 also praised the contribution of another bird who had come into its own during the war: the canary. Before the war they had been the miner's friend, during it they became the soldier's, the society commending them for their role as an early warning system of gas attacks. The idea of putting the canary down mines to detect the buildup of poisonous gases had first been trialled just before the war in 1913 by the eccentric Scottish physician and inventor, John Scott Haldane (1860–1936). Haldane was famous for his self-experimentation and big, unkempt moustache which at times resembled a bird's nest. He graduated from Edinburgh University Medical School in 1884 and from the late 1890s, he started to experiment with the effects of gases on mice and canaries. In the run up to the war he visited many mining disasters, carrying out post-mortems on miners who had died through a lethal buildup of poisonous gases. Haldane noticed most miners' bodies were stained cherry-pink – the result of a compound that formed in blood when carbon monoxide combines with haemoglobin.

To get 'live' results Haldane would famously lock himself in an airtight chamber and then fill it with a cocktail of different gases to record the effect it had on his mind and body. Lacking volunteers to take part in his extreme trials, he made it a family affair by experimenting on his son John Burdon Sanderson Haldane to see the effects that gases would have on a younger man. When war broke out, he visited the front at the request of Lord Kitchener, the Secretary of State for War, to identify the gases being used by the Germans, an experience which led to him inventing the first respirator or gas mask.

Haldane experimented on the domesticated form of the wild canary which occurs on the Macaronesian Islands (Azores, Madeira and the Canary Islands). The first canaries were brought to Europe by the Spanish in the seventeenth century and by the outbreak of the First World War they were a very popular pet. Haldane discovered the canary is far more sensitive to the colourless, odourless gas carbon monoxide and other poisonous gases than humans because of their complex respiratory system. Canaries require particularly large quantities of oxygen to fly, a characteristic which makes them a very good sentinel species. This is reflected in the size of their respiratory system, it accounting for 20 per cent of their body size in contrast to about 5 per cent in a human. As well as lungs, they also absorb oxygen through very small 'air sacs' which are distributed throughout their bodies. So, when the canary breathes out, the air stored in their sacs enters the lungs where another exchange of oxygen and carbon dioxide takes place. Canaries are therefore continuously breathing oxygen both when they inhale and exhale, making them extremely sensitive to any airborne toxins (it has been calculated that this makes canaries fifteen times more sensitive to poisonous gas than people). Haldane found that when exposed to poisonous gases they stopped singing, panted for breath and would then fall off their perch. So, on his advice miners took the canary with them deep underground to provide an early warning system. If the canary became ill the miners would know there was a buildup of poisonous gases.

As a result of Haldane's work, canaries were widely used during the war, both in the trenches and down the tunnels which crisscrossed the battlefield. Typically, two or three canaries were kept to test tunnels below the trenches for carbon monoxide, as recommended by the Government Mines Committee. Throughout the war both sides made extensive use of tunnelling, forming an underground network which could be packed with explosives to destroy the enemy lines from below. After an explosion the air was filled with poisonous gases, the tunnel only being accessible once the canary signalled it was safe. To ensure they were sufficiently sensitive, some birds were even given pedicures so that their claws could not grip their perches too tightly.

Serving with the soldiers on the front line many men became very attached to 'their canaries' who instead of being a working bird became a companion in the field. For many they also reminded them of home where before the war they had lived peacefully in an ornate cage in the living room, particularly in working-class families. In the trenches their stoicism and beautiful song lifted the spirits, to such as extent that many became regimental pets who were treated like the troops. One company commander, after a canary had been gassed three times in the line of duty, designated it 'P. B.' or Permanent Base. Officially retired by the army, the bird was kept at the headquarters dugout, where its only duty was to sing to the commanding officer.

The intimate relationship between canary and soldier soon attracted the Press Bureau, the propaganda department of the War Office. An official war photographer, Thomas Aitken, was sent to the front line to capture the bond between them, a series of photographs then appearing in the *Daily Mail* in May 1918. The pictures were designed to carefully capture the kindness and humanity of the Tommy in comparison to the cruelty and inhumanness of the Hun. As the war progressed many canaries suffered the same fate as the soldiers who cared for them, dying in the service of their country. To highlight their bravery, on 12 September 1918, the *Daily Mail* ran a further piece called 'V. C. Canaries'. It featured a canary called 'Dick' who had being gassed on numerous occasions while underground, the paper believing the bird should get the animal equivalent of the Victoria Cross for bravery [this was eventually instituted in 1943, when the Dickin Medal was introduced to honour the bravery of animals in the Second World War].'Many were the nights on which he was rudely disturbed from his slumbers, dumped unceremoniously into a sandbag, and carried through rain and snow up to the trenches,' it said, 'Here he would do his job underground, and as often as not reach the surface again a limp little form lying at the bottom of his cage. He never failed us, though … Hats off to the Canaries! Theirs is a V.C. job every time.'[13]

It was not just down mines that canaries saved lives. Walter Thorp was the radio operator on the steamship *City of Corinth*, a merchant vessel travelling from Singapore to London, when it was torpedoed twelve miles off the Cornish coast by the German submarine *UB-31* in May 1917. Thorp had purchased a canary in Singapore before he left which he had named Triller. After he had valiantly tried to radio for help, Thorp was the last person to jump overboard before the ship sank. He took Triller with him who was in a bamboo cage which on hitting the sea floated. Finding himself alone in the ocean, Thorp hung on to the cage but soon became cold and confused and struggled to stay awake. However, Triller kept chirping loudly every time his head started to drop, keeping him alive until he was rescued. Triller lived out the remaining thirteen years of his life in comfort at Thorp's parents' house in London.

Yet the true heroes of the war were the wild birds which had done so much to sustain the morale of the troops during over four years of fighting in the bloodiest conflict in British history. The RSPB marked the historic moment in its 1918 winter magazine, stating:

> Pigeon and Canary represent the trained and drilled force, doing their part like the army horses and dogs, because man has given it them to do. There are other divisions of the service in the V.A.D. [Voluntary Aid Detachment], most conspicuous perhaps being the Gulls. The help rendered by them in indicating the presence of

German mines and submarines has furnished exciting episodes in the war.[14]

Ten days after the armistice had been signed, on 21 November 1918, the German High Seas Fleet surrendered to the Royal Navy in the North Sea (led to anchorage in the Firth of Forth, they would later be scuttled at the Royal Navy's base at Scapa Flow in the Orkney Islands). The surrender, known as Operation ZZ, had been achieved after days of tense negotiation, a correspondent for *The Times* recording, 'The annals of naval warfare hold no parallel to the memorable event which it has been my privilege to witness today. It was the passing of a whole fleet, and it marked the final and ignoble abandonment of a vainglorious challenge to the naval supremacy of Britain.'

If the war on land had so often resulted in a bloody stalemate, at sea German U-boats had come perilously close to starving Britain into defeat. Now with the German High Seas Fleet, the second largest in the world, out of action, Britannia really did rule the waves. The surrender was celebrated in *Punch* magazine on 27 November 1918 with a cartoon of Britannia on her horse emerging victorious from the waves, trident in hand and looking to heaven. The RSPB was pleased to see that circling above Britannia's head were seagulls, commenting. 'It is good to find Gulls circling about the Britannia of the seas who personifies *Punch*'s tribute to the British Navy.' In its editorial the society also paid tribute to the contribution that birds like the brave house sparrow had played on the home front, part of 'the great land army of insect and vermin eating birds, clearing earth and air and plant of pests innumerable. Their part has been that of the home workers, essential to the success of the campaign abroad'.[15]

Yet it was the wild birds on the battlefields that had played the greatest part in helping to secure victory. At the end of the conflict long lists of birds seen during the war appeared in several ornithological magazines including the February 1919 issue of *British Birds*. Its editor, Harry Forbes Witherby, was a naval reservist who had been called up in November 1917, Witherby writing about the birds he had seen while stationed for a year as an intelligence officer at Dunkirk. In the May issue Captain Arthur de Carle Sowerby, the son of Christian missionaries in China, produced a comprehensive list of birds he had seen while travelling by car inspecting the Chinese Labour Corps in France (the Chinese Labour Corps was the largest foreign work force to serve the Allies during the war). A gifted ornithologist, he called the article 'Birds of the Battlefields' and in it wrote:

> Many of the readers of *British Birds* will agree with me when I say it is gratifying to find that in spite of the turmoil and stress of war, bird lovers have been able to devote part of their time, at least, to the study of bird life, even in the fighting zones. The recent contribution from Mr H. F. Witherby on 'Birds observed near Dunkerque' in north France, is particularly valuable, and should serve to stimulate others, who, alas, are forced to remain in France for some time to come, to follow along the same line of investigation. Such notes must inevitably prove of considerable value to British ornithologists, as throwing light upon the movements and seasonal distribution of our feathered friends.[16]

While bird observations, like those written by Witherby and Sowerby, are invaluable as a historical record, they did not convey what ornithology truly meant to so many soldiers serving in the trenches. Before the war birdwatching had been a popular British pastime but in wartime birds had come into their own, helping to define our national identity. It says a lot about Britain that in the trenches of the First World War the most popular hobby of many serving officers was not smoking, reading, writing, sports, playing games or gambling but birdwatching. The contribution of birds to maintaining the mental health of soldiers serving under the most horrendous conditions cannot be overestimated. From companions in the field to comrades in arms, they served by providing solace, succour and even divine inspiration to war-weary, shell-shocked and deeply depressed troops. In over four years of conflict they sung over the battlefields, nested in no man's land, plied the oceans in search of enemy vessels, carried top-secret messages while under intense enemy fire and lived cheek by jowl with the troops in the trenches. Both domestic and above all wild birds helped to turn the tide of battle and eventually win the war, playing their part with insouciance, verve and outstanding bravery.

The RSPB came closest to summing up their contribution when it wrote in the winter 1918 issue of *Bird Notes and News* that it was impossible:

to ignore the unconscious ministry of the wild birds of the battlefields – the Nightingales and Warblers and Blackbirds singing in wood and garden, the Skylarks rising up over the naked horror of 'No Man's Land', the Swallows nesting in the dug-outs, the Kestrels hovering by day. And the little Owls that call by night, the very Sparrows in the ruined walls; the strange birds and the familiar birds, heedless of thunder of gun and of shock and shell, and perishing, as they must have done, by myriads in the poisoned and shattered forests. For every moment of interest and relief afforded to many a man in the intolerable waiting hours; for every inspiring and inspiriting vision of home that has risen on the wings and songs of birds – surely for this too we are debtors to the First Flying Corps.[17]

1914 ✝ 1918

Roll of Honour

Aymer Edward Maxwell
Francis Algernon Monckton
Lord Brabourne
Lewis Neil Griffith Ramsay
Cecil Macmillan Dyer
Maxwell Green
Leoffer Beresford Mouritz
Richard Bowen Woosnam
Gerald Legge
Charles Hughes Tempest Whitehead
Alexander Douglas Gillespie
Charles Stonham
Frank Edward Southgate
Herbert Hastings Harington
Austin Geoffrey Leigh
Hugh and John Charlton
Boyd Robert Horsburgh
John Cyril Crowley
Lord Lucas

George Wilson Stout
Hector Hugh Munro
Frederick Courteney Selous
John Dighton Grafton-Wignall
Gustavus Arthur Perreau
Phillip Edward Thomas
Henry Edward Otto Murray-Dixon
Henry George Jesse Peavot
William Eric Brook Dunlop
Oliver Bernard Ellis
Leonard Gray
Edwin Ephraim Riseley
Godfrey Vassal Webster
Arthur Gerrard Davidson
Christopher James Alexander
Cecil Christopher Baring
John Bateson
Sydney Edward Brock

'Their name liveth for evermore'

Appendix

The Ornithological Roll of Honour

On landing in France, the Best Birdwatching Army Ever Sent to War counted among its ranks perhaps the greatest generation of ornithologists Britain has ever produced. While some survived the war and went on to greater achievements, for many others the battlefield was to be their last birdwatching expedition. Although most were officers and came from privileged backgrounds, some were privates while others, remarkably, choose to join the lower ranks instead of being commissioned (most of those serving were privately educated and after attending Officers' Training Corps at university were automatically enrolled as officers, with the rank of second lieutenant). Among the Ornithological Roll of Honour are scientists, explorers and professional ornithologists together with many amateur 'birders' and two winners of the RSPB's Silver Medal. Between them they were responsible for big strides in ornithological research, not just in Britain but across the world. From amateur studies to scientific papers and fieldwork at home to discovering new species abroad, they had already left their mark. Their achievements are all the more remarkable when you consider that many were only in their twenties or early thirties when they were killed in action or died of wounds sustained on the battlefield. Their future potential, had they survived, can only be guessed at but there is no doubt that the science of ornithology suffered a severe setback as a result of their deaths.

1914

Aymer Edward Maxwell

In the first major action of the war, the Battle of Mons, the British soon found themselves in retreat despite fighting bravely in Belgium. They regrouped and with the French Fifth Army stopped the German advance just outside Paris at the Battle of Marne. The following Battle of Alsne saw the Germans dig in and create a series of trenches which soon extended south to the Swiss border. By September the fighting had become focused around the front in Belgium where among the first to be killed was Lieutenant Colonel Aymer Edward Maxwell.

Maxwell was born in 1877 in Edinburgh and was the second son of the Right Honourable Sir Herbert Eustace Maxwell and his wife Mary. He was the Conservative MP for Wigtownshire from 1880 until 1909 and was an accomplished author, historian and naturalist who published several books on sea and freshwater fish. Aymer was educated at Eton and then went to military training college at Sandhurst before joining the Grenadier Guards in 1897. He took part in the Boer War (1899–1902) but was invalided out in 1900, retiring with the rank of captain in 1907 and joining the reserve. After he left the army Maxwell dedicated his life to the study of gamebirds, rapidly becoming an expert on grouse, pheasant and wildfowl shooting. An acknowledged world expert in his field, Maxwell contributed to and wrote many books on the subject including *Grouse and Grouse Moors* in 1910, *Partridge and Partridge Manors* in 1911, *The Gun at Home and Abroad, British Game Birds and Wildfowl* in 1912 and *Pheasants and Covert Shooting* in 1913.

On mobilization in August 1914, Maxwell immediately volunteered for active service despite being 36 years old and curtailed his bird research. After careful consideration given his age and experience, he was given command of the Collingwood Battalion, Royal Naval Division, with the rank of lieutenant colonel (the battalion was named after Vice-Admiral Cuthbert Collingwood, one of Lord Nelson's officers). The Royal Naval Division was formed at Walmer in Kent in September 1914 and was made up of reservists who at the time were not needed on ships. After six weeks' training, they sailed on the first Sunday in October 1914 from Dover to France, landing at Dunkirk. Ordered to relieve the Belgians fighting at Whybreck, they occupied a fort along the trenches at Antwerp and engaged with the enemy. However, the town came under heavy German bombardment and Maxwell was mortally wounded in the head by the first shell, on 8 October 1914, dying the following day in a military hospital where he was buried in the garden. In the ensuing action the battalion was annihilated: of the 700 men under Maxwell's command, only 22 returned safely to England.

Maxwell's legacy to natural history lies not just in the books he wrote on gamebirds but in his children. He married Lady Mary Percy in 1909, the fifth daughter of the 7th Duke of Northumberland, and they had four sons. The youngest, Gavin, was born in July 1914, just two months before his father left for France. Gavin Maxwell would serve with the clandestine Special Operations Executive during the Second World War and go on to become one of the most famous naturalists of his era, writing *Ring of Bright Water* in 1960 about an otter cub he raised. The book sold over a million copies and was made into a successful film in 1969 starring Bill Travers and Virginia McKenna.

Of his father Aymer, his commanding officer wrote in a letter to his mother, 'His death is a severe loss to my brigade. I personally have lost a friend, the whole brigade has lost one of its finest officers. His energy, earnestness and singleness of purpose inspired his whole Battalion, and both his officers and men were animated by his fine spirit from the moment he assumed command of them.' Aymer Maxwell was buried in the Schoonselhof Cemetery, Antwerp, and is commemorated on the Port William War Memorial in his home town of Wigtownshire. A member of the Marylebone Cricket Club, he is also one of the 330 names listed on their Great War memorial at Lord's pavilion.

Francis Algernon Monckton

On 8 November 1914, Staffordshire lost one of its most promising ornithologists with the death of Francis Algernon Monckton, a lieutenant in the 1st Battalion Scots Guards. The battalion's war diary for that day recorded his loss:

> 8th – do [Duty Officer] – Fairly heavy shelling. Enemy break through French and N. Lancs. get into communication trench and enfilade battalion trenches. L. N. Lancs. and our supports counter attacked and regained lost trenches. Germans remained in right trenches. Attempts made to turn them out with machine gun fire. Killed. Lt. R. N. Gipps, Lt. F.A. Monckton Wounded, Lt. B. W. Smith (died of wounds), J. S. Stuart (died of wounds), Lt. J. S. Dyer Bt. Missing, Lt. A. W. Douglas-Dick.

Monckton was born on 8 May 1890 in Granville Place, London, the eldest son of Francis Monckton and his wife Evelyn Mary Heber-Percy. The following year they moved to Stretton Hall, Stafford, a stately home with extensive grounds where they employed fifteen servants. Here Monckton had the opportunity to study birds, especially the wildfowl on the lake in Stretton Park, the River Penk which ran through the estate and a large body of water known as Bellfield's Reservoir. From the age of 15 he sent in regular bird reports to a local journal called *The Transactions of the North Staffordshire Field Club*, in the process recording many rare birds for the county.

He was educated at Eton where he wrote poetry and on their famous playing fields heard the corn bunting singing, a record which appeared in *The Field* on 14 November 1908. The following year he went on to study at Christ Church, Oxford. After graduating he joined the Scots Guards, obtaining his commission as second lieutenant in February 1912 and becoming a lieutenant the next year. On leave he sent the following record to the Staffordshire Field Club:

I saw 2 Knots on October 12th 1913 at Bellfields Reservoir. I watched them for some time through powerful glasses and when one flew close past me, I could distinctly see the grey rump. I believe the only previous satisfactory record of the Knot for Staffordshire is one shot at Tittensor near Trentham in December 1892. On the night of November 6–7th 1913, there was a large immigration of many different species and I saw three Ruffs at Bellfields on the 7th ... I believe there are only two previous records of the Ruff for Staffordshire – one which I saw at Bellfields in 1911 or 1912, and one which was shot at Norton Pool near Chasetown.

With the outbreak of war, Monckton continued to record the birds he saw in France. In a letter dated 22 October 1914 from St Nazaire, at the mouth of the Loire, where he was quartered before going to the front, he described the species he found there including those on migration:

On the 17th [October] there was a great rush of birds. I was out about 7.15 a.m. and the migration seemed to reach its height about 8.00 a.m. and had practically stopped by 10.30 a.m. It was a cold, overcast, hazy morning, with a fresh N.E. wind. The birds were flying up the river along the shore. They mostly passed straight on, but some dropped out here and there. The vast majority seemed to be Chaffinches, Linnets, Skylarks, and Goldfinches, with a certain number of Meadow Pipits. There were also a few Rooks, Jackdaws, Swallows, Martins and Wagtails.

On the 20th there was another strong migration, though hardly so many birds as on the day before. Mostly Chaffinches, Linnets, Skylarks and Goldfinches, but not so many Meadow-Pipits. A few Rooks, Starlings, Swallows, Martins, and Mistle Thrushes, one Redwing (or possibly a Song-Thrush), a Wheatear, a Merlin, and a good many Blue Tits.

Wednesday, 21st. I saw a Wheatear, and I think there was a slight migration: but it was difficult to tell owing to the fog. To-day (22nd), all migration seems to have stopped.

Monckton was killed two weeks later at Hooge, near Ypres and is commemorated at the Menin Gate. His name also features on a memorial in St John's Church, Stretton, with his younger brother, Geoffrey Valentine Francis Monckton, also a lieutenant in Scots Guards, who was killed in action at Cuinchy, near La Bassée in 1915 and his cousin, Christopher Monckton, killed at Mons-en-Chaussée, France in 1916.

The author of his obituary in *British Birds* wrote, 'The writer has lost in Monckton a valued and sincere friend and correspondent and the study of Staffordshire Ornithology will suffer much by his having given his life so nobly for his country.'

1915

Lord Brabourne
As the war entered its second year, attrition had set in with both sides confined to their trenches but still trying for a decisive breakthrough. One of the first offensives was the Battle of Neuve Chapelle in March 1915 in which the British breached the German lines at the eponymous village but were unable to exploit their success. On the penultimate day of the attack, 11 March 1915, the ornithologist Lord Brabourne was killed. The third Baron Brabourne, Wyndham Wentworth Knatchbull-Hugessen, was born on 21 September 1885, and inherited the peerage on the death of his father in 1909. As a young man he had spent several years in Paraguay, where he amassed a considerable collection of birds, which he presented to the British Museum on his return in 1908.

Lord Brabourne entered the Grenadier Guards in 1910 but resigned a year later to concentrate on ornithology, like Maxwell passing into the reserve. The same year he became a member of the British Ornithologists' Union and started to write a monumental six-volume work on the birds of South America in collaboration with the ornithologist Charles Chubb who worked at the British Museum. The first volume appeared in 1912 as *The Birds of South America*, detailing 4,561 species, nearly a thousand more than the only previous list published in 1873. In July 1912, Lord Brabourne left again for South America, collecting specimens in Peru for the next volume, returning home only when when war broke out to rejoin his old regiment.

In an article in the *Avicultural Magazine*, published in September 1914, Brabourne introduced British readers to the wonders of birds in Peru:

> To those acquainted with the Wealdon country, imagine the North and South Downs; imagine all the angles, breaks and irregularities immeasurably distorted and exaggerated. Here and there on the skyline are copses; replace these by jagged snow-peaks; in the middle of the plain is the rush-margined Lake Junin or Chinchaycocha about 22 miles long by 7 wide, the largest of the Andean Lakes except Titicaca and Poopoo ... The pale pinky smudge against the brown rushes not many hundred yards away is a long line of Flamingoes. Nearer at hand are the dark forms of small parties of Glossy Ibis (*Egatheus ridgwaym*), the bird of the neighbourhood most in evidence. An Andean Gull (*Larus serranus*), or a Carrion Hawk (*Ibyeter megalopterus*) in search of prey sails into view. The lake is not a mile away.

Lord Brabourne's untimely death aged just 30 meant the series was never finished and the first volume remains the only one ever written. However, a volume of thirty-eight hand-coloured lithographic plates of species which would have featured in the next volume was published posthumously in his honour by the book's artist and his friend, the Danish naturalist Henrik Grönvold. The Grenadier Guards war diary recorded his death in action together with 15 other officers and 325 soldiers during the battle. He has no known grave but his name appears on La Touret

Memorial in Béthune, France and his family erected a memorial to him in his parish church in Smeeth, Kent.

Lewis Neil Griffith Ramsay

Lieutenant Lewis Neil Griffith Ramsay survived the Battle of Neuve Chapelle but was killed in action shortly afterwards on 21 March 1915, aged 25, when he was shot by a sniper while repairing a trench. Ramsay was born in Aberdeen on 3 February 1890, the second son of Professor Sir William Ramsay and his wife. Educated at Merchiston School, Edinburgh, he later studied at Aberdeen University where his father taught, afterwards going on to Christ's College, Cambridge. Ramsey was preparing to study at the Imperial College of Science when war broke out. Just before the war he had acted as assistant to the Professor of Natural History at Aberdeen University where he took part in the first organized bird-ringing scheme in Britain with an ornithologist friend, Arthur Davidson, who would also be killed during the war, and another undergraduate, Arthur Landsborough Thomson. From an early age Ramsay had been fascinated by birds and on graduating he carried out detailed studies of many birds found near his home in Aberdeenshire. During his short life time he published scientific papers on the garganey, gadwall, blue-headed wagtail, spotted redshank, grasshopper warbler and mealy redpole, as well as completing a detailed study of the moult of the herring gull. In addition to his work on birds, Ramsay was a recognized expert on marine worms.

His legacy includes an analysis of the collections made by William Speirs Bruce on his Scottish National Antarctic Expedition 1902–4, he co-authoring the ornithology section and writing an account of the polychaete worms. Ramsay travelled on many birdwatching expeditions, notably across Asia Minor, publishing a paper on the birdlife of the Anatolian Plateau in Turkey in 1914.

As a young man he had served with the territorials, rejoining his old unit, the 4th Battalion Gordon Highlanders, in September 1914 and becoming a sergeant, later being promoted to second lieutenant. His obituary in *British Birds* was written by his friend and fellow ringer Arthur Landsborough Thomson. Ramsay is commemorated in the Estaires Communal Cemetery in Nord, France.

Cecil Macmillan Dyer

On 8 April 1915, Cecil Dyer was shot through the head while on lookout duty with the Rifle Brigade. Before joining up he had just finished his second year studying natural sciences at Cambridge University. A keen ornithologist, Dyer was buried behind a wood about four miles east of Ypres. He loved birds from boyhood and was delighted to be elected as a member of the prestigious British Ornithologists' Union in 1914 just before he went to war.

His obituary in *Ibis*, the journal of the BOU, said:

> He was one of the two leading spirits in ornithology during the time he was in Cambridge, and did a great deal of work in the neighbourhood, chiefly in estimating the number of each species of bird in the various districts and finding out in which spots they bred. He kept careful lists of the results, and his work was most accurate … He added a good deal to our knowledge of the birds of remote villages to the west of Cambridge.

On his brief time in the army one of his superior officers said of him, 'He did his work very well and was most conscientious,' and a private under his command reflected that he was 'a very brave officer, always forward'.

Dyer was the son of the late Louis Dyer, a professor at Balliol College, Oxford, and his wife Margaret Anne and the grandson of Alexander Macmillan, the publisher. He was born on 17 January 1894 at Sunbury Lodge, Oxford, and educated at Magdalen College School, Oxford, and later at Clifton College, Bristol. In October 1912, he went on to Christ's College, Cambridge, where he studied the Natural Sciences Tripos (degree course). He was also an active member of the boat club and served with the Officer Training Corps at both Oxford and Cambridge.

With the outbreak of war in August 1914 Dyer volunteered for the Special Reserve and received a commission as a second lieutenant in the 6th Battalion of the Rifle Brigade. He was then transferred to the 4th Battalion and went to the front with the 27th Division just before Christmas 1914. He was involved in heavy fighting and invalided out for a time with frozen feet. He fought at Neuve Chapelle and his last engagement was at St Eloi, a village about five kilometres south of Ypres, in March 1915. Dyer has no known grave but is commemorated on the Menin Gate. His obituary in the roll of honour at Christ's College Boat Club reads: 'To those who knew him best his future seemed to be one of bright promise, for he combined ability and enthusiasm with an affectionate and trustful disposition which had won him many friends, not only with his contemporaries but among men of older years.'

Maxwell Green

On 21 April 1915, Private Maxwell Green was killed instantly when he was shot in the head in the trenches at Ypres. Aged 19, he was described as an 'ardent naturalist' who took great solace from nature, especially on the battlefield. On Green's body was found an article he had been writing about the birds he had seen in Flanders for publication in the *Selborne Magazine* (the journal of the Selborne Society commemorating the life of the world-famous naturalist Gilbert White).

Green was the only son of Mr and Mrs Green who lived in Wembley, Middlesex. He was educated at Haberdashers' Aske's School, Hampstead, before doing a degree at the University of London. After graduating he joining the Commercial Union Assurance Company in the Foreign Fire Department. On the outbreak of war in August 1914, he enlisted with the Honourable Artillery Company and was posted to the Western Front in January 1915. His platoon officer said of him he was 'a good soldier and a friend'; his section commander, Sergeant H. P. Tate, wrote, 'Max had won for himself a place in all our hearts and will always be remembered as a brave and loveable comrade. We were proud of him.'

After his death his father wrote to the *Selborne Magazine* with the bird notes found on his body which were 'scribbled on several slips of paper lying between the pages of his copy of your March magazine, which were on him when he was killed and are evidently intended as a basis for a much more complete article'. His father added that he had made no attempt to edit them but still thought that the magazine may consider them worthy of publication. He concluded, 'It is some consolation to know that the simple soul of the naturalist could find relief and comfort for his leisure moments among such incongruous surroundings.'

Notes on birds I see out here
By Private Maxwell Green, No. 1 Company Honourable Artillery Company

Sunday, April 11th – There are some, but I have lost all my mental knowledge and cannot recognize them well. Down at my second resting-place I saw two Missel Thrushes, but there are, it seems, few small birds, except a few Sparrows at night.

It is curious how little the sound and turmoil of this great struggle has impressed itself upon the animal and birdlife of Flanders. One might have imagined that the daily sound of shells, plunging and bursting into the wood, might have driven the native inhabitants to forsake their accustomed haunts. But I have noticed how rapidly they have accustomed themselves to what is still to them a frequent annoyance.

The Hares can still be seen feeding upon the few unworn fields. The Blackbirds and Sparrows momentarily cease their chatter during a bombardment; then, as in becoming thankfulness, the danger over, burst anew into their songs. Whilst on both sides at night the sternness of vigils is kept, the guards will hear the hoot of the Owl as he flies over the fields, crossing trench and trench in search of prey.

How pathetic, indeed, was the death of a Pigeon I witnessed from my dug-out! A ruined cottage stood perhaps fifteen yards away, and all day two Pigeons had characteristically maintained their stations on the roof. A shell begins to come over; and, though the cottage is made an object of fire, the Pigeons continue to enjoy themselves. A small shell bursts in the the garden, and a piece of shell unfortunately strikes and kills a Pigeon. Unable, it seems, to realize what has happened, or where its mate has disappeared, the other remains for the remainder of the day in the same position, peering about in order to discover its mate, and occasionally emitting a soft coo. This seems to affect the bird more …

Four days later Green was killed, his article left unfinished but published posthumously by *Selborne Magazine*, the editor stating 'It is with melancholy pleasure that we print the letter above, together with the notes which accompanied it.' He was buried near Ypres, his colonel attending his funeral. Green's remains were later transferred to Voormezeele Enclosure No. 3 Cemetery in Belgium.

Leoffer Beresford Mouritz

It was not just on the battlefields of France and Belgium that ornithologists fell but across all theatres of the war. In 1915, Winston Churchill, First Lord of the Admiralty, launched the Allied Gallipoli campaign against the Ottoman Turks to gain control of the Dardanelle Straits which provided sea access to Russia. The amphibious landings which began in April 1915 saw Australian and New Zealand troops in combat for the first time, 16,000 of them supporting the Allied invasion force. However, the landings were a military disaster, the Turks inflicting devastating losses on the invaders and by the first evening 2,000 had been killed or wounded. For the next month there was stalemate, the Anzac forces advancing no further than the positions they had occupied on the first day. However, the campaign continued to take its toll and in May the ornithologist Leoffer Beresford Mouritz of the 2nd Light Horse Regiment, was reported as missing, later declared killed in action on 14 May 1915.

Mouritz was born in 1887 in Melbourne, Victoria, the son of Henry Joseph Mouritz who originally hailed from Chicago in the United States. A mining engineer by profession, he came to live in England and later worked in Rhodesia (Zimbabwe) and the Belgian Congo (Democratic Republic of Congo) before being joining the Australian Imperial Force on 1 September 1914. A keen ornithologist, he wrote an annual report on the birds of Surrey which in 1907 was published in *The Zoologist*. The same year a prestigious new monthly journal called *British Birds* was launched to appeal to the 'serious and scientific ornithologist' (in 1916 it incorporated *The Zoologist* due to its lack of subscribers). Seeing an opportunity to make a name for himself, Mouritz submitted a detailed article to the new journal. However, his keenness to impress was soon to plunge the publication into controversy and cause a minor ornithological scandal.

Mouritz and a friend, C. H. Bentham, wrote about the county's first breeding hen harriers (*Circus cyaneus*), the paper appearing in the 1 January 1908 edition of *British Birds*. Clearly delighted at his ornithological scoop he wrote:

> The breeding of the Hen-Harrier is undoubtedly to be regarded as the most important event; this bird unfortunately being, at the present time, almost entirely restricted, as a nesting species, to a few of the wildest and most extensive moorland districts, and it is therefore somewhat remarkable that a pair should have been successful in bringing off their young, in a comparatively populated neighbourhood within fifty miles of the metropolis, and moreover in a county in which game-preserving is extensively carried on.

The problem was that despite Mouritz's remarkable record, the hen harriers in question later turned out to be Montagu's harriers (*Circus pygargus*). What made the mistake particularly embarrassing was that it had been exposed in a competitor publication, *The Field*, a populist magazine about field sports. The founding editor of *British Birds*, the erudite Harry Forbes Witherby (1873–1943), was acutely embarrassed, especially as he had passed the paper for publication. So, Witherby faced a dilemma: should he come clean and accept the damage to the reputation of his beloved journal? Or should he write a face-saving article as a way out of the controversy?

In the end Witherby did the latter, after consulting with Mouritz writing a detailed defence in the 1 April 1908 issue. Choosing his words carefully, Witherby wrote, 'We regret very much, and we are sure that the authors of the article in question regret no less, that the readers of *British Birds* have been misinformed, and that the nest described and photographed was, without any doubt, that of a Montagu's Harrier (*Circus cineraceus*).' However, to salvage his journal's battered reputation he contended that the first nest had indeed been that of a hen harrier, only afterwards it being replaced by a Montagu's harrier. To prove his version of events Witherby asked the 'Last Great White Hunter', Frederick Courteney Selous, to identify two birds shot near the nest, the original female and one of the young (ironically, illegal shooting by game keepers was the reason why the birds were so rare). Selous was one of the most famous big-game hunters in the world and during breaks in his safaris resided in Surrey where he was an avid, bordering on obsessive, ornithologist. Relishing the challenge, he made 'exhaustive enquiries', from which Witherby concluded, 'There can be no doubt whatever by the test of the primaries as well as by the coloration that the bird shot in March is an adult female Hen-Harrier, and that the bird shot in August is a young Montagu's Harrier.' To prove his own ornithological credentials were still very much intact, Witherby finished his article with a detailed comparison of the primary feathers of both birds including two hand-drawn diagrams.

Mouritz left England in late 1907, no doubt pleased to leave the scandal and Witherby behind him and, despite it, was elected a member of the British Ornithologists' Union (BOU) in 1912. He subsequently wrote detailed papers on the birds he saw while prospecting for minerals in the Belgian Congo in 1914 and Rhodesia in 1915 but this time sensibly submitted them, not to *British Birds* but to *Ibis*, the BOU's journal.

Upon his death, the scandal was glossed over and his obituary in *British Birds*, written by the tactful Reverend Francis Charles Robert Jourdain (1865–1940), read:

> He was a keen and very promising young ornithologist, and while resident in England prior to going out to South Africa he did a good deal of ornithological work, chiefly in Surrey ... In collaboration with Mr. C. H. Bentham he also contributed an article to the first volume of *British Birds* on the breeding of what was believed at the time to be a pair of Hen-Harriers in Surrey in 1907, but which subsequently proved to be Montagu's Harriers (*Circus pygargus*).

Mouritz was 27 years old when he died on 14 May 1915; just over a year and a half later Frederick Selous would also be killed in battle. Mouritz has no known grave but is commemorated on the Lone Pine Memorial to the dead of the Gallipoli campaign in Turkey.

Richard Bowen Woosnam

Another victim of the Gallipoli campaign was Second Lieutenant Richard Bowen Woosnam. He was killed while gallantly leading his men in an attack on the Turkish trenches on 4 June 1915. Woosnam was a brilliant field naturalist, explorer and game warden who was a member of the British Ornithologists' Union and was awarded the prestigious silver medal by the Zoological Society of London in 1909 for his contribution to 'the understanding and appreciation of zoology'.

Woosnam was born on 17 November 1880 and at 18 joined the Worcester Regiment, taking part in the Boer War from 1899–1902, after which he resigned to concentrate on natural history. In 1903, he led a field trip to the Cape Colony (the Cape of Good Hope on the southern tip of Africa), the next year accompanying Arthur Bailward, a fellow Boer War veteran and member of the Royal Geographical Society, on an extensive journey through western Persia (now Iran) and Armenia. Here they took extensive photographs and collected a large number of animal specimens, including many small mammals and bats, donating them to the Royal Geographical Society and the British Museum.

In 1905, Woosnam led a successful expedition organized by William Robert Ogilvie-Grant, the head of ornithology at the British Museum, to the Ruwenzori Mountains in Uganda. Here, assisted by his friend Gerald Legge, they discovered twenty-nine new species and sub-species of bird to add to the Ugandan list. As a result, he had a number of birds new to science named after him including the wonderfully called trilling cisticola (*Cisticola woosnami*), fire-crested alethe (*Alethe castanea woosnami*) and the red-tailed bristlebill (*Bleda syndactylus woosnami*). Woosam also collected a wide variety of other wildlife and has the distinction of having a snake, mouse and a rat all named after him: the Great Lakes bush viper (*Atheris woosnami*), Woosnam's broad-headed mouse (*Zelotomys woosnami*) and Woosnam's brush-furred rat (*Lophuromys woosnami*).

In 1907, Woosnam returned to Persia, visiting the Elburz Mountains where he again collected specimens with Bailward. In 1909, he went on another expedition to Africa, this time exploring the Kalahari Desert with Legge. In honour of his work, he was appointed game warden for British East Africa (now Kenya) in 1910, only returning to England in order to rejoin his old regiment, the Worcesters, on the outbreak of war. He left an extensive collection to the British Museum, and accounts of the birds he discovered together with his field notes appeared in various volumes of the *Ibis* and in the *Transactions of the Zoological Society*. His life is commemorated on the Helles Memorial in Turkey to the dead of the Gallipoli campaign who have no known grave and in a plaque in his local church, St Idloes Church in Llanidloes, Powys. Woosnam's name lives on in the large number of species named after him from cisticolas to vipers.

Gerald Legge

Woosnam's colleague on his expedition to the Ruwenzori Mountains, Captain Gerald Legge, was killed shortly after him. The second son of the 6th Earl of Dartmouth, he was mortally wounded at Suvla Bay in the Dardanelles on 9 August 1915. The amphibious landing at the bay was the final British attempt to break the deadlock of the Gallipoli campaign and it proved another bloody defeat.

Legge was born in 1882 and was a keen naturalist all his life, taking a special interest in wildfowl which he both reared and studied in the field, putting his name to several scientific papers. At his father's home in Patshull in Staffordshire, like the Foreign Secretary, Sir Edward Grey, he bred a great many species of wildfowl, his collection including both tame and wild birds. His friend the zoologist John Masefield wrote of him:

> As an instance of his keenness in studying ducks I may relate that one day when I met him at Patshull he had just arrived from Northumberland, whence he had brought a nest of Teal just hatching out. By telegraphing forward to several stations en route he had secured a relay of hot-water bottles by means of which he had succeeded in keeping the ducklings warm. He gave me regular notes on the rarer Staffordshire birds, and especially the ducks, which he noted at Patshull.

Legge was a member of both Woosnam expeditions to Africa where he acted as a scout. In 1906, the short-tailed pipit (*Anthus brachyurus leggi*) was named after him. On the outbreak of war, he joined the 7th Battalion, South Staffordshire Regiment. An appreciation of him was published in *The Field* by his friend J. G. Millais who wrote:

> The rising sun, the beauty of a bird's wing, or a lovely flower were things before which he stood hat in hand, just as he held everything that was false or small of no account … Such a man was at once ready to defend his country. He was last seen lying mortally wounded on the ground, and cheering on the men of whom he was so proud. That was Gerald Legge.

Like Woosnam, Legge's name appears on the Helles Memorial in Turkey to the fallen in the Gallipoli campaign and he is also commemorated in St Mary's Church in his home village of Patshull, South Staffordshire. Gerald's brother William also served in the war with the Staffordshire Yeomanry where he fought in the Palestine campaign. He was promoted to lieutenant colonel in 1917 and survived the war, going on to become the 7th Earl of Dartmouth, a Conservative politician and Lord Great Chamberlain from 1928–36.

Charles Hughes Tempest Whitehead

In the autumn of 1915, the British again tried to break through the German lines during the Battle of Loos on the Western Front. The action was significant because it was the first time the British used poison gas and was also the first large-scale deployment of Herbert Kitchener's, the Secretary of State for War, 'New Army'. The offensive started on 25 September 1915 and on the first or the second day, Major Charles Hughes Tempest Whitehead was killed. Whitehead was born in 1881 and was the seventh son of George and Mary Whitehead, from York, five of his other brothers also serving, four in the army and one in the navy. Whitehead grew up in India and joined the 56th Punjab Rifles (Frontier Force) serving in the Boer War. In the First World War he was attached to the Highland Light Infantry. A keen ornithologist, he specialized in the birds of the North-West Frontier, in 1909, writing 'On the birds of Kohat and Kurram, northern India'.

His friend Edward Charles Stuart Baker, an officer with the Indian Police Service who catalogued the birds of India, in an obituary published in *British Birds* on 1 December 1915, said of him:

> Whitehead fell leading his men in a charge, being shot dead on the very parapet of the enemy's trench, which was taken. In person Whitehead was a singularly charming character, intensely earnest in everything he did, persevering and thorough, and most careful in all his work. He discovered the new Thrush [Whitehead's Mountain-Thrush], which I had the pleasure of naming *Oreoeincla whitehead* after him, and amongst other interesting discoveries he made were the breeding-haunts in the Himalayas of the Chinese Reed-Warbler.

He is commemorated at the Neuve Chapelle Memorial in France and in a brass plaque in St Helen's Church in Selby, North Yorkshire.

Alexander Douglas Gillespie

Another ornithologist soldier to die on the same day was Alexander Douglas Gillespie who was serving with the Argyll and Sutherland Highlanders. He was killed aged 26 while leading an attack at Cuinchy on the 25 September 1915, the first day of the Battle of Loos. Under heavy fire he fell just as he reached the German trench and according to his surviving men was the only officer to see the enemy that day. The bitter irony of his death was that he was killed by the poison gas that the British had previously released, which following a change in the wind, blew back in his face.

Gillespie was born in 1889 in Alveston, Gloucestershire, and was the eldest son of Thomas Paterson Gillespie who originally hailed from Longcroft, Linlithgow, near Edinburgh. His youngest brother, Lieutenant Thomas Cunningham Gillespie, also served in the war, joining the King's Own Scottish Borderers and was killed on 18 October 1914.

Gillespie was educated at Cargilfield School, Edinburgh, later going on to study at Winchester College where he excelled. In 1908 he won a scholarship to New College, Oxford, and graduated with a first-class degree in Classical Moderations and a second in *Literae Humanitores* (classics, philosophy, and ancient history) in 1912.

When war broke out, he was reading for the Bar (to become a barrister) but volunteered his services straight away, obtaining a commission in the 2nd Battalion Argyll and Sutherland Highlanders. He was sent to the front in February 1915 and wrote many letters home about daily life including the birds he saw there. These were published posthumously in 1916 with the title *Letters from Flanders* and contain this beautiful passage about the nightingale:

> Presently a misty moon came up, and a Nightingale began to sing ... and it was strange to stand there and listen, for the song seemed to come all the more sweetly and clearly in the quiet intervals between the bursts of firing. There was something infinitely sweet and sad about it, as if the countryside were singing gently to itself, in the midst of all our noise and confusion and muddy work; so that you

felt the Nightingale's song was the only real thing which would remain when all the rest was long past and forgotten. It is such an old song too, handed on from Nightingale to Nightingale through the summer nights of so many innumerable years.

In another one of his letters Gillespie writes movingly about his search for the chateau where his brother Thomas spent his last night before being killed. However, his most famous letter was written on 14 June 1915 to his old headmaster at Winchester, just three months before his death. It was about a remembrance project he wanted to create from the battlefield once the war was over. His dream was to transform no man's land into a *Via Sacra* – a sacred pathway – stretching 450 miles from the Belgian coast at Nieuwpoort to the Swiss border near Basel. In his letter, Gillespie said:

These fields are sacred in a sense and I wish that when the peace comes, our government might combine with the French government to make one long avenue from the Vosges to the sea. The ground is so pitted and scarred and torn with shells and tangled with wire that it will take years to bring it back to use again. But it would make a fine broad road in the No Man's Land between the lines, with paths for pilgrims on foot and planted trees for shade, and fruit trees, so the soil should not be altogether waste. Some of the shattered farms and houses might be left as evidence, and the regiments might put up their records beside the trenches which they held all through the winter. Then I would like to send every man, woman and child in Western Europe on a pilgrimage along that Via Sacra so that they might think and learn what war means from the silent witnesses on either side. A sentimental idea, perhaps, but we might make it the most beautiful road in all the world.

Gillespie's vision of a tree-lined walkway to honour the 3.3 million – Allied and German – killed on the Western Front is yet to be realized. However, The Western Front Way charity and his family are campaigning for the British, French and Belgian governments' approval for a joint walkway to honour his vision. With no known grave, Gillespie is commemorated on panels 125–7 of the Loos Memorial in the Pas de Calais, northern France.

1916

Charles Stonham

It was not just those ornithologists fighting at the front that gave their lives but also those treating their injuries. On 5 February 1916, the *British Medical Journal* announced the death of Colonel Charles Stonham, senior surgeon at Westminster Hospital. He had died five days earlier at his Harley Street home after having contracted dengue fever and dysentery while serving in Egypt. Born in 1858, Stonham was the eldest surviving son of T. G. Stonham of Maidstone in Kent. Educated at King's School, Canterbury, he studied surgery at University College and gained his Fellowship of the Royal Colleges of Surgeons in 1884. In 1887, he was appointed surgeon to the Westminster Hospital, two years later becoming senior surgeon.

As well as being an extremely skilful surgeon – Stonham was ambidextrous, his colleague Walter Spencer describing 'his long thin hands' and remembering that he was 'a very rapid operator, beginning and ending quickly, yet proceeding with all due caution at critical stages of the operation' – he was also an avid ornithologist who amassed a large collection of birds and eggs over his lifetime. He is best known for publishing the five volumes of the *Birds of the British Islands* from 1906–11. Stonham, who was a member of the British Ornithologists' Union, worked hard on the text, the illustrations being done by an artist and nurse he worked with, Lilian Medland.

An obituary in *British Birds* sniffily said of him:

> Stonham will be best known to ornithologists as the author of the *Birds of the British Islands*, 5 vols., 4to, London, 1906–11, a work which he undertook both from his deep interest in the subject and as an outlet for the indomitable energy which even the stress of a busy professional career was unable to subdue. The book achieved a popular success, but it cannot be said to have added much to our knowledge of the subject, and it would be idle to pretend that Stonham ranked high as a scientific ornithologist; a keen and painstaking field naturalist he was, and an ardent lover of Heaven's free air and the wildlife of the countryside. Where, however, he did excel was as an oologist, and had his inclination led him to

produce a book on the eggs instead of the birds of Great Britain, his knowledge of the subject and the remarkable series of eggs which he had personally obtained and added to his collections would have been of real importance.

Stonham served in the Boer War where he was the chief surgeon at The Imperial Yeomanry Field Hospital, being awarded the Military Medal, the Companion of St Michael and St George and being mentioned in dispatches. As a member of the Royal Army Medical Corps, he formed a field ambulance unit which was attached to the London Mounted Brigade. The brigade was mobilized at the outbreak of the war, and in April 1915 he was sent to Egypt with the rank of colonel. In his will he left his bird and egg collection to his old school at Canterbury.

His obituary in *British Birds* read:

As a man, Stonham was a striking personality, tall of figure, lean and saturnine of appearance, of a fearless and outspoken honesty, and the possessor of a biting tongue: he hesitated not to speak of men and things as he found them: of enemies therefore he did not lack, nor did he of very many friends, and those of us who were privileged to know him well, knew him for a man of the kindliest nature, true as steel, and with a heart of pure gold.

He was buried at Golders Green Crematorium with full military honours.

Frank Edward Southgate

Among the many ornithologists at the front were a number of bird artists including Frank Edward Southgate, who was serving with the 24th Battalion, Royal Fusiliers, a line infantry regiment. The 24th Battalion was part of the City of London Regiment which was one of the Pals battalions formed by Lord Kitchener at the outbreak of the conflict so that people who knew each other or had something in common could serve together. Southgate's 24th Battalion was one of three so-called 'Sportsmen's Battalions' which were composed of men up to the age of 45 who had distinguished themselves in sports, the arts and media. It was raised in London on 20 November 1914 and its eclectic mix included a number of famous recruits including the Liberal politician and baron Sir Herbert Rapheal (1859–1924), and the cricketer Charles Percy McGahey (1871–1935).

Southgate was born in 1872 in Hunstanton, Norfolk, to Samuel and Mary Southgate. From an early age he showed a great aptitude for painting and spent much of his childhood roaming the north Norfolk coast, a place of pilgrimage for many ornithologists, sketching and painting birds in both oil and watercolour. In 1903, he married Ethel Winlove and they lived just down the coast from his parents at Wells-next-the-Sea, later due to his success moving to London where they lived in upmarket Hampstead. He went on to become the art master at the Bideford Art School in Devon and the School of Art in Cambridge.

Southgate was a member of the prestigious Royal Society of British Artists (RBA) and specialized in Norfolk landscape scenes and birds, particularly waterfowl, waders and gamebirds. His work was widely exhibited, including at the Royal Academy and by the RBA. As well as undertaking commissioned paintings, Southgate illustrated a large number of books, including *The Norfolk Broads*, written by William A. Dutt, and published in 1903 for which he provided '48 coloured and 29 uncoloured' illustrations. These ranged from 'A Sparrowhawk calling her mate' to 'A successful shot at waders – The bird's end of a gun'. He also illustrated *Notes of an East Coast Naturalist: series of observations made at odd times during a period of twenty-five years in the neighbourhood of Great Yarmouth* by Arthur Henry Patterson, published in 1904, and provided sixteen illustrations for *Wild Life in East Anglia*, again written by Dutt and published in 1906.

He was killed on 23 February 1916 on the Western Front and is buried at the Lillers Communal Cemetery in the Pais de Calais in northern France.

Herbert Hastings Harington

The continuing war against the Ottoman Empire included the Mesopotamia (now Iraq) campaign in which the Allies, comprising British, Australian and Indian troops, took on the Turkish Army. On 8 March 1916, an Anglo-Indian force sought to relieve the town of Kut but was repelled, the Allies losing over 4,000 men in the attack. Among them was Lieutenant Colonel Herbert Hastings Harington who commanded the 62nd Punjabis. He was born at Lucknow in India on 16 January 1868, the son of Herbert Harington who was an administrator in the British Raj. Educated at Malvern College, he entered the army in 1888, two years later being appointed to the Indian Staff Corps where he joined the 92nd Punjabis.

Harington served with his regiment for over twenty years in Burma where he was attached to the Burmese Police. Here he became fascinated by the country's birds, carrying out a detailed inventory of them which was published in 1909 as *The Birds of Burma*. An obituary published in *British Birds* dated 1 June 1916 stated:

> Colonel Harington had always been a keen lover of nature and natural history generally, but it was not until he went to Burma that he really took up ornithology seriously. His first articles were written for the *Rangoon Gazette* and soon attracted notice on account of the careful and accurate observation they displayed. These articles he reproduced in book form in 1908–9, adding a valuable table showing the distribution of Burmese birds. He also contributed from time to time to the *Ibis*, the *Journal of the Bombay Natural History Society* and other periodicals, the most important of these contributions being his review of the Timeliidse [an ill-defined family of Babbling thrushes no longer used] which appeared in the last named Journal during 1914–15.

Harington is credited with discovering a number of new species and in his honour had several named after him including a sub-species of the Indian spot-billed duck (*Anas poecilorhyncha haringtoni* – formerly *Polionetta haringtoni*); a sub-species of the grey bush chat (*Saxicola ferreus haringtoni*), a sub-species of the rusty-cheeked scimitar babbler (*Pomatorhinus erythrogenys haringtoni*) and the white-faced jay (*Garrulus glandaris haringtoni*, a sub-species of the Eurasian jay found in the Chin Hills in Burma).

In 1909 Harington married Dorothy, the youngest daughter of the Honourable Walter Pepys, a relative of the famous diarist Samuel Pepys, with whom he had a son and two daughters. In December 1914 Harington was promoted to lieutenant colonel and in February 1916 was given command of the 62nd Punjabis who he was leading into battle when he died. He is commemorated on the Basra Memorial in Iraq.

Austin Geoffrey Leigh

On the 4 June 1916, a Warwickshire ornithologist by the name of Austin Geoffrey Leigh was killed in action in France, described in his *British Birds* obituary as 'a young and ardent worker'. Born in 1893, he was the youngest of four children of George and Emily Leigh who lived in the tranquil village of Hampton-in-Arden. His father was an artist and Austin grew up watching and sketching birds, after school training to be a dental apprentice. With the outbreak of war, his parents moved to Yardley in Birmingham and on 21 November 1915, he joined the 15th Battalion of the Royal Warwickshire Regiment, one of the Birmingham City 'Pal' battalions, as a private. He was promoted to lance corporal at the age of 21.

A keen ornithologist and ringer, he had been working on a history of the birds of Warwickshire when he died. According to *British Birds*:

> He was very early in life attracted by the birdlife around him and began making observations and collecting eggs. By the time he reached his eighteenth year this predilection had become a passion, and he conceived the idea of producing a history of the birds of Warwickshire. From that time, till he joined the Army towards the close of 1914, the greater part of his leisure was employed in collecting material for what he intended should be the great work of his life. He had already accumulated a considerable amount of matter, but had no intention of publishing for some years to come, for though such a work as he contemplated must necessarily be to a large extent a compilation, yet he wished it to be as far as possible a record of his personal experience and observation.

After war broke out Leigh 'threw himself into his military duties with the zest that characterized him in everything he did', quickly becoming an expert rifle-shot and getting his stripe as lance corporal. This unfortunately put an end to his systematic ornithological work, but he continued to send in records on birds whenever an opportunity arose. While training at Sutton Coldfield in Warwickshire, he found two Stonechat nests, confirming it as a breeding species in the county. His obituary in *British Birds* stated that this confirmed to 'his satisfaction that this bird is a Warwickshire breeder, statements on the subject by other authors being of too general a character to satisfy his very exact mind'.

He contributed various notes to *British Birds* magazine, his first one being in 1908 about his discovery of the redshank as a regular breeder in his parish of Hampton-in-Arden and nearby Packington. He later contributed records on the occurrence of the white-winged black tern and long-tailed duck in Warwickshire and in volume four, dated 1 March 1911, wrote a fascinating article about a kestrel chick he had hand-reared called 'On the Development of a Young Kestrel':

> As up to the present little seems to be recorded regarding the development and habits of nestlings and young birds, perhaps a few notes on two young Kestrels (*Falco tinnunculus*), which I reared last year, may be of interest to readers of *British Birds*.
>
> On May 23rd one of the keepers in the district where I live showed me a nest of this species containing five eggs, incubation having already commenced; these I examined occasionally during the next month, but it was not until June 20th that I found any young, the nest on that date containing two chicks and two addled eggs, the fifth having disappeared. One of the nestlings had its eyes well opened, and was covered with thick white down, with the exception of a small naked patch on the breast; from subsequent observations I concluded that it was seven days old. The other chick had evidently only been out of the shell a few hours, the down being much sparser and the eyes closed; from the fact of this bird being only just hatched, it is evident that in this case incubation lasted about twenty-eight days.
>
> Both adults being unfortunately killed, I took the two chicks, and placed them in a box filled with sticks, with a slight covering of dead grass, and for some time I fed them on liver and bird-meat; I had to have the elder killed, owing to its breaking a leg, but the other, of which I knew the exact age, I reared successfully.

Over six pages Leigh recorded in detail the kestrel's development including two photographs of the bird which he clearly loved but did not name. The kestrel was eventually returned to the wild, Leigh concluding:

The Kestrel always showed great interest in birds of all species, and especially Swallows and Martins; it made several unsuccessful attempts to capture these, but apparently concluding that they were too quick, it turned its attention to birds of less powerful flight, and at the age of forty-nine days succeeded in killing two – a Robin and a Warbler. From this age it fed itself entirely, and eventually disappeared on August 12th, being then fifty-four days old.

He also ringed large numbers of birds, his obituary stating:

From its inauguration Leigh took a great interest in the *British Birds* ringing scheme, and expected that in time great results would accrue from it. He himself ringed large numbers of birds in his district and was highly pleased when any of them were subsequently taken at places which seemed likely to throw light on migration, and he had several notable successes in this direction.

His friend T. Ground, who wrote his obituary, summed up his character:

Personally, he was one of those clean-souled men whom to know is to love. Fearless, upright, totally devoid of self-consciousness or conceit, he said and wrote nothing but what he believed to be absolutely true, without any regard to effect. Dubious or speculative statements on ornithological matters were ridiculed in no uncertain terms, he being of opinion that such were injurious to his beloved science, and he would have none of them.

He was 23 years old when he died and is buried at the Faubourg d'Amiens cemetery, Arras, in Pas de Calais, France and is commemorated on a memorial in St Edburgha's Church in Yardley, Birmingham.

Hugh and John Charlton

Within the space of one week, two birding brothers were killed on the Western Front, their joint ornithological knowledge and potential dying with them. Lieutenant Hugh Vaughan Charlton fell on 24 June 1916 just after having received a promotion, and a week later his brother Captain John Macfarlan Charlton was killed, on 1 July 1916, which was his birthday, having just been recommended for the Military Cross. Both brothers were artists and keen birders, Hugh was 32 years old when he died, his younger brother John was 25.

Their father was John Charlton, a well-known artist who painted military pictures, especially battle scenes. He exhibited at the Royal Academy and many of his pictures appeared in *The Graphic*, a popular weekly illustrated newspaper. Hugh was born in London in 1884 and John in 1891, the family then moving to the North East in 1901, with their father applying for membership of the Natural History Society of Northumberland two years later.

Hugh followed in his fathers' footsteps, becoming a skilled naturalist and artist. His obituary in *British Birds* read:

> He ... was a clever ornithologist, and the brothers worked much together, though Hugh's inclinations leaned towards animal painting, for which he studied in Newcastle, Edinburgh and London. Birds were his speciality; his work was very artistic, and he had a fine sense of colour and beauty in nature and in art, and was a sound critic. His paintings had already been hung in exhibitions in the cities where he had carried on his studies. One of his pictures, *The Home of the Dipper*, was exhibited in the Royal Academy of 1912.

Hugh was killed in action near Wytschaete, where he was mortally wounded by a bomb from a trench mortar. He had attended Officers' Training Corps while at Newcastle University receiving his commission in the 7th Northumberland Fusiliers in August 1915. Devoted to his regiment, his death drew warm tributes of affection from his colonel and comrades. According to *British Birds*, what made his 'death doubly sad, is the knowledge that he had, a few days before, received an important appointment on the Staff [promotion]'.

A week later his brother John was killed on the first day of the Battle of the Somme, 1 July 1916, a particularly tragic day as it was his twenty-fifth birthday. Shot through the head leading his company, he was charging a third line of trenches having taken the previous two under heavy enemy fire. According to his obituary in *British Birds*, his last words were shouted to his orderly: 'Is that you, B____? For God's sake, push on, I'm done.' The orderly stooped down and tried to help only to find him mortally wounded.

John joined the Northumberland Yeomanry in October 1914, receiving his commission in the 21st Northumberland Fusiliers (2nd Tyneside Scottish) later the same year, and then later was promoted to captain. He was educated at Uppingham School, where he was secretary of the Natural History club and took an active interest in taxidermy. His teacher wrote of him on 13 July 1915:

> For a boy, as he then was, he had a wonderful knowledge of birds, and quite remarkable powers of observation. Ornithology is my hobby and we spent many afternoons together, when his bright, sunny nature, his sense of humour, and his attractive personality made him a very pleasant companion. I remember the editor of the *Avicultural Magazine* was much struck by his work in our ornithological report for the year, which was entirely Charlton's writing.

John's ornithological potential was recognized at an early age when in 1903, at the age of 12, he wrote an illustrated essay on 'The Birds of the Farne Islands,' and entered it into the John Hancock prize run by the Natural History Society of Northumberland. Although he didn't win, one of the judges, Canon Tristram, was so impressed that he awarded him a special prize out of his own pocket. In December 1910, he won a bronze medal in the RSPB's Public School Essay Competition. Two years later, in 1912, he wrote 'The Birds of South-East Northumberland' for *The Zoologist*, which was subsequently published as a pamphlet with a map and illustrations. The next year he wrote an article about Norwegian birds which appeared in *Country Life* magazine and *British Birds*. As a soldier he won the respect of his senior officers and men alike for his courage under fire and before his death had been recommended for the Military Cross.

The brothers obituary in *British Birds* read:

> Both the Charltons were keen sportsmen, taking special interest in wildfowling, for which they had exceptional opportunities on the Northumberland coast. It may truly be said of them that they would have shone in whatever profession they chose; they were patterns of honour, integrity and gentlemanly character, as well as being charming companions. The writer deeply deplores their untimely death, a feeling that is shared by all who knew them, and lovers of

natural history will regret that ornithology has lost two students of great promise.

The Northumberland Natural History Society annual report for the year 1916/17 also recorded their passing:

Several of the younger members of the Society, men of promise and ability, have made the great sacrifice during the year under review. Of these, mention may be made of ... Lieutenant Hugh V. Charlton, a gifted artist and naturalist, whose brush cleverly depicted bird life, and his younger brother, Captain J. M. Charlton, a good ornithologist, who though not actually a member was a frequent visitor to the Museum, to which he presented specimens from time to time.

Their father John died on 10 November 1917, his obituary in *The Graphic* stating, 'He felt the loss of his two sons profoundly.' Hugh is buried at La Laiterie Military Cemetery in Ypres, Belgium, while John is buried at the Thiepval Memorial in northern France, with a memorial in Lanercost Priory, Cumbria. A memorial to both brothers is located in St Cuthbert's Churchyard, Cleveland.

Boyd Robert Horsburgh
On 1 July 1916, the British and French launched the Somme offensive against the Germans on the Western Front. The Battle of the Somme was the bloodiest battle in British history, over one million men being killed or wounded. Eleven days later, as the battle raged over 200 miles away, Lieutenant Colonel Boyd Robert Horsburgh died from his wounds at home in Surrey.

A member of the Army Service Corps supplying the troops at the front, he was fascinated by birds from childhood. As an adult he became an eccentric aviculturist keeping a large collection of wildfowl and other birds with him wherever he went in the world. At home in Surrey his collection was composed of a number of rare species from South Africa, America and India, including minivets, sunbirds and other species never previously seen in England. When he was posted abroad to South Africa, in 1904, he again established a large aviary at his new home on top of

Naval Hill, Bloemfontein. A contributor to the *Avicultural Magazine*, in 1912 he published his seminal work, *The Game Birds and Water-Fowl of South Africa*. The book was illustrated by a friend, Lieutenant Claude Gibney Finch-Davies of 1st South African Mounted Rifles, who also contributed a number of valuable field notes. Horsburgh also discovered a new sub-species of the South Africa red-necked falcon which was named after him (*Falco chicquera horsbrughi*).

He was the eldest son of Captain C. B. Horsburgh, a captain in the Central India Horse, a calvary regiment of the British Indian Army. Horsburgh was born at Poona (now Pune), India, on 27 July 1871. Educated at Wellington and Sandhurst, he joined the Warwickshire Regiment in 1893. He served for two years in Ceylon (now Sri Lanka) before transferring to the Army Service Corps. Hosburgh saw active service during the Sierra Leone Rebellion of 1898/9 where reportedly a local chief brought him birds to study, one of which was a hornbill that became a valued pet until it was killed by a large-spotted genet, another pet. He also raised two grey parrots that became his constant companions, teaching them to talk, and a turaco that used to share an early morning bath with him. He subsequently served in the Boer War, 1899–1902, before being invalided home, arriving back in England on the hospital ship *Nubia* in 1902. For his bravery he received the Queen's and King's South Africa medals with five clasps.

In the same year, 1902, he toured the United States, studying gamebirds and waterfowl and there met and married Elizabeth Mitchell from Philadelphia, who shared his love of ornithology. In 1904, he was again posted back to South Africa before he returned to England in 1907, bringing many new species with him, allegedly on the train trip from Bloemfontein to Cape Town, staying in the guard's van so he could feed and take care of his birds.

In 1912 he retired from the army with the rank of major and spent his time breeding wildfowl until he was recalled at the outbreak of war. Despite being 43 years old, he wanted to serve King and Country and saw action during the Battle of Loos, where he was mentioned in despatches. Horsburgh was wounded and returned home in November 1915, undergoing an operation from which he never recovered. He is buried in St Peter's churchyard, Tandridge in Surrey.

John Cyril Crowley

The Mesopotamia campaign claimed another victim on 11 September 1916 when Captain John Cyril Crowley was killed in battle. Crowley was in charge of a machine-gun company with the Guilford Battalion, Queen's Royal West Surrey Regiment, and was giving covering fire to a raiding party attacking Nasiriyah, a city on the Euphrates River, when he was killed.

Born in 1878 in Croydon and a local councillor before the war, Crowley was also a member of the British Ornithologists' Union and an accomplished amateur photographer, specializing in bird nests and their eggs. Despite the very real limitations of photographic equipment at the time, Crowley was proud of his results and would regularly give talks to bird clubs and schools. In 1902, he published an article called 'Bird Nest Photography and its Relation to Sport' in the *Badminton Magazine of Sports and Pastimes*.[1] The article was Crowley's brave attempt to stop birds being killed by 'sportsmen who shoot', children and egg collectors. Instead he promoted photography as a way to engage and interest them in conservation. 'I maintain that my ideal sportsman once indulging in this pursuit will become most attached to his small bird friends,' he wrote and so would 'see with disgust how much birdlife is annually destroyed, and in his own coverts, too, and will ultimately take steps to prevent this destruction.' The article gave Crowley's tips on photographing many different species from pheasants to chaffinches and stone curlews to snipes. In it he describes an unconventional technique for photographing the nest of a wheatear:

> Coming away from the hill tops you suddenly observe a wheatear dart out from an old rabbit hole ... A very pretty nest it proves to be, with a thistle-head built into the outside and seven pale blue eggs on the delicate lining ... so with the aid of a pocket-knife a sufficient opening was made to disclose it ... Although dug out and considerably disturbed, as the nest had to be, the bird, I am glad to say, was sitting again as cheer-fully as ever five minutes after I had patched up the opening and eventually she hatched six out of the seven.

The article concludes with Crowley blaming the decline of Britain's birdlife on 'two principal human enemies – the village children and the so-called scientific collector, both being utterly devoid of any sense of sport whatever'. Taking the children to task first, Crowley wrote, 'Their destructiveness arises from ignorance', his answer being to use slides to educate them about the wonders of birds – backed up by 'dire threats to be executed in the spring on any young scamp robbing a nest'. However, Crowley saved his harshest words for egg-collectors, 'Why cannot expert collectors be content with one or two eggs of a species? Why have hundreds?' he railed. 'I saw, this summer, over two hundred eggs of a rare British bird sold by auction, which bird is now practically extinct … This year again I know of four clutches of Kentish plover (a bird rapidly becoming scarce, needless to say)'. Crowley's answer was to 'take a good photograph and one egg, if a collector' and then 'jealously guard that nest until it has hatched off, and you will at least feel you have done your best, still remaining a true sportsman'.

By the time war was declared in 1914, Captain Crowley had turned down promotion for ten years so he could remain in charge of the machine-gun company in the hope of seeing action. Much to his frustration, he spent two years in India before finally leaving on 25 July 1916 to join the campaign in Mesopotamia where his role soon put him in mortal danger (as the British advanced the Turks had adopted a strategy of letting the enemy attack and occupy ground before surprising them and then counterattacking in strength as they retreated. Providing machine-gun fire to cover the rear of the attack was therefore a very dangerous role). Shot and dying almost immediately on 11 September 1916, Crowley was the first officer from his regiment to die in action and according to his commanding officer 'his loss was felt deeply'.

Crowley was also right to predict the decline of the Kentish Plover as a breeding species in Britain. Finally receiving full protection in 1904, its numbers built up slowly to forty pairs at Romney Marsh in Kent but the advent of seaside tourism meant that by 1931 it had stopped breeding in the county which gave the species its name. The last British breeding record was in 1979 when a pair fledged two young at Gibraltar Point on the Lincolnshire coast. A passage migrant, it is now considered extinct as a breeding bird in Britain. A lantern slide collection of Crowley's bird photographs is housed at the Natural History Museum and he is commemorated on the Basra First World War Memorial in Iraq.

Lord Lucas

On 3 November 1916 Lord Lucas was shot down flying over the German lines, bringing an end to a life that read like an adventure story in *Boy's Own* magazine. Auberon Thomas Herbert was born in 1876 and was the eldest surviving son of the Honourable Auberon Herbert. Bron, as he was known, succeeded to two baronies, the 9th Baron Lucas and the 5th Lord Dingwall, on the death of his elder brother and took up his seat in the House of Lords in 1907. Educated at Bedford School and Balliol College, Oxford, during the Boer War he was a correspondent for *The Times* newspaper but was wounded and had his leg amputated below the knee. Undeterred by his disability, he went on to serve with distinction, firstly as a captain in the Hampshire Yeomanry, then as a politician and finally as a pilot.

A Liberal politician, he was Private Secretary to the Secretary of State for War, Richard Haldane from 1907–8. When Asquith formed a government in 1908, he held several junior posts before in 1914 being appointed to the cabinet as President of the Board of Agriculture. Here he sat around the cabinet table with Winston Churchill but found political life tedious. He resigned on the formation of the Asquith coalition in May 1915 and, craving action, joined the Royal Flying Corps. Although at 39 he was far too old for the service, he quickly gained a pilot's licence, flying on active service in Egypt before becoming an instructor at Dover. In October 1916, he went to France where he was 'the oldest in years but the youngest in heart'. Leading a photo-reconnaissance formation of No. 22 Squadron, he was attacked by three enemy planes and shot in the head and leg, never regaining consciousness as the plane hurtled to the ground.

Lord Lucas's love of adventure also extended to a love of nature, especially birds, and in 1902 he was elected as a member of the British Ornithologists' Union. A keen ringer, his ornithological claim to fame was helping to bring back the marsh harrier as a breeding bird to Britain. In 1908, Lucas visited Hickling Broad in Norfolk accompanied by Lord Montagu where they met Jim Vincent, the son of a local gamekeeper. Impressed with the nature conservation potential of the site, the following year they returned joined by Foreign Secretary Sir Edward Grey, another passionate ornithologist. Negotiating with the landowners of Hickling Broad, Lucas leased it as a wildfowl shoot and nature reserve, installing

Vincent as the warden. He was determined to protect the marsh harriers, then extinct as a breeding bird in Britain, as well as other rare species like the bittern and Montagu's harrier. As a result, the next year marsh harriers attempted to breed on the broad but the eggs were stolen so Lord Lucas increased security at the site.

In 1915, while on military leave, he returned to Hickling Broad where Vincent proudly showed him a marsh harrier's nest with five eggs, the first confirmed breeding attempt in Britain in over twenty years. Lord Lucas was delighted, in Vincent's words he:

> dashed home to see the sight, for he adored the birds of prey. As we sat on the grassy bank and saw the Marsh Harrier go down to its nest on our right hand, and on our left a Montagu's Harrier settle on her eggs, his lordship turned to me with a sparkle in his eyes, and said, 'By Jove! Jim, this is the next greatest sight to the War.'

A memorial poem called 'For Lord Lucas' was written about him by the Irish playwright Katharine Tynan (1859–1931), a friend of the famous Irish poet and soldier Francis Ledwidge (1887–1917):

> Having found wings, he tossed, light as a feather,
> Airy as thistledown, 'twixt earth and sky,
> Oh, but the dark earth held his soul in tether!
> Could he come back who knew what 'twas to fly?
>
> His gravitation's now for stars and planets:
> These draw him, while the earth drops like a stone.
> Strong-winged beyond the flight of gulls or gannets
> He rises, ever rises; he is flown.
>
> When he came back all Spring was in his vision;
> Yet pined he like a wild bird in a net.
> His dreams were all of fields and groves Elysian
> Where he flew ever and no bounds were set.
>
> Did someone bring his body down? Then gaily
> He waved to his foe: 'Your luck to-day, not mine';

Shook himself free of bonds that irked him daily
With the last courtesy, so brave and fine.

He has o'erflown return in the wild rapture
What rumour of him in the unending space?
Flying so far, so fast, beyond recapture;
The flying ecstasy bright in his face.

At the outbreak of the war he offered his country house, Wrest Park in Bedfordshire, for use as a hospital and afterwards it became a home for disabled soldiers. Lord Lucas is buried at the Honourable Artillery Company cemetery in the village of Ecoust-Saint-Mein in France.

George Wilson Stout

On the first day of the Battle of the Ancre, on 13 November 1916, a private by the name of George Wilson Stout serving with the Royal Army Medical Corps (RAMC) was killed. The battle was the final big British push of the Somme campaign and it involved an attack on the German front line where it crossed the Ancre River. During the five-day offensive the British sustained over 22,000 casualties and the job of treating the wounded fell to the RAMC. Although non-combatants, it was a uniquely dangerous role, particularly during an offensive where bodies would have to retrieved from no man's land. The RAMC treated the wounded according to the British Army's triage system:

- Slightly injured – soldiers were given treatment on the spot and urged to carry on fighting.
- Requiring hospital treatment – after being recovered from the field, soldiers were taken by stretcher to the nearest field station or if available in a motorized or horse-drawn ambulance to a hospital.
- Beyond help – soldiers with mortal wounds or who stood little chance of recovery were made comfortable but received minimal treatment.

Stout was part of the 93rd Field Ambulance unit who were responsible for operating a number of field stations behind the front lines. The first of these were Bearer Relay Posts which were just 600 yards from the trenches, the unit also providing Walking Wounded Collecting

Stations. From here casualties were then taken rearwards through an Advanced Dressing Station to the Main Dressing Station. Stout was injured trying to recover a wounded comrade and died in his own dressing station.

Stout was born in 1888 on Fair Isle, the son of crofters, Robert and Tomima Stout of South Busta. Fair Isle, which is three miles long by one and half miles wide, sits midway between Orkney and Shetland in the Atlantic Ocean. It is a magnet for birds, particularly rare migrant ones, which due to its isolated location often use it a resting point.

The ornithological potential of Fair Isle was discovered by Dr William Eagle Clarke (1853–1938) who first visited the island in the autumn of 1905. There he met Stout who, despite a rudimentary education, Clarke found had a 'remarkable knowledge of the island's birds' which he had mainly obtained by shooting them. To encourage his interest in conservation Clarke provided him with books and binoculars and then set about training Stout in field identification. On his next visit the following year, Clarke gave Stout the title of the first official 'Fair Isle birdwatcher and recorder'.

As result the two became good friends and in 1909 Clark got Stout a full-time job on the mainland working for the Glasgow taxidermist Charles Kirk. To collect specimens the two would regularly return to the far north of Scotland, including a return visit to Fair Isle and St Kilda in 1910. Based on these visits, Clarke wrote a two-volume work, *Studies in Bird Migration*, in 1912, regarded as a 'milestone in the study of bird migration', it receiving a glowing eight-page review in *British Birds*. Following this in 1913, they visited Auskerry (a small island in eastern Orkney) and the following year the Butt of Lewis (the most northerly point of Lewis in the Outer Hebrides) before Stout was called up in 1916, joining the RAMC.

Fair Isle is world famous among birdwatchers for being the location of many firsts for the British list: the first record of a particular species for the country. Of the thirty-one additions the island has contributed to the list since 1900 Stout is credited with two records: a red-rumped swallow on 2 June 1905 and Blyth's reed warbler on 29/30 September 1910, in addition adding two to the Scottish list: Savi's warbler on 14 May 1908 and Icterine warbler on 1 June 1908. All apart from the red-rumped swallow were shot by Stout and were then sent off to the British museum by Clarke to confirm their identification.

As a result of its ornithological significance, a bird observatory was established on Fair Isle in 1948 by George Waterston a lieutenant in the Royal Artillery during the Second World War. He was captured after the Battle of Crete in 1941 and hatched the plan as a prisoner of war. It remains the location with more British 'firsts' than any other site and is now visited by hundreds of birdwatchers every year. Clarke lived to the grand old age of 85 and is credited with being one of the greatest ornithologists of his era. Stout died at the age of 28, all but forgotten apart from some old Fair Isle records, and is buried at the Couin British Cemetery in Pas de Calais, northern France.

Hector Hugh Munro

On the night of 14 November 1916, one of the most successful satirical short-story writers of his era was killed at the advanced age of 45 while sheltering in a crater in no man's land. Hector Hugh Munro fell at the fag end of the Battle of the Somme, his last words reportedly being, 'Put that bloody cigarette out!' before he was shot through the head by a German sniper. Munro as well as being a hugely talented gay writer was a keen ornithologist whose love of nature ran through much of his literary work.

Born in Burma in 1870, he was the youngest son of three children to Colonel Charles Augustus Munro (1844–1907), the inspector-general of police in Burma and his wife Mary Frances Mercer. Munro's mother died tragically in 1872 on a visit to England when she was trampled to death by a runaway cow. Afterwards his father sent him and his siblings to boarding school in Devon where they were brought up by their tyrannical aunts who regularly beat them. After his father retired in 1887, Munro initially followed in his footsteps joining the Indian Imperial Police in 1893 but successive bouts of fever forced his return home and three years later he moved to London where he started writing.

Under the nom de plume 'Saki', Munro was wildly successful, his short stories contrasting the banality and hypocrisy of Edwardian society with the life and death struggles of nature. They ranged from 'Gabrial-Ernest', a tale of disappearing young boys and wild beasts in woods (a radical revision of the children's story Red Riding Hood), to the semi-autobiographical 'Sredni Vashtar', a story of a sickly child called Conrad who rebels against his authoritarian aunt, his pole-cat eventually killing her after she tries to dispose of it. Munro, a closet homosexual, also enjoyed lampooning the political figures of the day, his stories appearing in many papers such as the *Westminster Gazette*, *Daily Express* and *The Morning Post* as well as popular magazines like *The Bystander*.

Entertaining and scandalizing Edwardian Society in equal measure, Munro was a great admirer of the poet Edward Fitzgerald (1809–83). Munros pen name 'Saki' was taken either from the cupbearer in the *Rubáiyát of Omar Khayyám*, Fitzgerald's most famous work, or was the name of a South American monkey which was a central character in his novel *The Remoulding of Groby Lington*, telling the story of a man who replaces his temperate parrot with a bad-tempered monkey. A creative, witty and prolific writer, in 1900 he published the *Rise of the Russian Empire*, a detailed history book tracing the empire's rise from 1721. Two years later Munro became a foreign correspondent on *The Morning Post* where he got to cover the Russian Revolution in 1905.

Munro also produced two novels, in 1912 publishing *The Unbearable Bassington*; described as 'an exquisite novel of manners', it is a poignant story of a broken mother-and-son relationship which painted Edwardian high society as being full of self-absorbed people with no moral conscience. The next year he wrote another novel, *When William Came*, subtitled *A Story of London Under the Hohenzollerns*, ironically a fantasy about a future German invasion and occupation of Britain. Underlying all his work was Munro's sexuality, his writing clearly influenced by another of his literary heroes, Oscar Wilde.

On the outbreak of war in 1914, Munro was 43 and far too old to fight but being a patriotic son of empire, he volunteered anyway. Refusing a commission, he joined the 2nd King Edward's Horse cavalry regiment as a private, later transferring to the infantry regiment of the 22nd Battalion, Royal Fusiliers where he rose to the rank of lance sergeant. At the front Munro took great solace in the birdlife he saw and his last dispatch was an article on 'Birds on the Western Front', which he contributed to the *Weekly Westminster* on 14 October 1916, a month before he died. In it he described the birds of prey he had seen catching rats and mice in the trenches, criticized gamekeepers at home for waging war on birds they considered vermin (stating their 'knowledge of wildlife usually runs on limited and perverted lines') and told the story of a hen chaffinch who stayed with the wounded after her wood was stricken by 'lyddite and shrapnel and machine-gun fire'. Munro has no known grave and is commemorated on the Thiepval Memorial in France and with a blue plaque on his former London home in Fitzrovia.

1917

Frederick Courteney Selous
As the war entered its third year the Ornithological Roll of Honour lengthened when one of the oldest participants in the war died. On 4 January 1917, the famous big-game hunter Captain Frederick Courteney Selous of the 25th Battalion Royal Fusiliers was killed in action at the ripe old age of 65. (The oldest soldier to serve in the war was 68 years old but he lied about his age, claiming to be 48. William John Paxton was born in 1846 and was a bricklayer who enlisted with the London Regiment on 21 October 1914. He was discharged on 19 July 1916 for health reasons.) Selous was one of the last of the African 'white hunters' and by the time of his death was one of the most celebrated adventurers of his era, counting President Roosevelt and the magnate Cecil Rhodes (1853–1902) as personal friends. He was also a prolific collector, during his lifetime donating over 5,000 animal and plant specimens to the Natural History Museum in London.

Born in 1851, his father Frederick Lokes Selous (1802–1892), was Chairman of the London Stock Exchange and his mother, Ann Holgate Sherborn, was a poet. Educated at Rugby, he was fascinated by natural history from childhood, one of his fellow pupils and big-game hunters Abel Chapman remembering how he used to enjoy plundering the nearby heronry at Combe Abbey, 'a place which, if I remember right, was quite ten or a dozen miles distant from Rugby and therefore quite outside all conceivable schoolboy range'. Chapman recalled how on the way home, his pockets bulging with herons' eggs and other oological plunder, Selous unexpectedly came across 'the tall figure and striking gait of our austere Headmaster [Dr Temple, Bishop of London] … he took prompt cover behind a friendly bush and watched the dreaded "Doctor" pass within a yard! Well I remember how the Bishop – soon to become Archbishop – joined in the laugh.'

Selous left Rugby in 1869, two years later travelling to South Africa where for the next twenty years he made a name for himself as an elephant hunter, shooting them to order for museums and private collections. As well as elephants, Selous collected a vast number of specimens from across the continent, Chapman describing him as a 'dashing rough-rider after every class of game, from elephants, giraffe, sable and oryx, down to cheetahs and wild dogs'. A prolific author, he published his first book in 1881 with the self-indulgent and protracted title, *A hunter's wanderings in Africa, being a narrative of nine years spent amongst the game of the far interior of South Africa, containing accounts of explorations beyond the Zambesi, on the river Chobe, and in the Matabele and Mashuna countries, with full notes upon the natural history and present distribution of all the large Mammalia.*

From 1890 until the outbreak of the First World War Selous alternated between expeditions to South Africa, Europe, Asia and North America, all in search of big game. In between he returned to the far more tranquil surroundings of Surrey where he swapped big-game hunting for the more sedate science of ornithology. On one trip home, at the age of 42, he married Marie Catherine Gladys Maddy, who was 22 years his junior. The daughter of a clergyman, despite the preacher's protestations, he had three sons with her. His friend Chapman recalled:

> But no sooner had he settled in Surrey – so far as such a wanderer settles anywhere – than the attraction of bird-study at once leaped to his mind and he threw himself into it with all the zeal and fierce energy of his nature. I remember him declaring that the field-craft involved in 'spotting' the nest of a single and scarce bird rivalled that of puzzling out a difficult spoor [track or scent of an animal] on African velt.

Selous's birdwatching trips were organized with the same military precision as his safaris and would even today put many obsessive twitchers to shame. His aim was to see as many nests as possible across the country in record time so he could catalogue and add them to his egg collection. Chapman commented:

One of those earlier springs, when he was coming to me here, he had written months beforehand fixing the precise dates and also specifying the birds whose nests he wished me to 'mark' for him in advance, though not an egg was to be taken save by his own hand alone ... It set forth in precise detail his programme from March to July, the pre-ordained routes including flying journeys to and fro across these islands from Orkney and Shetland, Caithness and Kent, Nottinghamshire, Northumberland and Norfolk – and I know not where else.

A member of the British Ornithologists' Union, Selous wrote for the magazine *British Birds* and as a result of his expeditions collected a huge number of eggs. 'In this way within a few years (aided by visits to Spain, Transylvania, Bosnia, Asia Minor, Iceland, etc.) he amassed an amazing collection of eggs of the rarer British birds,' remembered Chapman, 'and the methodical neatness of the collection was no less amazing than its amount. He collected solely in "clutches" and always insisted on having the full number in each selected clutch.'

When not hunting big game or adding to his egg collection, Selous took up arms on behalf of the British South Africa Company, taking part in the First and Second Matabele Wars, in the latter fighting alongside the founder of the Scout movement, Robert Baden-Powell. In 1907, he wrote the foreword to Africa's most popular man-eating lion novel, *The Man-eaters of Tsavo and other East African Adventures* by Lieutenant Colonel J. H. Patterson. A year later, on the suggestion of President Roosevelt, he wrote about his own remarkable life in *African Nature Notes and Reminiscences* and dedicated it to him.

In 1909/10 Selous acted as a guide to the former president on his African safari before Roosevelt was hosted by the Foreign Secretary Sir Edward Grey when he arrived in England. Clearly impressed, Roosevelt said:

Mr Selous is the last of the big game hunters of Southern Africa; the last of the mighty hunters whose experience lay in the greatest hunting ground which this world has seen since civilized man has appeared herein ... Mr Selous is much more than a mere big-game hunter however; he is by instinct a keen field naturalist, an observer with a power of seeing, and of remembering what he has seen; and finally he is a writer who possesses to a very marked and unusual degree the power vividly and accurately to put on paper his observations. Such a combination of qualities is rare indeed.

With the outbreak of war his addiction to high-risk adventure led him to rejoin the British Army at the grand old age of 64, joining the 25th (Frontiersmen) Service Battalion, Royal Fusiliers, fighting in the East Africa Campaign. A motley crew, they were a unit composed of Boer War veterans and other true eccentrics. Here the big-game hunter was in good company joining a millionaire, several cowboys, a Scottish lighthouse keeper, a circus clown, an Arctic explorer, an opera singer, a famous photographer and a lion tamer. Selous soon proved himself in battle, being awarded the Distinguished Service Order and promoted to captain.

He was shot dead by a German sniper while fighting on the banks of the Rufiji River in Tanganyika (now Tanzania), reportedly 'outnumbered five to one'. On hearing of his death, President Roosevelt proudly said:

> He led a singularly adventurous and fascinating life, with just the right alternations between the wilderness and civilization. He helped spread the borders of his people's land. He added much to the sum of human knowledge and interest. He closed his life exactly as such a life ought to be closed, by dying in battle for his country while rendering her valiant and effective service. Who could wish a better life or a better death, or desire to leave a more honourable heritage to his family and his nation?

Selous, as befitted a man who had achieved so much, left a lasting legacy. His life was the inspiration for the fictional big-game hunter Allan Quartermain made famous by the writer Sir Henry Rider Haggard. On 10 June 1920, a bronze bust of him was unveiled at the Natural History Museum by Sir Edward Grey where it stands in the Main Hall to this day, while a game reserve in south-eastern Tanzania is named after him. Lamenting his death, his friend Chapman wrote:

> Upon those who enjoyed it, Selous's friendship exerted a magnetic influence – strengthening, stimulating, straightening. Beneath that modest and gentle exterior – devoid of self assertion, disdainful of pride or pretence – none but realized the forcefulness of the soul

within, whole-hearted, true, and of single purpose – to 'make good'. His very death – 'killed in action' at 65 – epitomizes his whole career. Maybe it formed an appropriate climax, but alas! that never again shall we look into those straight blue eyes.

Selous is buried on the Rufiji River in the game reserve named after him.

John Dighton Grafton-Wignall

On Friday, 26 January 1917, the noted ornithologist Captain John Dighton Grafton-Wignall was killed in action fighting with the 82nd Punjabis in the Battle of the Hai Salient in Mesopotamia. He was born in Hampstead, London, on 25 January 1888. In 1906, he attended the Royal Military Academy, Sandhurst, where he trained to be an officer. In November, 1907, he went to India, firstly as part of the 'Fighting Fifth' before joining the Punjabis. At the outbreak of war, the 82nd was serving on the North West Frontier of India before being sent to Mesopotamia in January 1916.

His obituary in *British Birds* read:

> before reaching nineteen, he had closely studied such local species, amongst others, as Buzzard, Peregrine, Raven, Chough, Woodlark, Dartford Warbler and Water-Rail – a proud record for a boy; and even at that early age he was wonderful at identifying with certainty among a host of commoner waders some of the lesser-known sorts – a feat most of us, many years older, have yet failed to emulate. Indeed, I have seldom seen a quicker eye for woodcraft. For he had that perfect sight which enabled him to 'pick up' a sitting Woodcock or a clutch of shingle-laid eggs as quickly as (and he was quick) he could detect – and accurately name too – flying or at rest some bird a great way off. A rare combination, and one to be envied. Not until 1912 did he return home on leave, which he profitably spent studying Eagles, Peregrines, Short-eared Owls (finding a 'nest' in what I believe was a hitherto unrecorded locality), Dartford Warblers, Cirl Buntings, Greylag Geese, Kentish Plovers, Stone Curlews and so forth.[2]

As well as being an accomplished ornithologist, he was a 'fine boxer and shot and a capital cragsman'. According to his obituary, 'his loss is irreparable: ornithology, has lost a very accurate, first-rate and indefatigable observer.' He is commemorated on the Basra Memorial in Iraq and is buried in the cemetery of St Ffraidd Church, Carrog, Denbighshire in Wales. A memorial plaque in the church reads, 'Erected by his brother officers as a token of their esteem and regard.'

Gustavus Arthur Perreau

On 9 March 1917, Lieutenant Colonel Gustavus Arthur Perreau of the 2nd Battalion, 4th Gurkha Rifles was killed in Mesopotamia during an attack on Bagdad. Perreau was an experienced ornithologist and an expert on the birds of India who also kept a large wildfowl collection. He was a regular contributor to a number of prestigious ornithological publications including the *Avicultural Magazine* and *Ibis*, the journal of the British Ornithologists' Union.

He was born in 1873, the son of R. A. D. Perreau who worked for the Burma Commission. Perreau went to Hermitage House School in Bath and afterwards lived in Cheltenham where he married Ellen. He was a keen rugby player, appearing for Bath Rugby from 1891 to 1895. In 1894, he received his commission into the Royal Munster Fusiliers and after promotion in 1898, transferred to the Indian Army. He became a major in 1912 and was made a lieutenant colonel in early 1917.

His obituary in the *Avicultural Magazine* read:

> We very greatly regret that the war has claimed another of our members as a victim. Major G. A. Perreau has been killed. There was no one more enthusiastic and painstaking in aviculture. On more than one occasion he brought from India many insectivorous birds rarely seen in captivity, and which he had himself caught in the hills, some species being new to aviculture. We can ill afford to lose one who was not only a keen aviculturist, contributing to our Magazine from time to time, but who also impressed those who knew him with the courtesy of his manner and the diffidence with which he imparted his knowledge of the Indian birds that he so delighted in.[3]

Another obituary in *Bird Notes and News* said of him:

> He had a charming personality which drew all to him and the writer mourns the loss of a dear friend. He was an ardent aviculturist, and

keen bird-lover, and imported (when coming home on furlough), many rare species, and others quite new to aviculture. He will be greatly missed among aviculturists everywhere, and many of our members will feel a deep sense of personal loss. To Mrs. Perreau we extend our deepest sympathy in her great bereavement.

He was 43 years old and is commemorated at the Basra Memorial in Iraq.

Phillip Edward Thomas
Phillip Edward Thomas was a poet who was killed in action on 9 April 1917 during the Battle of Arras, a British push to break the stalemate on the Western Front. Although he wrote little of his war experiences, nearly all of his poems were produced during the war as the death toll in the trenches rose ever higher. Born in 1878 to Welsh parents, Thomas grew up in Lambeth, attending St Paul's school before going on to read history at Lincoln College, Oxford. By the outbreak of the war, he was already an established literary critic, biographer and author but like so many people with potential had failed to make much of a living from writing.

In a frenetic period from just before the start of the war until his untimely death two and a half years later, Thomas wrote over 140 poems motivated by his friend, the American poet Robert Frost (1874–1963). They included some of the finest poems of the early twentieth century, Thomas in particular excelling as a master of the short poem. Throughout his poetry birds feature as a reoccurring subject, Thomas using them to celebrate the beauty of nature and to explore themes from sorrow to spirituality.

His most famous poem was written on a train from Oxford to Worcester following an unscheduled stop at the sleepy old village of Adlestrop in the Cotswolds, on 24 June 1914. From his seat in the stationary carriage Thomas took nature notes looking out of the window, later turning them into a poem simply called 'Adlestrop'.[4] Written just six weeks before the start of war, in it he describes the beauty of the countryside and captures an innocence that would soon disappear forever:

> Yes, I remember Adlestrop –
> The name, because one afternoon
> Of heat the express-train drew up there
> Unwontedly. It was late June.

> The steam hissed. Someone cleared his throat.
> No one left and no one came
> On the bare platform. What I saw
> Was Adlestrop – only the name
>
> And willows, willow-herb, and grass,
> And meadowsweet, and haycocks dry,
> No whit less still and lonely fair
> Than the high cloudlets in the sky.
>
> And for that minute a blackbird sang
> Close by, and round him, mistier,
> Farther and farther, all the birds
> Of Oxfordshire and Gloucestershire.

In January 1915 Thomas wrote 'The Unknown Bird', a poem recalling a hauntingly beautiful bird song he had heard in a beech wood four or five years previously but could not identify. The poem explores his state of mind when feeling alone and 'sometimes suffering/A heavy body and a heavy heart'. It ends with Thomas celebrating how the memory of a bird song can help to overcome sadness and suffering:

> Three lovely notes he whistled, too soft to be heard
> If others sang; but others never sang
> In the great beech-wood all that May and June.
> No one saw him: I alone could hear him
> Though many listened. Was it but four years
> Ago? or five? He never came again.
>
> Oftenest when I heard him I was alone,
> Nor could I ever make another hear.
> La-la-la! he called, seeming far-off –
> As if a cock crowed past the edge of the world,
> As if the bird or I were in a dream.
> Yet that he travelled through the trees and sometimes
> Neared me, was plain, though somehow distant still
> He sounded. All the proof is – I told men
> What I had heard.

> I never knew a voice,
> Man, beast, or bird, better than this. I told
> The naturalists; but neither had they heard
> Anything like the notes that did so haunt me,
> I had them clear by heart and have them still.
> Four years, or five, have made no difference. Then
> As now that La-la-la! was bodiless sweet:
> Sad more than joyful it was, if I must say
> That it was one or other, but if sad
> 'Twas sad only with joy too, too far off
> For me to taste it. But I cannot tell
> If truly never anything but fair
> The days were when he sang, as now they seem.
> This surely I know, that I who listened then,
> Happy sometimes, sometimes suffering
> A heavy body and a heavy heart,
> Now straightway, if I think of it, become
> Light as that bird wandering beyond my shore.

Thomas's most haunting poem 'In Memoriam' was written during Easter 1915 when a generation of young men were being annihilated on the battlefields of Belgium and France. Deliberately produced at a time when the death and resurrection of Christ was being celebrated, it is particularly poignant because Thomas would also die two years later, on Easter Day. In it he contrasts the flowers in a wood with the death of the soldiers in the trenches who 'far from home' will never return to see them:

> The flowers left thick at nightfall in the wood
> This Eastertide call into mind the men,
> Now far from home, who, with their sweethearts, should
> Have gathered them and will do never again.

Thomas like many poets of his generation suffered from acute depression throughout his adult life and explored the emotion of loss that goes with it in his poem 'The Swifts' which was written in 1916. One of the last migrants to arrive in Britain in early May, swifts stay only long enough to breed, leaving again in late July. In the poem Thomas mourns their departure and at the same time contemplates his own mortality:

> How at once should I know,
> When stretched in the harvest blue
> I saw the swift's black bow,
> That I would not have that view
> Another day
> Until next May
> Again it is due?
>
> The same year after year –
> But with the swift alone.
> With other things I but fear
> That they will be over and done
> Suddenly
> And I only see
> Them to know them gone.

When war was declared, Thomas was already into middle age, being a 36-year-old married man with three children. He didn't have to volunteer but enlisted anyway with the Artists Rifles in July 1915, a Pals battalion which included painters, musicians, actors and writers. A year later he joined the Royal Garrison Artillery as a second lieutenant. He was killed in action soon after arriving in France on Easter Monday, 9 April 1917, the first day of the Arras offensive. By the end of it five weeks later, despite some early gains, the British had won little ground but had suffered 150,000 casualties.

As well as writing about birds, Thomas is credited by the author Tim Dee with being the first soldier to use binoculars on the battlefield for birdwatching.[5] He may also have the tragic honour of being the only person to be killed during the war while watching birds. As a forward observer for the artillery, Thomas was issued with a pair of binoculars for monitoring the enemy lines which he also used for surveying the birds in no man's land. However, there was a great risk in using field glasses as the sun would sometimes reflect off the lenses, the glint giving away the observer's position. This may have happened to Thomas who died by a clean shot through the chest from a German sniper. Buried in the Commonwealth War Graves Cemetery at Agny in France, he is commemorated in Poets' Corner in Westminster Abbey and in memorial windows at Steep Church in Hampshire and Eastbury Church in Berkshire. A blue plaque was also erected at the house where he was born in Stockwell and a study centre named after him at Petersfield Museum in Hampshire.

Like many war poets, Thomas would not live to see the publication of his work, his book *Poems* being published posthumously in 1917. Adlestrop station fared better, surviving for nearly fifty years until it was axed in 1966 as part of the infamous Beeching cuts.

Henry Edward Otto Murray-Dixon

On Easter Monday 1917, another artist by the name of Henry Edward Otto Murray-Dixon was also killed during the Battle of Arras. One of the most promising bird painters of his generation, he was mortally wounded at Vimy Ridge, the first attack of the Nivelle Offensive designed to draw German reserves away from the main battlefront. Moments after the attack began, a hail of German machine-gun fire inflicted heavy casualties on his battalion, the Seaforth Highlanders. By the end of the day 206 Seaforths including Otto Murray-Dixon had been killed, wounded or were missing.

Born in 1885, Otto Murray-Dixon's family were privately wealthy and he had a privileged upbringing. A year after his birth, James, his father, became the rector of Swithland Church near Loughborough in Leicestershire. Attending school at Swithland in 1894 with his two sisters, from an early age Otto Murray-Dixon showed a natural talent for drawing and painting. According to Anne Horton, a recent rector of Swithland, one of his earliest paintings was 'of a heron, labelled "for dear John" which was painted in 1897 when he was 12.' To develop his talent a top room in the rectory was converted into a studio where he painted the wildlife he saw around the vicarage. Like many children of his generation this included collecting eggs and shooting birds which he used to practise 'still life' paintings. From 1903 to 1908 he recorded all his wildlife observations in a book simply called *Nature Notes*.[6]

Otto Murray-Dixon went on to study drawing and painting at Leicester School of Art, Calderon's School of Animal Painting in Baker Street,

London, and the prestigious Royal Academy Schools founded in 1768. There he was tutored by the world-famous wildlife watercolour artist Archibald Thorburn (1860–1935). Thorburn was friends with another highly respected bird artist John Guille Millais (1865–1931) and as a result got Otto Murray-Dixon his first major commission, illustrating some of the species in Millais's book *British Diving Ducks* which was published in 1913. Otto Murray-Dixon's bird paintings also appeared regularly in many popular magazines of the day especially the *Illustrated Sporting and Dramatic News* and *The Field*.

Thorburn was responsible for getting Otto Murray-Dixon a second important commission, to design the RSPB's Christmas card. Thorburn was vice-president of the RSPB and had designed their first card issued in 1899 and every one subsequently. With the outset of war in 1914, he recommended that Otto Murray-Dixon should be given the opportunity. The RSPB agreed and commissioned him to do a painting for their 1914/15 Christmas card on the theme of a 'Bird of Good Omen', Otto Murray-Dixon choosing a white dove, the classic symbol of peace. Announcing the commission in the RSPB's magazine, *Bird Notes and News*, the society said it 'will be of a character peculiarly appropriate to the terrible events which are engrossing all thought at the present time'.[7] In order to help the RSPB's finances Otto Murray-Dixon waived his reproduction fee and after it went on sale the card sold extremely well, the painting also being exhibited at an art gallery on 140 New Bond Street in London thanks to the generous sponsorship of 'Messrs. W. E. Hill and Son'.

At the start of the war, Otto Murray-Dixon volunteered with the Seaforth Highlanders, a Scottish infantry regiment and in 1915 he was commissioned as a second lieutenant. Despite hailing from Leicestershire, he joined them because, like his mentor Thorburn, so much of the wildlife he painted and loved came from the Highlands of Scotland. While serving at the front, he continued painting and in the autumn was commissioned to produce the RSPB's next Christmas card, for 1915/16. To illustrate it he was asked to paint a bird to go with the poem 'Into Battle' written by Captain Julian Grenfell (1888–1915).[8] Grenfell had served with the Royal Dragoons, a cavalry regiment, and had been killed in action at Ypres earlier in the year, on 26 May 1915. His poem had been published posthumously with the announcement of his death in *The Times* and had made a big impact on the public. In it Grenfell and his men are waiting to go up to the front and the poem expresses the close, almost mystical, connection between the fighting man and the natural world.

> The naked earth is warm with spring,
> And with green grass and bursting trees
> Leans to the sun's gaze glorying,
> And quivers in the sunny breeze;
> And life is colour and warmth and light,
> And a striving evermore for these;
> And he is dead who will not fight;
> And who dies fighting has increase.
>
> The fighting man shall from the sun
> Take warmth, and life from the glowing earth;
> Speed with the light-foot winds to run,
> And with the trees to newer birth;
> And find, when fighting shall be done,
> Great rest and fullness after dearth.
>
> All the bright company of Heaven
> Hold him in their high comradeship,
> The Dog-Star, and the Sisters Seven,
> Orion's Belt and sworded hip.
>
> The woodland trees that stand together,
> They stand to him each one a friend;
> They gently speak in the windy weather;
> They guide to valley and ridge's end.
>
> The kestrel hovering by day,
> And the little owls that call by night,
> Bid him be swift and keen as they,
> As keen of ear, as swift of sight.
>
> The blackbird sings to him, 'Brother, brother,
> If this be the last song you shall sing,
> Sing well, for you may not sing another;

Brother, sing.'
In dreary, doubtful, waiting hours,
Before the brazen frenzy starts,
The horses show him nobler powers;
O patient eyes, courageous hearts!

And when the burning moment breaks,
And all things else are out of mind,
And only Joy of Battle takes
Him by the throat, and makes him blind,

Through joy and blindness he shall know,
Not caring much to know, that still
Nor lead nor steel shall reach him, so
That it be not the Destined Will.
The thundering line of battle stands,
And in the air Death moan and sings;
But Day shall clasp him with strong hands,
And Night shall fold him in soft wings.

To illustrate the poem Otto Murray-Dixon chose a kestrel with the title 'Swift and Keen', the RSPB stating it was a 'Message of Greeting and High Courage for Soldier Friends at Home and Abroad and for all bearing in their thoughts the Men who are fighting for King, Country and Freedom'.[9] The card again proved extremely popular, two special editions being produced with the badges of the 3rd City of London Regiment (Royal Fusiliers) and the Seaforth Highlanders.

On 6 April 1917, Otto Murray-Dixon sent his last letter to his former colonel, Colonel MacFarlane, the sender's address simply stating 'trenches 1917'. In it Otto Murray-Dixon mentioned that he had completed three black and white paintings for the *Illustrated Sporting and Dramatic News*. These were 'Hooded crows on French corn stack', 'Rats in the trenches' and 'Partridges in No Man's Land'. Otto Murray-Dixon noted, below the latter's title, that 'on many parts of the British front covies of partridges are often seen, right up to the front line trenches, even in no man's land it is a strange cheering thing to hear their well known call at dusk mingling with the thundering of heavy guns and exploding shells, by which they now seem to be little disturbed'. He went on, 'these are precarious days! and will be yet more certainly so in the very near future, but I trust I may show a brave front when the time comes, it's all very appalling.' Mentioning with joy that he had recently seen a barn owl, he signed off, 'The Seaforths will do great things when the time comes and you will know I'll be trying to do my duty and proud to be one of them! P.S. Do you see any prospect of a fairly early termination of hostilities? We can't help thinking it will be a long time yet.'[10]

Three days later Otto Murray-Dixon was mortally wounded by a splinter from a shell, dying the next day. He is buried in Aubigney Communal Cemetery Extension in the Pas de Calais, France, and remembered on the Swithland War Memorial. Thorburn published an appreciation of him in *The Field* magazine, dated 23 March 1918, saying that Otto Murray-Dixon's work 'showed careful study ... from life', while Millais commented that 'his excellent draughtsmanship, delicate handling of details, and close observation proved him to be one who in time would have taken a high place among artists of bird life'. A fellow soldier, Lieutenant Norman Collins of the Seaforth Highlanders, whose memoir, *Last Man Standing*, was published by Pen & Sword in 2002, remembered him as a charming man, but one who was unable to remember to lead off on the left foot on parade. Otto Murray-Dixon's father simply wrote, 'by someone, somewhere in France, a man of peace he fell in war, giving his life for others.'

Henry George Jesse Peavot

It was not just ornithologists who joined the Roll of Honour but also those who helped them in their research. On 21 April 1917, Henry George Jesse Peavot was killed in action at the Battle of Arras serving with the Honourable Artillery Company on the Western Front. Peavot was the librarian at the Zoological Society of London (ZSL), a job he loved. The ZSL was founded in 1826 and is a charity devoted to the worldwide conservation of animals and their habitats. It is situated on the Outer Circle of Regent's Park, adjacent to London Zoo's main gate. The society houses one of the major zoological libraries in the world, Peavot being responsible for over 200,000 volumes including books dating back to the sixteenth century, together with the zoo's extensive archive.

Born in 1882 in Islington to Henry and Mary Peavot, he later lived in Cricklewood where he married Maude Odette Schneider in 1912. She was a typist at the library and they had one son together, Leslie, a year later.[11] Peavot attested to the Honourable Artillery Company on 9 December 1915 under the so-called 'Derby scheme'. Named after Lord Derby, it was the last voluntary campaign before conscription was introduced with the Military Service Acts in January 1916. He was called up to B Company, 1st Battalion, Honourable Artillery Company, as a private nearly a year later, on 6 December 1916. Peavot, like a lot of men, attested on the understanding that as a married man he would not have to serve until all the single men had been called up. Lord Derby had stated that 'the men in the married groups can only be assumed to be available if the Prime Minister's pledge to them has been redeemed by the single men attesting in such numbers as to leave only a negligible quantity unaccounted for'. As a result many came forward on the assumption that they would not have to serve.

A colleague who worked with him, Edwin Ephraim Riseley, also died in the war a few months later. Peavot was 35 years old and has no known grave. He is listed at the Arras Memorial in Pas de Calais and commemorated on the Librarians Memorial in the British Library and the ZSL, London Zoo Memorial.

William Eric Brook Dunlop

Following the Battle of Arras on 19 May 1917 one of 'the most promising young ornithologists of the north' was killed, according to his obituary in *British Birds*. Second Lieutenant William Eric Brook Dunlop of the 5th Battalion, Border Regiment was killed barely a month after having arrived in France. The eldest son of Arthur Brooke Dunlop, a justice of the peace from Windermere in the Lake District, he was born in 1887 and was educated at Rugby and Carlisle where he became a keen ornithologist, after graduating working for Carlisle Museum.

Touring the hills and dales of the Lake District, he monitored the resident breeding birds, making copious notes on the behaviour of the common buzzard, peregrine falcon and the raven. Dunlop was also one of the first ornithologists to record barn owls hunting during the day 'whilst the sun is yet high in the heavens' and made a special study of the roosting habits of crows. According to *British Birds* this showed 'that the whole of the British members of this group of birds congregated for roosting at certain seasons'.

In 1913 Dunlop updated the ornithological section of the *Fauna of Lakeland*, a seminal work first published in 1892 by the Reverend H. A. Macpherson, adding new species and records. Like a lot of ornithologists of the time, many of Dunlop's records were based not just on observation but on birds he or others had shot. For the honey buzzard he wrote, 'In October, 1908, a Honey Buzzard was shot at Scotby, and is now in Carlisle Museum. Another was trapped in Cumberland last summer, and … some time later a bird of this species was seen about the same locality, there cannot be much doubt that they would have nested if left alone.'

In his account Dunlop took particular pleasure in solving an ornithological mystery which had been raging in the national press about a bird that had been attacking people on the fells near Windermere. The bird had even featured in a column in the mass-circulation *Daily Dispatch*, a very popular tabloid launched in Manchester in 1900. In 1910 it had published a tabloid scoop with the sensational title 'Clergyman's fight with Great Bustards, Exciting adventure in the Lake District, Savage Birds beaten off with Stick'. It told the story of a God-fearing clergyman who like Wordsworth had been wandering lonely over the hills when he was suddenly and viciously dive-bombed from above by an angry bird. Despite putting up a terrific fight, swinging his walking stick at the marauding bird, he was forced to flee, the *Daily Dispatch* reporting breathlessly, 'As the encounter was assuming a perilous phase, the clergyman, being singlehanded in the combat, thought it best to retire, and so he beat a hasty retreat.' The reverend's photograph appeared in the paper, the *Daily Dispatch* concluding solemnly that he 'narrowly escaped serious injury' and compelling its readers to find the avian marauder before it had the chance to attack again.

Dunlop decided to investigate and retraced the clergyman's steps over the fells. When he finally located the area he was also attacked, the bird dive-bombing him, making 'two stoops to within two yards of me, coming past with a great rush. He then rose to a good height, finally making a perfectly magnificent stoop from fully 200 yards above me'. Watching the bird rise, Dunlop said, 'He closed his wings, so that the shoulders were only just separated from the sides, and with his legs an inch or two from his body, he dropped headlong to within two yards of me, then passing over my head with a regular roar of wind.' Dunlop discovered that the avian marauder was not a great bustard but a very dark male buzzard who had lived on the fell for over a decade. Despite solving the ornithological mystery, sadly Dunlop's scoop was not reported in the *Daily Dispatch* which, being the media, soon moved on from the story. Instead, his paper was published in 1923 in the *Transactions of the Carlisle Natural History Society* where despite all his hard work it was assigned to an appendix.

Afterwards Dunlop moved to Canada and when war was declared in 1914, he was studying birds in northern Manitoba, in particular looking at the little known ovitegous (incubation from the laying of the first egg) habit in birds. His observations appeared in the pages of *British Birds* on 1 October 1915 where he stated:

> As the best means of ascertaining the value of the ovitegous habit to birds, I devoted some time during the breeding-season to watching the Herring Gull (*L.argentatus*), which I had previously found normally incubated from the laying of the first egg. Various experiments were also made ... sufficient evidence is brought forward to make, I believe, the value of the ovitegous habit undeniable.

He also collected an extensive series of birds and mammal skins showing changes and variation with the season. Although enjoying his work in Canada, he wanted to serve King and Country so in 1915 he joined the army, enlisting in the 78th Canadian Grenadiers before joining the Border Regiment in April 1917 at Monchy. Before leaving for the front, Dunlop appointed the well-known ornithologist Reverend Francis Charles Robert Jourdain (1865–1940), assistant editor of *British Birds* magazine, as his his literary executor, depositing all his manuscripts with him.[12] Jourdain subsequently drew on his work in many of his books including his seminal five-volume *Handbook of British Birds* published between 1938 and 1941. Dunlop was just 30 when he died and is buried at the Arras Memorial, Pas de Calais in northern France.

Oliver Bernard Ellis
On the same day that Dunlop was killed on the battlefield, another promising ornithologist Oliver Bernard Ellis was killed in the air over the Western Front near Arleux. A pilot with the Royal Naval Air Service, Ellis was just 18 years old when he died.

Born in 1898 in Leicester to Bernard and Isabel Ellis, from 1912 to 1916 he attended Bootham School, a private Quaker boarding school in York, following in the footsteps of his father and brother. Here he excelled at athletics and became famous among the boys for climbing the North East Railway headquarters in York in the middle of the night and painting his initials on the roof for a dare. However, the railway company didn't realize the graffiti was a prank and instead launched an inquiry fearing it was the work of a spy who was trying to identify the building to Zeppelin bombers. After the story generated headlines in the press, Ellis eventually owned up to his headmaster, Arthur Rowntree, who initially did not believe him. When he finally did, Rowntree severely punished Ellis but he became a hero to the other boys.

When not scaling buildings, Ellis liked to watch birds and it was at Bootham that he developed a passion for natural history photography. On a visit to Strensall Common in Skipworth, over ten miles from the school, he found a cuckoo egg in a house sparrow nest. Ellis decided to photograph the development of the cuckoo chick and show how it had usurped the house sparrow young from the nest. To do this he would cycle there every other day, often having to get up before dawn so he was back in time for school which started at 6.30 a.m.

In 1914 he entered his pictures into a school photography exhibition run by the Natural History Exhibition Committee and won a prize. The committee report said:

> After the absence of competitors last year we are pleased to welcome the work of three ornithologists. O. B. Ellis, of Leicester, shows an extensive series of observations, illustrated by photographs and lantern slides. These include an excellent series, starting with the cuckoo's egg in the hedge sparrow's nest, and showing the development of the cuckoo and the fate of the young hedge sparrow. The black-headed gulls and other water-fowl at Skipwith have been studied and illustrated by a further series of creditable photographs. There were extensive fatalities among young gulls, but some suspicion cast upon owls seems to have been dispelled by careful examination of their pellets. A long essay on 'How Birds Protect their Eggs' shows that O. B. Ellis has tried to arrange his observations and make them of value. We award him an exhibition of £7.

Ellis had hoped to take up his place at St John's College, Cambridge University, in the autumn of 1916 but instead he joined the Royal Naval Air Service in the June. He did his initial training at Redcar before transferring to the Royal Flying Corps air training school at Cranwell where he gained his pilot's wings, being awarded the rank of Flight Sub-Lieutenant in March 1917. He was based at No. 1 Squadron, near Arras and went down in a dogfight over German lines east of Arleux. In a letter home his Squadron Commander R. S. Dallas wrote, 'your son gave a very fine account of himself indeed. He had already shot down one of his opponents when I saw him attacked by another. Your son was very tenacious and fought it out, and went down out of control through the clouds.'

His loss made a deep impression at his old school, his headmaster writing:

Oliver Ellis came to Bootham from Sidcot with a reputation for genial friendship and for holding the junior sports championship two years in succession. He proved himself a fearless football player, a brilliant and daring gymnast. He took a good position in class, and did excellently in his pilot's examination a few months ago. He was a keen ornithologist and a forceful reeve – full of the spirit of adventure when he left school less than a year ago. His loss will be felt in a large circle of friends, for he has left behind him that worthier thing than tears, the love of friends without a single foe.

One of his former classmates simply said, 'We could scarcely believe that one who possessed his gifts had been taken so soon. His energy and spirit, combined with remarkable thoroughness, made him a leader in every undertaking; and his open honesty made him the true friend of all who knew him.'[13]

In his last letter home to his parents, dated 3 May 1917, Ellis wrote, 'thank God that I've got the safest job in this war. Don't worry about me, I'm having the time of my life and am enjoying myself hugely, and the war can't last for ever.' Ellis is remembered on the Arras Flying Services Memorial, Pas de Calais, and in the archives of Bootham School.

Leonard Gray

On 31 July 1917, in the early hours of the morning, the British and French launched the first assault in the Battle of Passchendaele, the torrential rain and mud making the troops easy targets for the German machine guns and artillery. Nearly 2,000 miles away on the same day Captain Leonard Gray of the 1st/5th battalion, Essex Territorial Regiment died in hospital at Alexandria in Egypt from heart failure and typhoid contracted during the Palestine campaign.

Born in 1872, he was educated at Eastbourne and attended Pembroke College, Oxford University, afterwards training to be a solicitor and establishing his own practice. Like so many of his generation Gray's interest in ornithology sprang from collecting eggs in his childhood, his obituary in *British Birds* stating, 'From his schoolboy days, Captain Gray had taken a keen interest in ornithology and had been an active collector of birds eggs, often visiting Scotland and other districts favourable for collecting.'[14]

He gained an officer's commission in October 1915 and a year later arrived in Gallipoli to join his battalion in battle against the Turks. Before enlisting he had been a keen amateur birdwatcher, contributing notes to *British Birds*. In 1908 these included one of the first ever records of breeding lesser redpoll in Essex which he recorded in his garden:

A pair built a nest this year at the very top of a standard pear tree in my garden at Chelmsford. On July 28th the pair of old birds were accompanied by two young ones, and this little family party, a rather noisy one, remained about here for two or three weeks off and on, but have now apparently quite disappeared. The nest, on examination, proved to contain one much decomposed young one, so that apparently the clutch consisted of three eggs.

The next year he updated the readers of *British Birds* on his garden nest and in 1912 provided a note on nesting crossbills in Suffolk.

Gray fought bravely in both the first and second battles of Gaza in 1917 but he was was plagued by ill health. On his death, his commanding officer, Lieutenant Colonel T. Gibbons, said:

On July 9th [1917] Gray was obliged to go to hospital. He had hung on longer that he should have done, but we were always short of officers, and his sense of duty was always strong. It was with great grief to all ranks to hear about a month afterwards, that he had succumbed to enteric [intestinal infection] at Alexandria. Modest to a fault, without the slightest assumption of virtue or trace of 'goody-goody', no man ever came nearer to my ideal of a Christian and a gentleman than Leonard Gray.[15]

The *Essex County Chronicle* said of his death:

The news will be received in the County Town and far beyond the limits with great regret, for he was a keen and kindly officer, and in civilian life a quiet unassuming gentleman. In November, 1914, he responded to the call for volunteers, and was given a commission in the Essex Regt. He served through a large part of the Gallipoli campaign, but although laid up with dysentery and jaundice, he did not come home on sick leave. He was pronounced fit again in February, 1916, and returned to active duty, going through one of the most terrible tasks ever faced by the Essex Regiment without a scratch. For a time he was Acting Captain.

He bequeathed his extensive egg collection to Chelmsford Museum and is buried at Alexandria (Hadra) War Memorial Cemetery in Egypt. He is also commemorated on the Civic Centre Memorial in Chelmsford, in Chelmsford Cathedral and on the parish memorial of his local church, St John's in Moulsham. A month after his death his solicitors practice was renamed in his honour and continues to operate to this day from its office in Chelmsford.

Edwin Ephraim Riseley
On 1 August 1917, Edwin Ephraim Riseley, a librarian colleague of Peavot who had died a few months earlier, was killed in action. The two had worked together at the Zoological Society of London before Riseley got his dream job as Head Librarian at the prestigious Linnean Society of London. However, it was a position he got only after the previous incumbent, a German-born librarian, had been unceremoniously sacked by the society as an 'enemy alien' and suspected spy.[16]

Born in 1889 in Pimlico, Edwin was the only son of Ephraim and Emily Riseley, the couple two years later having a daughter, May Emily. When he was 10, his parents split up following a notorious divorce case in which his father accused his mother of sleeping with all three of their lodgers, a case which scandalized Victorian Society.[17] Brought up by his father, he left school at 15 and began work as a clerk at the ZSL. According to his obituary published in the *Proceedings of the Linnean Society in 1918*, here he 'acquired an excellent knowledge of library methods and of zoological literature. In the spring of 1914 an assistant was wanted in our library, and Mr Riseley was chosen for the post, and from the outbreak of war in that year the charge of the library and of our publications devolved upon him.' His starting salary was £100 a year, working 10 a.m. to 6 p.m. on weekdays and 10 a.m. to 1 p.m. on Saturdays and on nights when the society met. Riseley was good at his job but was promoted in controversial circumstances when his salary was increased to £125 a year.[18]

The Linnean Society of London is the world's oldest active biological society and it counts among its former members Charles Darwin and Alfred Russel Wallace, the fathers of evolution. It was founded in 1788 by Sir James Edward Smith (1759–1828), who was its first president. The society takes its name from the world famous Swedish naturalist Carl Linnaeus (1707–78) whose botanical, zoological and library collections were donated to it in 1829. Riseley was therefore in charge of one of the most unique biological collections in the world. His promotion to the role followed an internal inquiry into the society's previous librarian, a German by the name of August Wilhelm Kappel. At the time war broke out Kappel was on holiday visiting his relatives near Düsseldorf, returning in the middle of August 1914 to the society where as a senior librarian with years of loyal service he expected to resume his role. However, on arrival he was arrested by the police and, according to the *Proceedings of the Linnean Society in 1918*:

> For some undisclosed reason he came back about the middle of August, and was permitted by the police to stay at Teignmouth, in Devonshire. Having been informed that Kappel, an enemy alien and not naturalized, had not been registered by the police, the officers of the society remaining in Britain suspended Kappel from his functions, and when on the 1st September he presented himself for duty he was forbidden to enter.

A council was held on 15 October and on the 'evidence' presented to it, Kappel was sacked from his role. The 'evidence' presented to the council was provided by the general secretary who strongly suspected Kappel of having German sympathies and spying. To investigate further he had examined Kappel's desk and had discovered 'certain drawers kept locked against the Society by the Librarian'. As a result, it was unanimously decided that Kappel should be dismissed immediately and in place of working out his notice should be provided with three months' salary amounting to £91.13s.4d.

Kappel's treatment by the some of the most learned members of the society, including professional scientists, naturalists, historians and artists, entirely reflected the xenophobic attitudes prevalent at the time. His summary dismissal, based on very flimsy and probably fabricated evidence, was typical of the way that many Germans living in Britain were treated in the months following the declaration of war. On 5 August 1914, the Aliens Restriction Act was passed by Parliament requiring all 'enemy aliens' like Kappel to register with the police. However, Kappel, being away in Germany at the time, may not have known this although he cannot have failed to realize it when he returned. By the beginning of September, just under 67,000 foreign nationals from Germany, Austria and Hungary had been registered with the police. Those deemed to be a threat to national security or an enemy of the state were much more closely monitored but Kappel assumed that as a librarian of the world's oldest biological society that did not apply to him. He also probably had a misplaced faith in his erudite colleagues being above the nationalist clamour then sweeping the country.

Despite mirroring the worst excesses of anti-German sentiment, the society did at least do the right thing by Riseley who in his absence was paid £45 of his salary while on active duty. While training in Kent, on 26 June 1916, he wrote to the officers of the society thanking them and commenting, 'To see the battle planes here every day and the firing that goes on, one would think it impossible for any more raids to take place in London [the capital then being subjected to regular Zeppelin raids].'

Following Kappel's dismissal Riseley was appointed to the role from 1 September 1914 although he was not confirmed in post until 21 January 1915. According to his obituary:

> He began energetically to improve the arrangement of the books, checked them with the catalogue, and set up card catalogues for

accessions, although he was unable fully to carry out his plans for overtaking the arrears which the previous Librarian had suffered to accumulate. He rapidly gained a knowledge of the botanical volumes in our possession, which, added to his attainments gained at the Zoological Society, made him an admirable officer of the Society. He enlisted in the 9th Battalion of the Rifle Brigade and, after training, was drafted to France, where he met his death by a shell on the 1st August, 1917.

To honour his memory, the council commissioned a memorial tablet of beaten copper with an inscription in Latin which when translated reads:

In memory of Edwin Ephraim Riseley, born on the 15th February, 1889, in charge of this library from 1914 to 1917, during which period, by universal consent, he endeared himself to the Fellows by the energetic and able discharge of his duties; he laid down for his country a life of high promise on the 1st August, 1917, in the 29th year of his age.[19]

The plaque was hung in the library as a permanent reminder of Riseley's contribution to the work of the society and still hangs there to this day. Riseley was also remembered on the Linnean Society's Roll of Honour with seven other members of staff who were killed, his name also appearing on the British Library Memorial.

In contrast to Riseley's treatment, Kappel found himself ostracized following a surge in anti-German sentiment after the sinking of the RMS *Lusitania* on 7 May 1915. This led to a week of unprecedented rioting across the country in which virtually every German-owned shop had its windows broken. Bowing to public pressure, the government then began interning all foreign nationals despite believing most like Kappel posed no military threat. Severely depressed at his predicament and unable to return home to Germany, he died a broken man and an enemy alien on Christmas Eve 1915 at his adopted home in East Ham.

Godfrey Vassal Webster
On 4 August 1917, King George V and Queen Mary attended a special service at Westminster Abbey commemorating the third anniversary of

the war. On the same day Godfrey Vassal Webster, an award-winning young ornithologist, was killed at Ypres after being hit by a shell. Born in 1897, Webster was the only son of Major Sir Augustus Frederick Walpole Edward Webster (1864–1923), the 8th Baron of Battle Abbey in Sussex and his wife Lady Mabel (née Crossley) Webster (1876–1917). Educated at Eton, he later attended the Royal Military Academy at Sandhurst and was commissioned on 1 November 1916 as a second lieutenant in the 3rd Battalion, Grenadier Guards.

Ibis, the journal of the British Ornithologists' Union, said of him:

A born naturalist, at Eton he was placed in charge of the school Natural History Collections, and early in his last year the writer of this notice spent a day with him at Eton and saw the really good work put in by him in arranging and classifying the specimens in the Museum, and also in restoring some of them, for he was a really expert hand in taxidermy.

Fascinated by birds, in 1914 Webster won second prize in the RSPB's Public School Silver Medal competition for his essay on 'Our Summer Migrants'. The next year he won the first prize with an essay called 'The Flight of Birds'. Drawing on the aeronautical design of birds, his writing showed a professional understanding of bird flight way beyond his years:

The bird is a perfect flying machine. The shape of the body is calculated to offer little resistance to the air, the curve of the wings from front to back is almost mathematically perfect for giving lifting power. The curve has the further advantage of adapting itself to the pace of the bird, for the faster the bird travels the more the feathers bend, giving the slighter curve which aviators find necessary on high-speed machines. Aviators have also found that an upward incline of their planes is productive of greater stability. Many birds have found this also, for when flying the tips of the primaries bend slightly upwards. This is specially noticeable in the Rook. Lateral stability is ensured by the flexibility of the flight feathers. Equilibrium is also obtained when necessary by the bird giving more powerful strokes with one wing than with the other. This is very difficult to see; the best instance I know of is that of the Lapwing when disturbed from her nest.[20]

Summing up his life, *Ibis* reported:

> As modest as he was clever, his name – in conjunction with other members of our Union who have also given their lives for King and Country – will be respected and revered for all time, and his death, coming so soon after the tragic death of Lady Webster in June last, will, I am sure, cause the sympathy of our Members to go out to his father – Sir Augustus Webster, and to his two sisters, in this their hour of deep sorrow. Godfrey Webster had only this year been elected a member of the British Ornithologists' Union.[21]

In its obituary *British Birds* said Webster 'was one of the younger students of ornithology from whom much was hoped'. He was 20 years old when he died and is commemorated on the Eton Roll of Honour and the Menin Gate Memorial at Ypres in Belgium.

Arthur Gerrard Davidson

On 8 May 1909, the first organized bird-ringing scheme in Britain was 'hatched' at the University of Aberdeen, one of the ringers being Arthur Gerrard Davidson. The scheme was the brainchild of an undergraduate student at the university called Arthur Landsborough Thomson and another friend, Lewis Ramsay. Thomson had come up with the revolutionary idea of putting metal rings on to birds' legs with information on them so they could be identified and if recaptured their journey could be tracked.

To test Thomson's theory the three friends had headed out to the Sands of Forvie in Aberdeenshire, a popular nature reserve. There they found a lapwing (*Vanellus vanellus*) nest and placed unique rings on each of the six young fledglings in it. Just over a month later, on 13 June 1909, they recaptured one of the lapwings nearby, marking a historic first from a ringing scheme in Britain. Since then, bird ringing has done more than any other branch of ornithology to transform our understanding of bird behaviour throughout the world.

Thomson, Ramsey and Davidson all grew up in Aberdeen and had been friends since childhood. As boys they loved exploring the countryside together in search of nests, often cycling up to the Ythan Estuary or along Deeside. Ramsay's and Thomson's fathers were Regius professors at the University of Aberdeen and they both lived on the campus in Old Aberdeen, Thompson's father running the large natural history museum there where the boys would take the eggs to be identified.[22]

Born in 1890, Davidson was fascinated by natural history from an early age, he later attending the same grammar school as Thomson, Ramsey being educated in Edinburgh. Both Thomson and Ramsey then went on to study natural history at Aberdeen University. However, Davidson came from a more working-class background, his father being a tailor with a small business in the town. As a result following school, rather than going to university, he went to work in his father's shop and then later with a tailor in London. However, he remained good friends with Ramsey and through him became involved in the bird-ringing scheme at the university.

Following the declaration of war, Davidson joined the Gordon Highlanders as a private before rising to sergeant and then gaining a commission. On 21 March 1915, he learnt that his friend from childhood and fellow ringer Lewis Ramsey had been killed. Davidson was devastated by the news and decided to retrain, applying to the newly formed Royal Flying Corps. Here he again excelled and gained his pilot's wings in April 1917. A few months later he and his observer were shot down and killed in a dogfight with four enemy planes, on 9 September 1917. Davidson was 27 years old and his remains were buried in the Zuydcoote Military Cemetery near Dunkirk in France.

Thomson also fought in France with the Argyll and Sutherland Highlanders and was the only one of the three to survive the war. Afterwards he collaborated with another ornithologist, Harry Forbes Witherby, the editor of *British Birds* magazine, to develop a joint ringing scheme. This was transferred to the British Trust for Ornithology in 1937 who run it to this day. Over his lifetime Thomson produced over 70 books and papers and received many awards, including a knighthood in 1953. He died on 9 June 1977 at the age of 86 but never forgot his boyhood friends and fellow ringers.

Christopher James Alexander

The Battle of Passchendaele claimed another ornithologist on 5 October 1917 when Christopher James Alexander was killed at the Battle of Broodseinde. Although he could have been commissioned as an officer, Alexander preferred to enlist as a private, believing it was better to get promotion on merit rather than privilege. This made him very popular with his fellow soldiers who came to view him with great affection and admiration.

Born in 1887 in Croydon, he was the son of Joseph Gundury Alexander and the brother of ornithologists Wilfred Backhouse Alexander (1885–1965) and Horace Gundry Alexander (1889–1989). From 1900 to 1904 he went to Bootham School, a private Quaker school in York, where he excelled at natural history (Oliver Bernard Ellis, also killed in action, later attended the same school). In 1903, Alexander won the school natural history prize for lepidoptera (the study of butterflies and moths) and became curator of the school's extensive natural history collection. In 1903, in the school debate he defeated a motion that egg-collecting wasn't cruel, instead promoting photography and birdwatching as a way of appreciating birds. In the same year he also won the Old Scholars' Natural History Exhibition with a prize of £5 for his 'voluminous and very careful diary illustrated with unusual ability and extending over three years; with great variety of observation, especially in the fields of Entomology, Ornithology, and Botany'.

After leaving Bootham, Alexander studied agriculture at Wye College, gaining a science degree in 1909, following which he became Berkshire recorder for insect and fungal diseases. In 1911, he was voted a member of the British Ornithologists' Union and moved to Rome to be *Rédacteur* (editor) at the International Institute of Agriculture where he stayed for five years, dedicating all his spare time to the study of birds.

Alexander joined the Buffs (Royal East Kent Regiment) on 29 February 1916 before transferring to the Queen's Royal Regiment (West Surrey). He did his military training at Dover, where he 'chased Dark Green Fritillaries and watched Shrikes [as] in his first school-days, eighteen and twenty years before'. In June 1916, his regiment sailed for France where he took part in the fighting on the Somme.

According to the obituary written by his brother in *British Birds*, Alexander was 'always able to banish something of the gruesome surroundings by looking and listening for the birds – and often rewarded by the sight of good things, such as a Green Sandpiper put up from a flooded trench, a Great Grey Shrike on the cheerless downs at Christmastime, and a Bustard that flew over the camp one day in February, 1917'. After breaking his leg, he was sent back to England to convalesce before returning to France in July, the last letter he ever wrote being received by his brother on 30 September 1917, in which he wrote, 'of a Quail they had put up, which, with Pied Flycatcher, Woodchat and Melodious Warbler seen passing a few days before, made 107 species for the year – a wonderful total under such conditions.' [23]

His obituary in *Ibis* read:

> He was always shy and retiring, and did not easily make friends: he preferred to enlist as a private in the Army, where he soon became generally loved for his universal kindness and modest generosity to all whom he could help. It was typical of him that it was only after his death that any of his family learn't, from one of his Italian friends, that in one of the battles in which he took part he had captured a German prisoner and shared his last biscuit and water with him. In advancing through the barrage to support the front line in one of the great Passchendaele battles on 4 October, 1917, he was hit by a shell and severely wounded; he appears to have died or been killed later the same day, after being put on an ambulance.[24]

Alexander was 30 years old is buried in Hooge Crater Cemetery in Ypres, Belgium.

1918

Cecil Christopher Baring

As the war entered its fourth year the third Baring brother to die in battle occurred when Cecil Christopher Baring was killed on 21 March 1918. A second lieutenant in the 8th Battalion, Queen's Own (Royal West Kent Regiment), he was the son of the Reverend Francis Henry and Amy Baring, who lived in Chandler's Ford, Hampshire. One of seven children, two of his brothers had already been killed in action, Charles on 4 September 1916 and Ernest on 2 April 1917.

Baring was born in Simla, India, and educated at Haileybury College in Hertfordshire. A very keen ornithologist from an early age, in 1914 he won the Silver Medal in the RSPB's Public School Competition on the subject of 'Our Summer Migrants' recording detailed notes on the arrival of twenty-nine species in Haileybury and Sudbury. In the autumn of 1916, he sent in a remarkable bird diary from the Western Front in France which was published in *Bird Notes and News*:

April. – Out in rest at last, after an 'over the top with the best of luck'.

11th. – The first Swallow has turned up, and in the lane behind the farm we are billeted in is a Blackbird's nest with one egg.

23rd.– The House-Martins, Chiffchaffs, and a few Willow-Wrens are here.

26th. – This afternoon I watched a small Warbler hopping about in the creeper outside the farmhouse. From its note and general appearance, I am convinced it was an Icterine Warbler.

28th. – To-day I saw a fine cock Wheatear; it was probably still on migration.

May 5th. – This morning I put up a hen Meadow Pipit from her nest, while doubling across a field on 'open warfare' manoeuvres. It had five eggs in.

7th. – All the Magpie and Carrion Crows nests which I have found so far in at all accessible positions have been robbed. The Meadow Pipit has deserted, I am sorry to say. There are five or six Sandpipers passing up and down the river here. They are very shy and I have not been able to get a good look at them. I am almost sure they are not Common Sandpipers, as their note seems to me quite different. Along the same river there are a number of small bushes in which several pairs of Whitethroats have begun to build their nests. If one is lucky one can see a Kingfisher flash by in all the glory of its breeding-season plumage.

8th. – I have located the Kingfisher's home quite by chance. I put the hen bird off the nest of fish-bones, on which reposed seven pearly white eggs. She was just beginning to sit, and the eggs had lost the beautiful pink glow that suffuses them when newly laid. I found nests of the Robin, Yellowhammer, Hedge-Sparrow, Wren, Linnet, and Garden-Warbler containing eggs; Nightingales are fairly plentiful in suitable spots, but I have found no nest as yet.

June. – An end to rest and peace; we have moved up to the ill-fated 'Salient'. We are in a once-famous town, now sadly smashed about. There is a fine tower still left standing. At least five pairs of Kestrels nest in it, besides Jackdaws, Pigeons, and Starlings, so there is everlasting war in the air round it; how they all fit in together I can't think. The air seems full of screaming Swifts. They don't seem to mind the tower being shelled, but rejoice in the additional nesting-places the ruins afford. Last night on patrol I ran into a flock of Redshanks in 'No man's land', which is a marsh in this part of the line. Fortunately for us they did not scream out and only displayed a certain vague restlessness. One full-throated alarm call, and we should have had a dozen Hun lights at us. – We are in a place where the front line is in the middle of a wood, now a mere ghost of itself. But a pair of Nightingales still haunt it, and Chaffinches, Hedge-Sparrows, Blackbirds, and Whitethroats are singing everywhere ... Last night I heard a Great Reed-Warbler singing beside a lake I had to pass. Its song dominated the whole night as the Nightingale's does, but of course it is not quite so melodious ... This morning I had a most delightful adventure. I stumbled across a ruined chalet surrounded by most beautiful grounds, which were full of syringa bushes in full bloom, while Golden Orioles called from the tall trees or flashed by in the sunshine.

Later. – We are in the middle of the offensive, the shelling is almost incessant, and there is very little cover. Naturally there are not many birds up here now. I have seen several Sparrows suffering from 'shell shock'. A most beautiful cock Pied Wagtail haunts a large shell-hole full of water near one of my posts. Besides these a few Swifts and Swallows occasionally come over.

July. – I am far away from the battle on a course. I have discovered a pleasant little wood. In it I have found a nest full of young Carrion

Crows, several nests of Blackcap and Garden Warblers with young nearly ready to fly, and eight different species of orchis. – Today I saw several Wheatears; they must have nested here. I also discovered a Partridge's nest with twelve eggs. – Today, in manoeuvres, I found four Partridge's nests. A Tank missed one of them only by inches! They are nesting very late this year.

August. – During August I was too busy to make any observations beyond the following –

3rd. – Saw several large flocks of Starlings, rather an early date for really large flocks to be found.

25th. – Yesterday I passed by a lake where there were still quite a number of Great Reed-Warblers about.[25]

His obituary in *Bird Notes and News* read:

by his death a most promising naturalist is lost to this country ... He had hoped that his last leave in England would extend long enough to allow him to attend the Society's Annual Meeting, and was full of pleasant anticipations of the study of fresh bird-life in his prospective new home in Hampshire. He died a fortnight after his regiment went to the front. His ornithological work was always notable for its directness and accuracy, and the same frank sincerity in manner and speech gave charm to a fine character.

A friend of his father's, the Reverend. J. G. Tuck, also wrote of him: 'Birds, butterflies, and flowers all had their own charm for him, and his notes from France printed in *Bird Notes and News* a few months ago testify to the keenness and accuracy of his observations. At Haileybury he gained a good scholarship at Hertford College, Oxford, but his military duties prevented him from going up to the University.'

Cecil's death was not to be the last tragedy in the family. Two months later another brother, Reginald, who was in the Royal Air Force, was missing presumed killed on 9 June 1918 flying his Sopwith Camel. Cecil is commemorated at the Roye New British Cemetery on the Somme and on the Sudbury War Memorial in Suffolk.

John Bateson

On 14 October 1918, Lieutenant John Bateson was killed near Passchendaele and despite being only 20 had already been singled out as a 'naturalist of exceptional promise'. For his bravery attempting to rescue wounded comrades under fire he was posthumously awarded the Military Cross.

Born on 22 April 1898, he was the eldest son of three boys born to William and Caroline Beatrice Bateson who lived in Merton, London. His father was a world-famous geneticist who was credited with being the first person to use the term genetics to describe the passing on of traits or heredity between generations. He attended Charterhouse School in Godalming, Surrey, where he became a very good amateur ornithologist, being awarded the school's Poole Prize in Natural History in 1914, 1915 and 1917, a remarkable record. He had won a place at St John's College at Cambridge University before the war intervened.[26]

Following the outbreak of hostilities, Bateson was commissioned into the Royal Field Artillery and was killed in action while serving with his battery. Further family tragedy followed four years later when his second brother Martin committed suicide on his birthday. However, his youngest brother Gregory (1904–1980) would go to become a distinguished anthropologist and social scientist who wrote many important works including *Steps to an Ecology of Mind* in 1972 and *Mind and Nature* in 1979.

In 1918 Bateson was awarded the Military Cross, the citation reading:

> When his battery was being heavily shelled, he twice went through an intense barrage to find a medical officer and assist a wounded man to the dressing station. On the same night, while helping a wounded man to the dressing station, his party was caught in a heavy barrage and all of them were wounded. Though wounded himself, he went forward to the dressing station and brought back help. He showed splendid courage and self sacrifice.

Bateson is buried at the Dadizeele New British Cemetery in Belgium

Sydney Edward Brock

Of all the ornithologists to join the Roll of Honour, perhaps the most poignant is the death of Captain Sydney Edward Brock, on the very last day of the war. Like Bateson, he was posthumously awarded the Military Cross, his injuries resulting in him passing away on Armistice Day and not living to see a peace for which he had fought so bravely.

Brock was born in 1883 at Overton near Kirkliston, West Lothian, his memorial stone stating he was a 'farmer, naturalist and scholar'. In 1904, he took over the tenancy of the family farm, volunteering for active service a decade later when war broke out, joining the 8th Battalion, Royal Scots (Lothian Regiment). A cyclist battalion, Brock rode into battle with his rifle and his binoculars and during lulls in the fighting made detailed notes from the trenches of the birdlife he saw in the Peronne district of the Somme.

His obituary in *British Birds* read:

> there is reason to believe that he had in his mind the preparation of a Fauna of Linlithgowshire, where the greater part of his life was spent. Although chiefly interested in birdlife, he had acquired considerable knowledge of some of the lesser worked groups of insects, and of late years had devoted special attention to ecological problems. Most of his contributions to science appeared in the *Annals of Scottish Natural History* from 1906 onward, but he also wrote for *The Zoologist*, and the volume for 1910 contains some original observations on the fledging periods of birds, and a very careful paper on 'The Willow Wrens of a Lothian Wood'. His most important contribution to *British Birds* was a thoughtful and suggestive paper on 'Ecological Relations of Bird-Distribution'. There was every reason to expect much good work in the future from such a careful and good observer.[27]

On 17 October 1918, he was severely wounded in action at Courtrai in Flanders, and was transferred to a military hospital in Aberdeen where he died from his wounds on the morning of 11 November 1918, hours before hostilities ended. Awarded the Military Cross for bravery, his citation read:

> Captain Sydney Edward Brock, 10th Bn., R. Scots. T.F. (attd. 12 Bn.) For most conspicuous gallantry at the bridgehead at Cuerne on 17th Oct., 1918. He led part of his company over the bridge, under very heavy enemy fire, in an entirely exposed position, displaying

great coolness and disregard of danger, and setting a most inspiring example to his men.

Brock is buried at Kirkliston cemetery in West Lothian. The peace treaty he never lived to see was signed between the Allies and Germany at Le Francport near Compiègne, coming into effect on 11 November 1918. This would bring to an end the fighting on land, sea and air which had raged for four years, three months and one week. The sheer scale of sacrifice during the Great War can perhaps best be judged by the fact that over 850 Allied soldiers would, like Brock, lose their lives that morning before peace was finally declared at 11 a.m.

Notes

Chapter 1: The Charm of Birds
1. Statement by Sir Edward Grey in the House of Commons, 3 August, 1914 HMSO.
2. Ibid.
3. Ibid.
4. Edward Grey (Viscount Grey of Fallodon), *Twenty-Five Years* Vols. 1& 2, London: Hodder & Stoughton, 1925. p. 20.
5. Theodor Wolff, *The Eve of 1914*, New York: Alfred A. Knopf, 1936, p. 92.
6. Statement by the Prime Minister in the House of Commons, 6 August, 1914 HMSO.
7. Royal Society for the Protection of Birds, *Bird Notes & News*, Spring 1914 Vol., 6 p. 17.
8. Edward Grey (Viscount Grey of Fallodon), *The Charm of Birds*, Hodder & Stroughton, 1927, p. 5.
9. https://en.wikipedia.org/wiki/Grey%27s_Monument.
10. Edward Grey (Viscount Grey of Fallodon), *The Charm of Birds*, Hodder & Stroughton, 1927, p. 3
11. Edward Grey (Viscount Grey of Fallodon), *Fallodon Papers*, London: Constable & Co Ltd., 1926, p. 136
12. Michael Waterhouse, *Edwardian Requiem: A Life of Sir Edward Grey*, London: Biteback Publishing, 2013, p. 8
13. https://en.wikipedia.org/wiki/Henry_Percy,_7th_Duke_of_Northumberland.
14. Edward Grey (Viscount Grey of Fallodon), *Fallodon Papers*, London: Constable & Co Ltd., 1926, p. 115.
15. Ibid., p. 116.
16. Michael Waterhouse, *Edwardian Requiem: A Life of Sir Edward Grey*, London: Biteback Publishing, 2013, p. 10
17. Ibid., p. 23.
18. Edward Grey (Viscount Grey of Fallodon), *Fallodon Papers*, London: Constable & Co Ltd., 1926, p. 34.
19. Edward Grey & Michael Waterstone, (ed.) *The Cottage Book: The Undiscovered Country Diary of an Edwardian Statesman*, London: Weidenfield & Nicolson, 1999, p. 38.
20. Edward Grey (Viscount Grey of Fallodon), *Twenty-Five Years* Vol. 2, London: Hodder & Stoughton, 1925, p. 87.

21. Royal Society for the Protection of Birds, *Bird Notes & News*, Spring 1919, Vol. 8, p. 34.
22. Ibid.
23. Edward Grey (Viscount Grey of Fallodon), *Twenty-Five Years* Vol. 2, London: Hodder & Stoughton, 1925, p. 134
24. Ibid.
25. Edward Grey (Viscount Grey of Fallodon), *Fallodon Papers*, London: Constable & Co Ltd., 1926, p. 123.
26. The 'John Bull' portfolio of war celebrities 1914 Containing 16 mounted photogravure portraits with biographical notes, Oldhams Ltd.
27. Jonathan Parry, 'A Regular Grey', *London Review of Books* Vol. 42 No. 23, 2020.
28. Edward Grey (Viscount Grey of Fallodon), *Fallodon Papers*, London: Constable & Co Ltd., 1926, p. 131.
29. Gordon Seton, 'Lord Grey: The Naturalist', *The Scottish Field* 1933 p. 146.
30. Robert Self (ed.), *The Neville Chamberlain Diary Letters: Volume 1: The Making of a Politician 1915–20*, Oxford: Routledge, 2000, p. 80
31. Alex Danchev, & Daniel Todman, (eds.), *War Diaries 1939–1945 Field Marshal Lord Alanbrooke*, London: Weidenfeld & Nicolson, 2001, p. 160.
32. https://history.blog.gov.uk/2015/12/07/sir-edward-grey-a-fitting-tribute/

Chapter 2: The Great War on Birds
1. Ministry of Agriculture, 'Wild Birds and Their Land', Bulletin No. 140, London: HMSO, 1948, p. 51.
2. http://media.freeola.com/other/19969/westfarleighanddistrictratandsparrowclubmodifid.pdf.
3. Royal Society for the Protection of Birds, *Bird Notes & News*, Spring 1915 Vol. 6, p. 78.
4. Royal Society for the Protection of Birds, *Bird Notes & News*, Winter 1914 Vol. 6, p. 55.
5. Royal Society for the Protection of Birds, *Bird Notes & News*, Autumn 1914 Vol. 6, p. 44.
6. Ibid.
7. Royal Society for the Protection of Birds, *Bird Notes & News*, Autumn 1914, Vol. 6, p. 108.
8. Royal Society for the Protection of Birds, *Bird Notes & News*, Autumn 1915, Vol. 6, p. 117.
9. www.ww1worcestershire.co.uk/key-dates/1917/03/local-footballer-killed/.
10. http://media.freeola.com/other/19969/westfarleighanddistrictratandsparrowclubmodifid.pdf.
11. Royal Society for the Protection of Birds, *Bird Notes & News*, Spring 1917 Vol. 7 p. 57
12. Royal Society for the Protection of Birds, *Bird Notes & News*, Summer 1917 Vol. 7 p. 78

13. Ibid., p. 75.
14. Derek Ryan & Stella Bolaki (eds.), *Contradictory Woolf*, Liverpool: Liverpool University Press, 2012, pp. 281–2.
15. Royal Society for the Protection of Birds, *Bird Notes & News*, Summer 1917, Vol. 7, p. 73
16. Ibid., p. 75.
17. House of Commons Debate 25 April 1917 'Sparrows (Destruction)', Hansard.
18. Royal Society for the Protection of Birds, *Bird Notes & News*, Autumn 1917, Vol. 7, p. 103
19. www.shipleyww1.org.uk/1917-11-16.htm.
20. Hugh S. Gladstone, *Birds and War*, London: Skeffington & Son, 1919, p. 33.
21. www.poemhunter.com/poem/to-a-sparrow/.
22. Royal Society for the Protection of Birds, *Bird Notes & News*, Spring 1918, Vol. 8, p. 3.
23. *The Times*, 25 April 1918
24. www.arborfieldhistory.org.uk/WW1/WW1_Agriculture.htm
25. www.bbc.co.uk/programmes/p02b3drh

Chapter 3: The Best Birdwatching Army Ever Sent to War
1. https://guidedbattlefieldtours.co.uk/education/british-expeditionary-force-bef-1914/.
2. Ronald Hickling, *Enjoying Ornithology*, London: Bloomsbury, 2010, p. 161.
3. *The Avicultural Magazine* Vol. 5 No. 11, September 1914 pp. 337–8.
4. Royal Society for the Protection of Birds, *Bird Notes & News*, Autumn 1914, Vol. 6, p. 42.
5. Royal Society for the Protection of Birds, *Bird Notes & News*, Winter 1914, Vol. 6, p. 43.
6. Ibid., p. 57.
7. Royal Society for the Protection of Birds, *Bird Notes & News*, Spring 1915, Vol. 6, p. 79.
8. Arthur Guy Empey, *Over the Top*, London: G.P. Putnam's Sons, 1917, p. 45
9. www.worldwar1postcards.com/smokes-for-the-troops.php.
10. Wills's Cigarettes British Birds: A Series of 50: No. 9 House-Sparrow, The Imperial Tobacco Co., 1915.
11. Royal Society for the Protection of Birds, *Bird Notes & News*, Summer 1915, Vol. 6, p. 87.
12. Ibid.
13. Ibid., p. 88
14. Ibid.
15. Ibid.
16. *British Birds* Vol. 9, 1 June 1915, p. 32.
17. Royal Society for the Protection of Birds, *Bird Notes & News*, Summer 1915 Vol. 6, p. 89.

18. Ibid.
19. Royal Society for the Protection of Birds, *Bird Notes & News*, Spring 1915, Vol. 6, p. 84.
20. Royal Society for the Protection of Birds, *Bird Notes & News*, Summer 1915, Vol. 6, p. 92.
21. N. Gullace, 'White Feathers and Wounded Men: Female Patriotism and the Memory of the Great War', *Journal of British Studies*, 36(2), 1997, pp. 178–206.
22. https://spartacus-educational.com/FWWfeather.htm
23. www.bbc.co.uk/news/uk-england-birmingham-15684022
24. Royal Society for the Protection of Birds, *Bird Notes & News*, Winter 1916, Vol. 7, p. 67.
25. Royal Society for the Protection of Birds, *Bird Notes & News*, Spring 1915, Vol. 6, p. 78.
26. Ibid., p. 79.
27. Ibid.
28. https://en.wikipedia.org/wiki/Edward_Fitzmaurice_Inglefield.
29. www.ijnhonline.org/wp-content/uploads/2012/01/article_wilson.pdf.
30. Ibid.
31. Thomas Mills, *The Fateful Sea-Gull. [Reminiscences, Including an Account of Gold Mining Experiences in Australia and of the Author's Scheme for Training Seagulls to Locate German Submarines in World War I. With Illustrations, Including Portraits]*, Bradley & Son, 1919.

Chapter 4: Birds at the Front
1. Royal Society for the Protection of Birds, *Bird Notes & News*, Autumn 1915, Vol. 6, p. 102.
2. Ibid., p. 103.
3. Ibid., p. 97.
4. Royal Society for the Protection of Birds, *Bird Notes & News*, Spring 1916, Vol. 7, p. 3.
5. Ibid., p. 1.
6. *The Avicultural Magazine*, March 1916, Vol. 7, p. 132.
7. Philip Gosse, *A Naturalist Goes to War*, London: Penguin, 1934, p. 87.
8. Royal Society for the Protection of Birds, *Bird Notes & News*, Spring 1916, Vol. 7, p. 17
9. Ibid., p. 15.
10. www.poemist.com/john-william-streets/a-lark-above-the-trenches.
11. www.ymca.org.uk/wp-content/uploads/2017/11/Betty-Stevenson-YMCA-Womens-Auxiliary-The-Happy-Warrior.pdf.
12. Annual General Meeting of British Ornithologists' Union, April 1916, *Ibis*, p. 367.

Chapter 5: Birds and Enemy Aliens
1. Royal Society for the Protection of Birds, *Bird Notes & News*, Autumn 1916, Vol. 7, p. 30.
2. Clarke H. Thoburn. 'Swallows at the Front', *Country Life*, 7 October 1916.
3. H.H. Munro, 'Birds on the Western Front', *The Westminster*, 14 October 1916.
4. Royal Society for the Protection of Birds, *Bird Notes & News*, Winter 1916, Vol. 7, p. 45.
5. Ernest Pollard & Hazel Strouts (eds.), *Wings over the Western Front: The First World War Diaries of Collingwood Ingram*, London: Day Books, 2014, p. 17.
6. Royal Society for the Protection of Birds, *Bird Notes & News*, Spring 1917, Vol. 7, p. 69.
7. www.teignheritageworldwar.org.uk/index.php/miss-constance-teschemaker.
8. W. Teschemaker, 'The Influence of German Aviculture', *The Avicultural Magazine*, February 1917.
9. A. Buxton in *The Times*, 10 January 1917.
10. M. M. Oyler, 'What the Kingfisher knew' *Punch*, 28 July 1917.
11. Royal Society for the Protection of Birds, *Bird Notes & News*, Summer 1917, Vol. 7, p. 77.
12. J.C. Richardson in *The Times*, 28 July 1917.
13. Royal Society for the Protection of Birds, *Bird Notes & News*, Winter 1917, Vol. 7, p. 107.

Chapter 6: The First Flying Corps
1. Royal Society for the Protection of Birds, *Bird Notes & News*, Winter 1916, Vol. 7, p. 106.
2. Philip, Gosse, *A Naturalist Goes to War*, London: Penguin, 1934, p. 125.
3. Royal Society for the Protection of Birds, *Bird Notes & News*, Winter 1917, Vol. 7, p. 105.
4. Ibid., p. 114.
5. https://nationalpoetryday.co.uk/poem/returning-we-hear-the-larks/.
6. Royal Society for the Protection of Birds, *Bird Notes & News*, Spring 1918, Vol. 8, p. 15.
7. Pollard, Ernest & Hazel Strouts (eds.), *Wings over the Western Front: The First World War Diaries of Collingwood Ingram*, London: Day Books, 2014, p. 234.
8. Royal Society for the Protection of Birds, *Bird Notes & News*, Winter 1918, Vol. 8, p. 25.
9. Ibid
10. 'Sea Heroes, Thomas Crisp VC, DSC, Hero of the Q–Ships', Suffolk Records Office.
11. Gosse, Philip, *A Naturalist Goes to War*, London: Penguin, 1934, p. 31.
12. www.lrb.co.uk/the-paper/v41/n07/jon-day/operation-columba.

13. https://pethistories.wordpress.com/2018/05/02/love-in-the-air-canaries-on-the-western-front/.
14. Royal Society for the Protection of Birds, *Bird Notes & News*, Spring 1918 Vol.8, p. 26.
15. Ibid.
16. A. de C. Sowerby, 'Birds of the Battlefields', *British Birds*, 1 May 1919, Vol. 11, p. 266.
17. Royal Society for the Protection of Birds, *Bird Notes & News*, Winter 1918, Vol. 8, p. 25.

Appendix: The Ornithological Roll of Honour

1. 'Bird Nest Photography and its Relation to Sport', *Badminton Magazine of Sports and Pastimes*, No. LXXXVI. Vol. XV, September 1902, pp. 251–61.
2. Obituary Captain John Dighton Grafton-Wignall in *British Birds*, October 1917, Vol. 10, p. 245.
3. Obituary in *The Avicultural Magazine*, May 1917, Vol. 8, p. 208.
4. https://interestingliterature.com/2015/10/a-short-analysis-of-adlestrop-by-edward-thomas/.
5. An interview with Tim Dee, 24 July 2014, Little Toller Books, www.littletoller.co.uk/the-clearing/an-interview-with-tim-dee/.
6. www.thurcastoncropstonhistory.org.uk/report_mar2017/.
7. Royal Society for the Protection of Birds, *Bird Notes & News*, Autumn 1914, Vol. 6, p. 52.
8. Royal Society for the Protection of Birds, *Bird Notes & News*, Autumn 1915, Vol. 6, p. 105.
9. Royal Society for the Protection of Birds, *Bird Notes & News*, Winter 1917, Vol.7, p. 114.
10. https://livesofthefirstworldwar.iwm.org.uk/lifestory/1646629.
11. https://livesofthefirstworldwar.iwm.org.uk/lifestory/3457262.
12. https://livesofthefirstworldwar.iwm.org.uk/story/50664.
13. http://blogs.boothamschool.com/archives/index.php/2017/06/29/in-memoriam-oliver-bernard-ellis/.
14. Obituary in *British Birds*, 1 March 1918, Vol. 11, p. 239.
15. www.chelmsfordwarmemorial.co.uk/first-world-war/chelmsford/gray-leonard.html.
16. www.linnean.org/news/2014/01/06/january-2014-edwin-ephraim-riseley.
17. www.criminalhistorian.com/the-man-whose-wife-had-sex-with-the-lodgers/.
18. www.linnean.org/news/2017/08/01/1st-august-2017-remembering-e-e-riseley.
19. https://worldwarzoogardener1939.wordpress.com/2017/08/01/remembering-edwin-ephraim-riseley-zsl-and-linnean-society/.
20. Royal Society for the Protection of Birds, *Bird Notes & News*, Summer 1916, Vol. 7, p. 9.
21. Obituary in *Ibis*, 1917, Vol. 5, p. 614.

22. BB eye 'In memoriam', *British Birds*, July 2014, Vol. 107, pp. 282–3.
23. C. J. Alexander in *British Birds*, February 1918, Vol. 11, pp. 204–9.
24. Obituary Christopher James Alexander in *Ibis* XVII, Vol. 6, 1918, pp. 301–2.
25. Royal Society for the Protection of Birds, *Bird Notes & News*, Winter 1916, Vol. 7, pp. 90–1.
26. https://charterhousewarmemorial.org.uk/RollofHonour.aspx?RecID=730&TableName=view_WarTable&fromTimelinePage=true.
27. https://worldwarzoogardener1939.wordpress.com/2014/03/04/lost-ecologists-of-the-first-world-war/.

Bibliography

Danchev, Alex & Daniel Todman, (eds.), *War Diaries 1939–1945 Field Marshal Lord Alanbrooke*, London: Weidenfeld & Nicolson, 2001.

Empey, Arthur Guy, *Over the Top*, London: G.P. Putnam's Sons, 1917.

Gladstone, Hugh S., *Birds and War*, London: Skeffington & Son, 1919.

Gosse, Philip, *A Naturalist Goes to War*, London: Penguin, 1934.

Grey, Edward & Michael Waterstone, (ed.) *The Cottage Book: The Undiscovered Country Diary of an Edwardian Statesman*, London: Weidenfield & Nicolson, 1999.

Grey, Edward (Viscount Grey of Fallodon), *Fallodon Papers*, London: Constable & Co Ltd., 1926.

Grey, Edward (Viscount Grey of Fallodon), *The Charm of Birds*, Hodder & Stroughton, 1927.

Grey, Edward (Viscount Grey of Fallodon), *Twenty-Five Years* Vols. 1 & 2, London: Hodder & Stoughton, 1925.

Hickling, Ronald, *Enjoying Ornithology*, London: Bloomsbury, 2010.

Mills, Thomas, *The Fateful Sea-Gull. [Reminiscences, Including an Account of Gold Mining Experiences in Australia and of the Author's Scheme for Training Seagulls to Locate German Submarines in World War I. With Illustrations, Including Portraits]*, Bradley & Son, 1919.

Osman, A.H., *Pigeons in the Great War*, The Racing Pigeon Publishing Company Ltd, 1928.

Pollard, Ernest & Hazel Strouts (eds.), *Wings over the Western Front: The First World War Diaries of Collingwood Ingram*, London: Day Books, 2014.

Ryan, Derek & Stella Bolaki (eds.), *Contradictory Woolf*, Liverpool: Liverpool University Press, 2012.

Self, Robert (ed.), *The Neville Chamberlain Diary Letters: Volume 1: The Making of a Politician 1915–20*, Oxford: Routledge, 2000.

Waterhouse, Michael, *Edwardian Requiem: A Life of Sir Edward Grey*, London: Biteback Publishing, 2013.

Wolff, Theodor, *The Eve of 1914*, New York: Alfred A. Knopf, 1936.

Index

Alexander, Christopher James xii, 147, 213, 227
American robin 22
Andean gull 153
Asquith, Herbert Henry 4, 5, 9, 19, 20, 24, 25, 33, 179
Avicultural Magazine 53, 54, 84, 85, 107, 111, 153, 174, 176, 190
Avicultural Society 53, 54, 69, 106, 107, 110

Balfour, Arthur 19, 71
Baring, Cecil Christopher 147, 214–17
Barn owl 76, 102, 121, 199
Bateson, John 147, 218
Bee-eater xii, 117
Berlepsch, Baron von 56–7
Bird Notes and News viii, 34, 36, 53, 60, 65, 68–9, 82, 90, 93, 131, 136, 145, 190, 196, 215, 217
Blackbird xii, 8, 22, 37, 46–7, 60–2, 64, 79, 84, 89, 90–1, 100, 105, 146, 157, 192, 197, 215–6,
Blackcap 22, 30, 82, 89, 217
Black-headed gull 203
Blue-headed wagtail 98–9, 154
Blue tit 49, 152
Blyth's reed warbler 182
Board of Agriculture vii, viii, xii, 33–4, 36, 40–2, 44, 48–9, 50–1, 179
Brabourne, Lord 95, 147, 152–4
British Expeditionary Force xi, 52–3, 63
British Ornithologists' Union (BOU) vii, 53, 94–5, 96, 106, 108, 153, 155, 160, 166, 177, 179, 187, 190, 210–11, 213
Brock, Sydney Edward 147, 216–20
Brooke, Alan 30
Bullfinch 37, 46–7, 57, 64
Buzzard 84, 102, 117, 189, 200–2

Campbell-Bannerman, Henry 19–20, 52
Canary 69, 140–3
Carrion crow 216
Carrion hawk 153
Chaffinch 57, 59, 634

Chamberlain, Neville 112
Charlton, Hugh 147, 172–5
Charlton, John 147, 172–5
Chiffchaff 215
Chinese reed-warbler 163
Chough 189
Church Army 93
Churchill, Winston 30, 80, 158, 179
Cirl bunting 189
Common sandpiper 215
Creighton, Mandell 9–10, 26
Crested lark 83–4, 105, 133
Crowley, John Cyril 147, 177–8
Cuckoo 17, 91, 98, 203
Curlew 128

Daily Chronicle 39, 61
Daily Mail 47, 142–3
Daily Telegraph 48
Dartford warbler 21, 189
Davidson, Arthur Gerrard 147, 211–12
Defence of the Realm Act (1914) 33, 137
Dipper 173, 59
Dove 69, 118, 131, 136, 138, 196
Dunnock 17
Dunlop, William Eric Brook 147, 200–2
Dyer, Cecil MacMillan 95, 147, 155–6

Eagle owl 86
Ellis, Oliver Bernard 147, 202–4, 213
Egret xiii, 68

Falcated duck, Siberian 13
Fieldfare 84
Fire-crested alethe 161
Flamingo 153
French, John 52

Gadwall 154
Gallipoli 80, 82, 94, 158, 160–3, 205–6
Garden warbler 18, 30, 82, 121, 216–7
Garganey 13, 154
George V, King 25, 58, 77, 209
Gillespie, Alexander Douglas 147, 164–5
Gladstone, William 10

Glossy ibis 153
Goldcrest 212
Golden-crowned kinglet 22
Golden eagle 26
Golden oriole 64, 83, 90, 97, 216
Goldfinch 59, 152
Gosse, Philip 86–8, 127–8, 139–40
Grafton-Wignall, John Dighton 147, 189–90
Grasshopper warbler 82, 154
Gray, Leonard 147, 204–6
Great bustard 201
Greatgrey shrike 135–6, 214
Great reed warbler 82, 216–17
Great Reform Act (1832) 6–7, 10
Green, Maxwell 147, 156–8
Green sandpiper 214
Grey-backed warbler 82
Grey bush chat 169
Grey, Charles 6–7
Grey, Dorothy (née Widdington) xiii, 10, 12, 14–19
Grey, Edward xiii, 1–31, 32, 52, 54, 162, 179, 187–8
Grey, George 7, 9
Grey heron 128, 185, 195
Greylag goose 117, 189
Grey parrot 176
Grouse 149

Haig, Douglas 52, 134
Haldane, John Scott 141–2
Haldane, Richard 19, 52, 179
Harington, Herbert Hastings 147, 168–9
Harrier (spp) xii, 76, 117, 121,
Hedge sparrow *see* sparrow
Heligoland 68
Hen harrier xii, 84, 158–60
Herbert, Auberon Thomas (Lord Lucas) 147, 179–81
Hinton, Thomas 1
Hornbill 176
Homing pigeon 64, 137–9
Hooded crow 198
Horsburgh, Boyd Robert 147, 175–6
Hoopoe xii, 112
Honey buzzard 201
House martin 35, 63, 77, 100, 215
House sparrow *see* sparrow

Ibis 53, 55, 94–5, 106, 155, 160–1, 169, 190, 210–11, 214
Icterine warbler 182, 215
Indian spot-billed duck 169
Inglefield, Edward Fitzmaurice 71
Ingram, Collingwood 'Cherry' 105–6, 133, 135

Jackdaw 64, 118, 120, 128, 152, 216
Jackson, Peter xi
Jay 37, 46, 64, 89, 169
Jutland, Battle of 89

Kennedy, Reverend Geoffrey Studdert 59
Kentish plover 178, 189
Kestrel 63, 84, 102–3, 118, 121, 123, 131, 146, 171–2, 197–8, 216
Kingfisher 16, 84, 114–16, 215
Kitchener, Lord 25, 52, 66, 141, 163, 167
Knatchbull-Hugessen, Wyndham Wentworth (Lord Brabourne) 152
Knight, Captain Charles 26
Knot 151

Lapwing 211
Ledwidge, Francis 47, 180
Leigh, Austin Geoffrey 147, 170–2
Legge, Gerald 95, 147, 161–3
Leighton Moss 51
Lesser redpoll 205
Lesser whitethroat 18
Linnet 152, 216
Little owl 121, 146, 197
Lloyd George, David 36, 105, 129, 139
Long-tailed duck 171
Long-tailed tit 15, 17, 171
Lucas, Lord Herbert, Auberon Thomas 147, 179–81
Lumber Jills 130

Magpie 63, 65, 81, 89, 98, 215
Mallard 1, 13
Mandarin, duck Chinese 13, 28–9
Marsh harrier 51, 117, 179–80
Marsh warbler 82
Mary, Princess 58
Maxwell, Aymer Edward 147, 148–50, 153
Meadow pipt 152, 215
Mealy redpole 154
Melodious warbler 214
Merlin 152
Mills, Thomas xiii, 72–4
Mistle thrush 152
Monckton, Francis Algernon 147, 150–2
Montagu harrier 113–14, 159–60, 179–80
Moorhen 1, 78, 84
Munro, Hector Hugh 102–4, 147, 183–5
Mouritz, Leoffer Beresford 147, 158–60

National Farmers' Union vii, 32
Nightingale xii, 16–17, 22, 59, 62, 64, 82–3, 89–91, 97, 110, 118, 123, 129, 146, 164–5, 216

Osman, Alfred H. 137
Osprey 66, 79

Otto Murray-Dixon, Henry Edward xiii, 131–2, 147, 195–9
Ovenbird 35

Parrot 69, 176, 184
Partridge xii, 76, 103, 149, 198, 217,
Passchendaele, Battle of xii, 47, 125–6, 204, 213–14, 218
Peavot, Henry George Jesse 147, 199–200, 206
Pelican 1
Percy, Henry 11
Peregrine falcon 84, 189, 200
Perreau, Gustavus Arthur 147, 190–1
Pheasant 62, 66, 69, 88, 128, 149, 177
Phillip, Edward Thomas xiii, 147, 191–5
Pied wagtail 81, 84, 216
Pike, Oliver 48, 120–4
Pintail 13, 27
Pintail, Bahaman 13
Pintail, Chilean 13
Plover (lapwing) 104
Plumage Bill vii, 4–5, 55–6
Pochard 1, 13
Pochard, red-crested 13

Quail 214

Ramsay, Lewis Neil Griffith 147, 154
Rat xi, 32, 35, 36–8, 40, 44, 46, 49–50, 85–8, 92, 102, 127–8, 139, 161, 184, 198
Rat and Sparrow Club vii, xii, 33, 36–8, 44, 46, 49–50
Red Cross 93, 107
Red-legged falcon 102
Red necked falcon 176
Red-rumped swallow 182
Redshank 128, 171, 216
Redstart 16, 81–2
Red-tailed bristlebill 161
Redwing 84, 152
Reed warbler 182
Riseley, Edwin Ephraim 147, 200, 206–9
Robin xii, 8, 22–3, 28, 57–8, 61, 81, 84, 89, 107, 131–2, 172, 216
Rook 152, 210
Roosevelt, Theodore x, 20–4, 185, 187–8
Rosenberg, Isaac 133–4
Rosy billed pochard 13
Rothschild, Lionel Walter 95
Royal Flying Corps vi, 48, 104–6, 120, 122, 135–6, 179, 204, 212
Royal Society for the Protection of Birds (RSPB) vii–viii, ix, xii, xiv, 4, 28, 32–51, 53, 55–8, 60, 65–6, 68–9, 75–6, 78, 82, 89, 91, 93, 95, 97–9, 103–4, 106, 128–9, 131, 134, 136, 138, 140, 143–5, 148, 174, 196, 198, 210, 215
Ruff 151
Rufous warbler 82
Rusty-cheeked scimitar babbler 169

Sassoon, Siegfried 126
Savi's warbler 182
Scotsman 117, 126–7
Scott, Peter 27
Seagull (spp) xiii, 69, 72–3, 144
Sedge warbler 82
Selous, Frederick Courteney 21, 147, 159–60, 185–9
Shell shock 88, 125–7, 145, 216
Short-eared owl 189
Short-tailed pipit 162
Shoveler 1, 13
Shrike, red-backed 18, 59
Skylark xii, 21, 63, 79–80, 84, 90, 92, 212, 146, 152
Song thrush 17, 22, 78, 152
Southgate, Frank Edward 147, 167–8
Sparrow vii–viii, xii, 32–51, 57, 59–60, 63–4, 76, 84, 89, 100, 103, 105, 127, 129, 144, 146, 157, 168, 203, 216
Sparrowhawk 102, 168
Spender, John 3
Spotted-bill duck 13
Spotted redshank 154
Starling 17, 45–7, 49, 59, 89, 92, 117, 126, 129, 152, 216–7
St. James's Park 1, 5, 24, 29–30
Stonechat 170
Stone curlew 177, 189,
Stonham, Dr Charles 95, 147, 166–7
Stout, George Wilson 147, 181–3
Streets, John William 92–3
Swallow xii, 35, 63, 75–6, 100–1, 104, 117, 119, 129, 134–5, 146, 152, 172, 182, 215–6
Swan xiii, 68
Swift 100, 120, 193–4, 216

Tawny owl 86
Teal 13, 162
Teal, Brazilian 13
Teal, Chilean 13
Teal, Japanese 13
Teal, silver or versicolor 13, 24
Teschemaker, William xiii, 107–11
The Times 40, 48, 62, 82, 85, 88–91, 107, 112, 118, 144, 179, 196
Thomas, Edward (Phillip) xiii, 147, 191–5
Thorburn, Archibald xiv, 131, 196, 199
Thoburn Clarke, H 99–102

Thomas, Edward xiii
Tree sparrow vii–viii, 41, 50–1
Trevor-Battye, Aubyn 132
Trilling cisticola 161
Tufted duck 1, 13
Turaco 176

U-boat xiii, 36, 48, 69–74, 129, 137–8, 144

Via-Sacra (Sacred Way) 99, 165

Water rail 189,
Webster, Godfrey Vassal 147, 209–11
Westminster Gazette 3, 184
Wheatear 215, 217
White Feather Brigade viii, xiii, 66–7
Whitehead's mountain-thrush 163
Whinchat 81
White-faced jay 169
Whitehead, Charles Hughes Tempest 147, 163–4
Whitethroat 17–18, 81, 123, 215–6
White-winged black tern 171
Wigeon 13
Wigeon, Chilean 13

Willow wren *see* wren
Witherby, Harry Forbes 110–11, 144–5, 159–60, 212
Women's Timber Service 130
Woodbine cigarettes 58–9
Woodchat 214
Woodcock 189
Wood duck, blue-winged 13
Wood duck, Carolina 13
Woodlark 21, 84, 189
Wood pigeon 137
Wood thrush 22
Woosnam, Richard Bowen 95, 147, 160–3
Wren 16, 21, 30, 63, 89, 215–16, 219
Wyndham, Pamela Adelaide Genevieve 27

Yellowhammer 63, 121, 216
Yellow wagtail 84
Young Men's Christian Association 93

Zeppelin airship xiii, 69, 77–8, 128, 137, 203, 208
Zoological Society of London (ZSL) 53–5, 72, 94, 108, 160, 199–200, 206–7, 209